# PARADE MEDAL BARS OF THE THIRD REICH

# PARADE MEDAL BARS OF THE THIRD REICH

Thomas M. Yanacek

**Schiffer Military History**
Atglen, PA

*Acknowledgments*

I would like to sincerely thank everyone who has helped me with this project. Without your support and assistance, this book would not have become a reality: Jody Beltram, Bob Biondi, Gary Boward, John Buling, Richard Lundström, Edward Maroli, Dick Reimer, George Robinson, Peter B. Schiffer, Andreas Schulze Ising.



*Dedication*

This book is dedicated to those most special in my life:

To my wife: for tolerating my hobbies and for always encouraging me to pursue my interests. Your love and support have made me a happy man.

To my daughter: for being my pride and joy.

To my parents: for raising me and for guiding my footsteps along the path of life. Thank you for always being there for me.

A special dedication goes to my late father, who served in the U.S. Marine Corps during World War II, and the Korean War. Also to my two deceased uncles, who served in the U.S. Army during World War II. May they and all deceased veterans rest in peace forever.

Book design by Robert Biondi.


Library of Congress Catalog Number: 2008931199.



Printed in China.
ISBN: 978-0-7643-3091-9



Published by Schiffer Publishing Ltd.
4880 Lower Valley Road
Atglen, PA 19310
Phone: (610) 593-1777
FAX: (610) 593-2002
E-mail: Info@schifferbooks.com.
Visit our web site at: www.schifferbooks.com
Please write for a free catalog.
This book may be purchased from the publisher.
Please include $5.00 postage.
Try your bookstore first.

In Europe, Schiffer books are distributed by:
Bushwood Books
6 Marksbury Ave.
Kew Gardens, Surrey TW9 4JF
England
Phone: 44 (0)20 8392-8585
FAX: 44 (0)20 8392-9876
E-mail: info@bushwoodbooks.co.uk
www.bushwoodbooks.co.uk
Free postage in the UK. Europe: air mail at cost.
Try your bookstore first.

# CONTENTS

# INTRODUCTION

Writing and compiling this book has truly been an enjoyable experience for me. This is actually my first attempt at writing a book and I hope that you, the reader and collector, will find this to be a valuable supplement to the already numerous and excellent reference works dealing with German military collectibles of World War II. Although many books have covered the subject of German medals, I feel that this book is a first of its kind. No book in print to date has ever examined the subject of German medal bars, and that will be the focus of this book. Not individual medals, but mounted medal groupings that were worn by the recipients on their dress uniforms for formal and special occasions. Whereas a single medal is interesting by itself, it only represents a single act or accomplishment. A grouping of medals is far more interesting because it reflects not just a single accomplishment, but numerous accomplishments or even an entire career. It is therefore a much more significant and desirable piece of history.

I have been interested in military history as far back as I can remember. For the past thirty-plus years, I have studied and collected German military artifacts. My interest was probably first sparked when I was ten years old. My uncle showed me a German Iron Cross and a Luftwaffe (German Air Force) dagger that he had sent home during World War II. Seeing these items, and being able to handle them was fascinating. I knew then, that I wanted to start collecting German military items. As soon as I got my first job, I began to save money so that I could build a collection. Now, over thirty years later, I still find it as fascinating as when I first began. For me, collecting German militaria is not just a hobby; it is a historical experience as well as being my favorite hobby.

This book will illustrate and discuss numerous parade-mounted medal groupings. However, it will not show every single kind of medal awarded by Germany during World War II, nor every possible combination of awards. Many of the medals shown in this book are quite common as individual pieces. As part of the larger, mounted group though, they are scarce. There were a far greater number of medals produced than actually ever awarded. Even with awarded medals, the recipient seldom wore the medal. In lieu of the actual medal, the recipient wore the medal's ribbon, either diagonally through the second buttonhole of the tunic, or as a small ribbon bar pinned to the tunic above the left breast pocket. Moreover, many of the recipients of these awards died in action and never had the chance to get their medals mounted for wear on parade.

The medal bar is a display of the actual awards to an individual. Just looking at a medal bar will tell you quite a bit about the person who wore it. Medal bars will show bravery, meritorious service, branch and length of service, particular campaigns, and other special accomplishments. In some very rare instances, a medal bar is traceable back to the original owner if the grouping is unusual enough. Mounted groups are quite rare when compared to individual, un-mounted medals. They are far more interesting than an un-issued medal in mint condition. Mint condition medals are the pieces that sat out the war in some factory or storehouse, and never saw part of the action. As you examine the medal bars pictured in this book, you will see how each one is a unique piece of history. These medal bars are as unique as the persons who once wore them.

It is my sincere hope that you will enjoy this book, study its contents, and continue to refer to it for many years to come. If you are a collector, I wish you much success and enjoyment in your quest for historical artifacts.

### A Note to Collectors

For anyone who collects, or is contemplating the collection of World War II German military artifacts, I cannot over-emphasize the importance of having a good working knowledge of the subject. It is safe to assume that every kind of medal or award, produced by Germany during World War II, has been reproduced to some degree. This goes for the common medals as well as the very scarce ones. The value of the originals has increased to the point where it is now profitable to reproduce even the most common of items. Some fakes are very crude and obvious to even the novice. Other fakes are quite convincing, and detecting them requires close scrutiny. Some fakes are so close to perfect that they can even fool an experienced collector. We need to be on constant guard against fakes or we are liable to spend hard-earned money on worthless junk. It is very important that we continue to refine our knowledge and skills. Fake military items are everywhere, and the fakes are getting better and better.

Having books on the subject is a matter of necessity, and the more books the better. Collectors should periodically study the photographs in their references and reread the text so that the information remains fresh. Of course, no collector reference book is perfect, and that goes too for this book you are reading now. Every book written on the subject has a few mistakes. From my own personal experience over the years, I have purchased reproductions because of something I read in a book that turned out to be wrong. I have also passed up items because a book led me to believe they were fakes, only to learn later that the items were genuine. This happens not because the author is trying to mislead the reader, but because no one knows everything there is to know about this very complex subject. In fact, the longer I study and collect, the more I realize how much I don't know. A book is only a reflection of the author's own knowledge and personal experience on the subject, so it is not infallible. It is important not to rely entirely on any one book in particular.

The internet is also a very valuable resource for collectors. There is a wealth of information on German military collectibles available online. Because of the internet, more information is being shared than ever before, and the knowledge and expertise from around the world is now at our fingertips. Check out some of the collector forums on the internet. You will see that medals are continually being discussed and evaluated by serious collectors. Many of the fakes are being revealed as such, almost as soon as they hit the collector market. The internet is a great benefit to the collector. It has also made things harder for the forger and fake peddler, which of course is a good thing. Our individual knowledge and collective knowledge is increasing thanks to the fast pace of information being shared on the internet. Forgers' wares are being spotted immediately, and the whole collector community is being made aware of what to look out for. Fake peddlers, who use to make a living by ripping people off, are finding it harder and harder to sell their junk. I know of a few of these unscrupulous characters who have actually been driven out of business because everyone is now on to their swindle.

Experience is also an important factor in collecting. Unfortunately, experience cannot be gained by reading books or using the internet. Experience takes time to acquire, and usually there are some hard lessons to learn along the way. I remember several occasions where I spent money on something that I thought was real, only to find out later that it was a fake and worthless. I am sure that most collectors can recall similar mistakes. These bad experiences can really discourage a collector. Sometimes, they even cause the collector to give up the hobby altogether. Over the years, I have tried to remain positive about the hobby. I learn from the mistakes made along the way and try not to repeat them. Looking back, I see that the mistakes made were minimal when compared with the many pieces of original militaria that I have acquired.

Rather than buying everything off the internet, I recommend going to military collector shows, gun shows, and antique shows. Look at and handle as many items as possible. Ask many questions and talk to other collectors. A serious collector is always happy to share information with others. With a little time and patience, you will gain experience and confidence in the hobby. Collectors say that original items have a certain look and feel to them. This is something that even the best made fakes cannot duplicate perfectly. Collectors develop a "gut feeling" for items and they learn to trust their gut feeling more than anything else. This is a collector's experience, knowledge, and senses all working in perfect unison. If your gut feeling tells you something is not right with an item, you will not feel any better by paying money for the item and taking it home. Don't try to convince yourself that an item is good. If an item is real, you should not have to ignore your senses and talk yourself into believing it. For the experienced collector, the majority of fakes are immediately recognizable and the genuine items equally obvious.

If buying on the internet, deal only with reputable businesses that offer a full-refund and a reasonable time period for returns. Those that do not stand unconditionally behind what they sell are not worth your time and money. Before buying, many people will post images of an item on a collector forum and solicit opinions from others. This is a great idea, especially if you lack experience in the hobby. Fellow collectors will tell you who the good dealers are, and which ones to avoid at all cost. Do not hesitate to ask questions and request help from others. There are many wonderful people in this hobby and most will go out of their way to assist you. Whenever in doubt, do not buy an item. Remember that you and you alone must be satisfied with the item. To sum it all up: Know what you collect and collect what you know. I wish everyone the best of luck and happy hunting. May your collecting experience be as enjoyable as mine has been.

With regard to the values shown in this book, please bear in mind that they serve only as a guide. I have made every effort to show fair market values and not over-inflated prices. The prices reflect value at the time of printing for the items illustrated and in the condition shown. For the most part, values should increase with the passage of time. However, as with any other collectible, prices can fluctuate too. Collector interest propels the market and determines the values. In future years, if no one is interested in collecting German medals, the prices could plunge. A collectible is only worth what someone is willing to pay for it.

Where measurements are given, I have used the metric system. Dimensions are shown in millimeters and weight is shown in grams. While this might not be standard for a book published in the United States, it is certainly standard for anyone that collects medals of a foreign country that uses the metric system. To give dimensions of German medals in inches and weight in ounces would be contrary to the standards of the collecting community. The measurements given are for the actual specimens pictured and are not to be considered absolute. Because many different manufacturers produced these medals, the measurements will vary to a degree.

I have made every effort to show only original medals, documents, and photographs in this book. Also, unless otherwise noted herein, all of the medal bars shown in this book are to the best of my knowledge, Third Reich Period assemblies.

## CHAPTER ONE

# GERMAN MEDAL BAR CONSTRUCTION

### Examining the Medal Bar for Authenticity

Before starting to collect medal bars, a person should at least have some basic knowledge and experience in collecting individual medals. In other words, if you are new to this hobby, collecting medal bars is not a good place to begin. Don't jump in too fast, too soon. Start out with common medals, which are less expensive and not faked to the degree of the scarcer awards. By doing this, any mistakes made along the way should not be too costly. Once you gain some experience, you will have a better feel for original items and the confidence to make a larger purchase.

The "big picture" is the first thing to look at when trying to determine whether the medal bar is original or not. Does the medal bar as a whole seem logical and believable? Is the combination of awards something we would expect to see, or even possible? Does the placement of the medals on the bar follow the established regulations on the wearing of awards and their order of precedence? This does not mean that there cannot be a mistake in the placement of an award or something contrary to regulations, but you should avoid any bar that shows a total disregard for the rules and regulations. Also avoid any bar that depicts some "fantasy super hero" that was fighting simultaneously on all fronts, winning every kind of medal imaginable, and still finding time to be an active party member while putting out fires on weekends. Some bars I have seen are just that ridiculous. They are usually large monstrosities, having ten, twelve, or even more medals on them. On some of these bars, the total amount of service time required to theoretically earn all the awards represented would exceed a person's lifetime.

If the bar passes the first test, then we can move on to the next step. Examine each medal on the bar to insure that they are all original. For the most part, medals were die-struck, just as coins are. They should not display pockmarks, seams, or other signs of casting. Insure that the medals are made from the proper materials. Original medals were made of iron, steel, nickel-silver, genuine silver, bronze, tombak bronze, aluminum, and zinc. They were not made from soft metals such as lead or tin, or from brittle alloys such as white metal. Medals should not bend or snap in half if pressure is applied. Many of the newer fakes are made from better-quality metals, but these modern alloys do not produce the look and feel of originals. Artificial aging is often used in an attempt to make the fake appear old. Fortunately for us, the artificial aging is usually obvious. It is very difficult to duplicate the look of natural wear and aging. Although anything old should show some signs of the passage of time, it is not unusual to find medal bars in excellent condition. They do not necessarily have to be faded, dull, corroded, and broken in order to be real. Some original medal bars have stood the test of time quite well, shining almost as brightly as when they were first made. Most medal bars were worn only a very limited number of times for ceremonies such as weddings, funerals, parades, or other formal functions. When not worn, they were probably stored away in a drawer or even a protective case. Any bar that was well cared for will show only subtle signs of age.

At the same time you check the medals, check the ribbons as well. Ribbons were made from silk, artificial silk, or mercerized cotton. The ribbons should not glow when examined under black light. Look especially at the whites in the ribbon. If they glow neon bluish-purple, it is definitely a bad sign. This should also hold true for the thread used to stitch the bar together. Cotton or other natural fibers were used for the most part, but synthetics were also being used during the Third Reich Period. Whether natural or synthetic, the materials should not give off a glow. Insure that each medal is suspended from the correct colored ribbons. The color dyes should not bleed or run on original ribbons. Fading may or may not be present. Many original ribbons look as bright as when they were new. Other original ribbons can show quite a bit of color loss, most notably in the reds. It probably depends somewhat on the quality of the dye and the pigments used by the particular ribbon manufacturer. I have seen some ribbons where the colors are almost completely bleached out. This could occur if the ribbon was exposed to too much sunlight. The effect of bleaching is seen more frequently on ribbon bars than on medal bars. This is because ribbon bars were worn on a daily basis, being continually exposed to the weather. Medal bars were only worn occasionally, so they received far less exposure to the elements. While not in use, they were stored away indoors.

Once you are satisfied that the medal bar shows a believable combination of awards, and that each of the medals and ribbons are original, you are off to a good start. The evaluation should not end at this point though, for the medal bar may still not be one-hundred percent original. For instance, it could be a post-World War II assembly made using all original parts. Or it might be a bar assembled with a mixture of original and reproduction parts. Close examination is always required. At times, it might be near impossible to make a determination with absolute certainty.

The final determination rests solely on your knowledge, experience, and gut feeling as a collector.

### Good Indicators of Authenticity

1. Consistent aging: The medal bar must look uniform in regard to the amount of wear and age. Beware of medal bars that have worn and aged medals combined with bright-colored and new-looking ribbons. Also beware of medal bars that have faded and worn ribbons combined with medals that are in mint condition.

2. Chemical reactions between medals: Medal bars were mounted in such a way that the medals will overlap one another to some degree. Because of the overlap, medals composed of different base materials and finishes are in constant contact. Over time, the different metals will react with one another, causing darkening or a corrosive effect at the point of contact. This effect is usually subtle, but it can also be very distinct.

3. Abrasion at areas of overlap: This is due to the overlapping medals rubbing against one another over time, creating scratches in the surface. Again, this effect is usually subtle and it can be almost non-existent, especially on medal bars that are sewn up tightly and have the cross arms tied down with heavy thread. If the medals are tightly secured, there will be very little abrasion from metal on metal contact.

4. Ribbon wear at areas of contact with medals: This happens due to the medals rubbing against the ribbons over a long period of time. It is most noticeable with crosses, where the slight swinging of the top cross arm wears a path into the ribbon and even starts to poke holes into the ribbon. This will not occur to a significant degree if the medals are securely mounted, but the more a medal can swing or sway on the mounting, the more likely it is to cause wear.

### Types of Medal Bars

German parade medal bars were hand-assembled products and as such, no two will look exactly the same. The end result was a reflection of the skills and creativity of the assembler. Although each medal bar is unique, all medal bars can be classified into one of seven general styles of construction.

1. **Traditional German Parade Mount**: This style is characterized by double-wrapped ribbons and large ribbon rosettes at the bottom. The medals rest completely upon the ribbon rosettes.

2. **Modified Traditional Parade Mount**: This style is similar to the traditional. The ribbon rosettes are usually smaller though, and the medals will hang down partly below the rosettes rather than nesting on them.

3. **Bavarian Parade Mount**: This style features a furled ribbon wrapping instead of the double-wrap fold as used on the traditional parade mount. This style has no ribbon rosettes.

4. **Trapezoid Clasp**: This style was used often for enlisted medal bars during the Imperial Period. It was also used during the Third Reich Period, but to a lesser degree. This style is not too attractive looking. The ribbons are usually wrapped in a simple manner and have a flat appearance. The medals are clipped onto hooks on the back plate and can be removed. The

*An example of the traditional German style medal bar.*

*A modified traditional style medal bar.*

*A Bavarian style medal bar.*

medals hang down in such a way that alignment and balance are lacking. The tops of the medals are partially obstructed from view. This style also has no ribbon rosettes.

5. **Bavarian Trapezoid Clasp**: This style also features removable medals that are clipped onto the back plate. It is essentially the same as the trapezoid clasp, except that the ribbons are furled in the Bavarian style.

6. **Ribbon Bar/Medal Bar Combination Clasp**: This style was designed to serve a dual-purpose. The medals were hooked onto the reverse of the back plate, just like on the trapezoid clasps. For special occasions, the medals were attached. At all other times, it was worn without the medals as an oversize ribbon bar.

7. **Frack Bar Parade Mount**: This type of medal bar shows a complete departure from the other six types. Whereas most medal bars were worn horizontally on the uniform, the frack bar was worn at an angle. In addition, the medals were worn in order of importance from the viewer's upper right to lower left. On all other types of medal bars, the medals were placed in order of importance from the viewer's left to right. The frack bar was worn most often on naval, double-breasted tunics. It was much more common in the Imperial Period than during the Third Reich.

*An example of the trapezoid clasp.*

*An example of the Bavarian trapezoid clasp.*

*A ribbon bar/medal bar combination clasp.*

*An example of a frack mount medal bar.*

**Medal Bar Mounting Plates and Backing Materials**

Medal bar mounting plates were made primarily from sheet steel and zinc. Steel plates will attract a magnet while zinc plates are non-magnetic. Steel plates will usually have some type of finish on them. The most common finish was bright, nickel-silver plating. This type of finish is very durable and it remains shiny (almost mirror-like) over the years. Steel mounting plates can also be found with brass, bronze, and copper finishes. Painted and even chemically anodized finishes have also been observed on steel plates. Bare steel plates were also used, but in most cases a finish was applied to inhibit rust. Zinc mounting plates usually had no finish applied to them. They appear dull and dark gray in color. Occasionally, a mounting plate might be seen that is made from a material other than zinc or steel. They could be made from other non-magnetic alloys such as brass, tombak, and copper. Keep in mind though, that these were very rare exceptions, especially during the Third Reich Period. All of the better quality metals were tightly controlled as they were vital to the war effort. Brass was used often for small components such as pins, hinges, and catches, but almost never for an item like a mounting plate. As the war went on though, even the use of brass for small items like pins probably came to a halt. From the mid to end of the war period, steel plates with steel pins and zinc plates with steel pins were the standard.

Size of the mounting plates varied depending on whether the plate was for a ribbon bar, combination clasp, or medal bar. Also, the sizes probably varied to a degree depending on the specific manufacturer of the plates. The Lüdenscheid firm of F.W. Assmann & Söhne produced plates in standard heights of 10mm, 20mm, 30mm, and 40mm.[1] They also produced some sizes in between. 10mm was used for narrow ribbon bars, 15mm to 18mm was for normal size ribbon bars, 20mm to 30mm was for oversize ribbon bars and combination clasps, and the 30mm to 40mm sizes were for medal bars. Of course, the length of the mounting plate depended on the number of medals that were to be mounted. Typical length of a single-place medal bar plate ranged from about 38 to 45mm. A two-place mounting plate ranged between 63 and 70mm long. Three-place bars were about 90 to 108mm, four-place 114 to 127mm, five-place 133 to 146mm, and six-place 140 to 170mm. These dimensions are not to be considered precise or absolute. The length of a medal bar can vary outside the given ranges, so this serves only as a guide.

On many medal bars, a backing cloth was used over the mounting plate. The backing cloth was stitched in place. It not only gave the medal bar a more finished look, but also served to protect the uniform while the medal bar was being worn. The materials and colors of the backing cloth could vary considerably. Wool and cotton seem to have been the primary materials. In some cases, silk or silk-like ribbon was used. I have seen a few examples that used the ribbon from an actual medal. Even synthetic fibers like rayon were contemporary to the period. Typical fabric textures were broadcloth, twill, and grosgrain. In many cases, a non-woven fabric such as wool felt was used for backing the medal bar. Yes, that is correct! Felt was used during the Third Reich, so it does not necessarily mean fake. As much as the backing materials varied, the colors varied even more. Anything is possible, from the dark and drab to the bright and colorful. Red seemed to be a popular color for backing the medal bar. In some cases, a color that matched the uniform of the wearer seems to have been used: dark blue for the navy, field-gray for the army, and blue-gray for the air force. This was not the standard practice though, and for the most part the assemblers used whatever they had on hand. I have heard some collectors suggest that medal bars were backed with the color of the wearer's *Waffenfarbe* (arm of service color) used on collar tabs and epaulette piping. For example, in the German Army: white for infantry, red for artillery, black for engineers, pink for panzer, golden-yellow for cavalry, and blue for medical to list only a few. While it is possible that some may have asked the uniform shop to use a particular color to match their *Waffenfarbe*, it was in no way a standard practice.

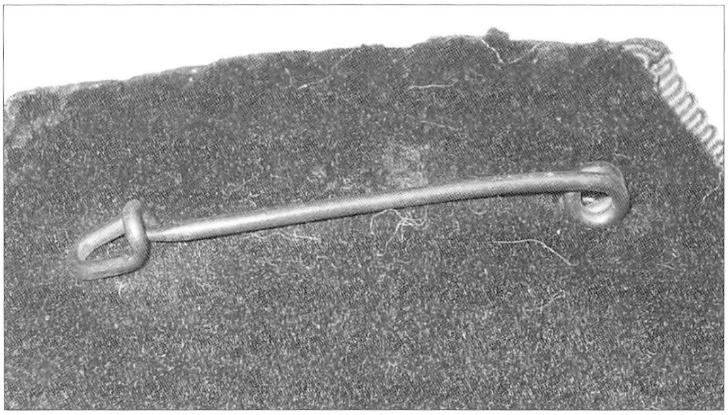

*The "tinnie" or "day badge" type safety pin was sometimes used on small medal bars.*

*The conventional type safety pin might be encountered on a medal bar. Almost anything is possible with a homemade assembly. The pin shown here is attached to the ribbon of a Medal for the German/Italian Campaign in Africa.*

*A sheet steel back plate showing an integral pin hinge.*

### Pins, Hinges, and Catches

Medal bar attachment pins were made from steel and brass. Most were formed from round wire stock, but occasionally you will encounter a pin formed from flat metal stock. Usually the end of the pin is pointed, but it can also have a blunt, rounded end. From measuring the pins on numerous medal bars, I have noted that the pin diameters range between 1.14mm and 2.33mm. The smaller gauge pins were typically made of spring steel and used in combination with sheet steel back plates, having integral hinges and catches. These pins do not bend easily, and they are sometimes brittle and prone to breakage. Larger gauge pins can be brass or steel. These larger gauge pins are usually found on zinc back plates, having separately applied hinges and catches. In many cases, it seems that the gauge of the pin increased in relation to the length of the back plate. Obviously, the longer plates had more medals mounted on them so the pin had to hold more weight. I consider a magnet to be an essential tool for the collector. Consequently, I am always checking medals, back plates, pins, and any other metal objects to see if they are magnetic or not. This may seem unnecessary to some, but over the years it has given me a good sense about what I now come to expect with specific medals. A magnet tells me whether a medal is the usual base metal, whether it is unusual or scarce, or whether it is highly suspect. Check things with a magnet and you will get surprised from time to time. Sometimes you will see a pin or a back plate that you would swear is made of brass, but when you take a magnet to it you will realize that it is actually steel with a brass plating.

*A zinc back plate with an applied, brass hinge.*

*Another example of a brass hinge, soldered to a zinc mounting plate.*

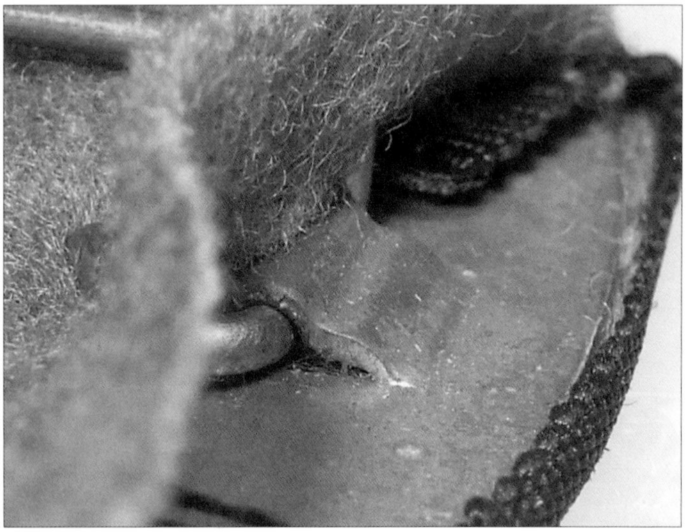

*A zinc back plate with an integral hinge. Some zinc mounting plates also had integral catches.*

*A sheet steel back plate showing an integral catch. The shape was cut into the back plate and then bent outwards to form the catch.*

*A sheet steel back plate with a round, steel wire catch. The catch was fed through the two, integral mounts and crimped in place.*

*This round, brass wire catch was soldered to a zinc mounting plate. Brass catches made from flat metal stock were also used frequently with zinc mounting plates.*

Here is an interesting tidbit of information for collectors: Hopefully you will know that Czech Annexation Medals were made from tombak and are therefore non-magnetic. But did you also know that a small number of original Czech Medals were struck from iron and are magnetic? Check out your Czech Annexation Medals. If you have one that is magnetic, you have a very scarce variation of a "common" medal.

For single-place or small, multi-place bars, safety type pins were sometimes used. These pins were made of brass or steel. They were the same style of pin that was used on German "tinnies" or "day badges." Occasionally, a more conventional type of safety pin might be found. These were probably used seldom, if at all, by the uniform and insignia shops. The conventional safety pin is more indicative of a homemade assembly.

Hinges and catches were made from brass, steel, and zinc. They were either separate components soldered to the back plate, or they were made from the back plate itself. Hinges and catches fashioned from the back plate are referred to as integral components. Integral components were formed by cuts made into the back plate. For integral catches, the cut shape was bent outwards from the plate, thus forming the catch. For integral hinges, pressure was applied to the cut areas so that the hinge would protrude from the surface of the back plate. Mounting plates with integral hinges/catches were used extensively during the Third Reich Period. This type of setup was simple to manufacture. The cutting and forming was probably accomplished by a single stamping process. Production time and cost was saved since there were no separate parts to make and no soldering required. Integral hinge/catch setups are most common on plates made from sheet steel, but some zinc plates featured them as well. Some sheet steel plates were made without an integral catch. Instead, they featured integral catch mounts. On this type of plate, a round wire steel catch was used. The catch was fed through the mounts of the back plate, and then crimped in place. Since the catch was a separate piece, it did take more time to produce. It still saved some time though, as there was nothing that had to be soldered. The advantage of this setup was that it provided a much stronger catch than the integral type. Integral catches were thin sheet metal and inherently weak at the bend point.

Separately applied hinges and catches were made from brass and steel. Zinc was not used for small, applied components. Hinges were formed from sheet metal and catches were made from round wire or flat metal stock. These parts had to be soldered to the mounting plates. Since the soldering process is time-consuming, the use of separate parts was inefficient from the manufacturing standpoint. Companies were always looking for more cost-effective ways of producing a product. As time went on, the use of integral hinges and catches increased while the use of separate pieces decreased or may have even been eliminated by some manufacturers. Still, there was probably such a large stockpile of parts that both methods remained in use throughout all of World War II.

### The Order of Precedence for Mounting Awards

Regulations were established with regard to the proper order in which medals were to be displayed on the medal bar. This is usually referred to as the order of precedence. On medal bars, the award having the highest precedence was mounted to the far left when viewing the bar. The other medals were then placed in descending order of importance from the viewer's left to right. Because of the many different awards that were instituted during the Third Reich Period, and the large number of existing Imperial Period awards, these regulations were never as simple as one would think. The regulations were actually complicated, leading to confusion, misinterpretation, and frequent errors in the placement of awards. In addition, the regulations had to be modified from time to time as new awards were created. Even without the complication of new awards, there were changes made in the regulations because of decisions to elevate the status of a particular award while lowering the status of other awards. Because of some of these changes, a medal bar that was completely correct in the pre or early-war period could be incorrect in the mid to late-war period. The following is a listing of award precedence in a simplified form to account for most of the ribboned awards of the Third Reich Period. It is therefore the regulations that were in effect from around 1942 until the end of the war. Please keep in mind that this list has been simplified and is by no means complete.

1. **Iron Cross Second Class:** Either the 1914 or 1939 Iron Cross, but not both. If the recipient won the Iron Cross Second Class in both world wars, the 1914 Iron Cross would be worn with a 1939 Clasp attached to the ribbon of the 1914 Iron Cross. Two Iron Crosses would never be worn side by side. If you see such a thing, be assured that something is amiss with the medal bar and avoid it at all cost. On a medal bar of the Third Reich Period, the Iron Cross should be placed to the extreme left when viewing the bar. During the Imperial Period, it was common to see some state awards placed before the Iron Cross, if the recipient was from a German State other than Prussia. However, during the Third Reich, the Iron Cross was given the highest order of precedence on the medal bar.

2. **1939 War Merit Cross Second Class:** Either with or without swords.

3. **Medal for the 1941/42 Winter Battle in the East:** Even though only a campaign award, the Russian Front Medal was given a high placement on the medal bar.

4. **1939 War Merit Medal:** This was strictly a civilian merit decoration. The medal by itself is very common, but it is not seen often on a medal bar. It is not likely to be found on a medal bar in combination with the War Merit Cross or with military decorations of the Third Reich Period. Prior to 1942, the War Merit Medal was ranked below the 1914-1918 Cross of Honor.

5. **Imperial State Awards for Valor/Merit:** This includes the wide range of state orders, decorations, and medals that were given for valor and military merit in World War I.

6. **Other Imperial State Awards:** These were placed on the medal bar by class and date of award.

7. **1914-1918 Cross of Honor (Hindenburg Cross):** This award was instituted during the Third Reich as a commemorative medal to recognize service in World War I and to replace the individual state commemoratives.

8. **Silesian Eagle:** A Freikorps award instituted in 1919 for Germans defending Silesia against Polish Nationals.

9. **Life Saving Medal:** Rarely seen on a medal bar and unusual that a medal awarded for saving human life was given such a low placement.

10. **Long Service Awards of the Armed Forces:** Up to two of these could be worn by qualified members of the armed forces. The highest class would be placed first. Awarding of these medals apparently ceased in late 1940.

11. **Other Long Service and National Awards:** This would include awards for the NSDAP, Police, SS, RAD, Luftschutz, Fire Brigade, etc. These awards were also to be arranged by class and award date.

12. **Medal for the Annexation of Austria**

13. **Medal for the Annexation of Czechoslovakia:** Either with or without the Prague Castle Bar.

14. **Medal for the Return of the Memel District**

15. **Defense Wall Honor Award (Westwall Medal)**

16. **1936 Olympic Games Commemorative Medal** (There was also an Olympic Games Decoration Second Class that ranked above the annexation medals.)

17. **German Red Cross and Social Welfare Decorations**

18. **Foreign Awards**

In addition to arrangement according to the order of precedence, the medals were usually aligned to give a neater appearance. Most medal bars were aligned so that the bottoms of the medals formed a single plane. However, some medal bars were aligned by the tops of the medals, or by the medal centers. With medal bars/clasps having hooks for removable medals, alignment was usually lacking. The placement of the hooks, as well as the size of the medal and its suspension ring would determine how low the medal would hang. Since the medals were different sizes, a staggered effect was created.

### Assembler Labels on Medal Bars

The following pictures show only a small sampling of maker labels that can be found on medal bars. Most medal bars that are encountered will not have any maker label on them. Based on my own collecting experience over the years, I would estimate that only about five to ten percent of the medal bars were labeled by the assembler. If you do find a medal bar with a label on it, the quality of the assembly should be first-rate. Shops would never want to advertise their name on anything showing sub-par workmanship, so the quality should be apparent. Because only a small percentage of medal bars are found with labels, it is always a nice bonus when you do find one. Keep in mind though, that a label is no guarantee that the medal bar is genuine. Just as a fake tailor label can be made for a reproduction uniform, a fake label can be added to a fake medal bar to make it appear more authentic. Always be on guard and scrutinize everything. Remember that the label will tell you the name of the shop that assembled the medal bar, but it in no way represents the manufacturer that produced the medals. Assembler labels are usually cloth, with either embroidered or woven lettering on them. There are also assembler tags that are made of metal. The label will identify the tailor or uniform shop, as well as the city where the shop was located. In many cases, the label will also include the street address for the shop. Natural materials were used for the labels and lettering so once again, there should be no glowing effect if the label is examined under black light.

*An embroidered label for the medals/decoration shop of Bruno Görlich, located at Rathenower Street 8 in Berlin Northwest.*

*This woven label is one of the more common ones seen. It is for the shop "ECK" located on Liebfrauen Street in Frankfurt on the Main.*

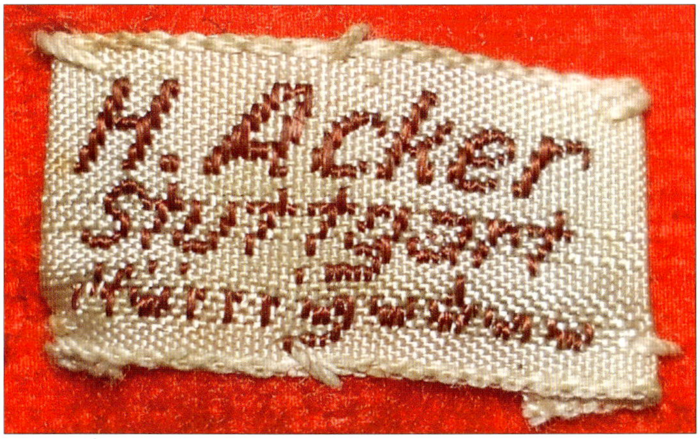


This is a very small stitched label for the shop of H. Acker, located in Stuttgart. The street address is not legible.

Maker labels were also made from metal. This label is pressed aluminum with the lettering in relief and paint filling the recessed areas. There is a metal tab at each end that secures it to the backing. The label is for the military equipment shop of Fr. Ackermann, located on Balduin Street 1 in Koblenz on the Rhine. Courtesy of George Robinson.

This stitched cloth label is from the uniform shop of C. G. Ulrich, located in Hamburg. The German word "Nachfolger" indicates that the shop is actually owned by Ulrich's successor.

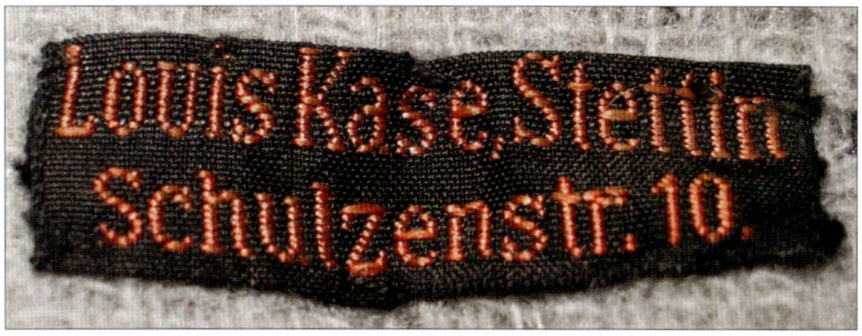


This stitched label is for the shop of Louis Kase, located at Schulzen Street 10 in Stettin.

This is another example of a metal label: an aluminum button with stenciled markings in black. A metal rivet secures the button to the backing material. The shop is that of Wolfgang Robert Schwarz. Courtesy of George Robinson.

## CHAPTER TWO

# SINGLE-PLACE MEDAL BARS

Single-place medal bars are an interesting facet of medal collecting. While nowhere near as impressive as a medal bar displaying multiple awards, they still reflect a special moment in the life of the recipient: the time when they received their first medal. I would think that most were proud of their accomplishment. They probably had the medal mounted at their earliest convenience, so that it could be worn on the uniform at the next formal function. Single-place medal bars are scarce when compared to the same medal in the un-mounted form. They are sought after by the collector who prefers to have medals that were actually worn rather than medals that were never worn or even issued. This chapter will illustrate some of these medals of the Third Reich Period. Wherever possible, more than one example is shown in order to illustrate variation in mounting style, pins, plates, backing materials, etc. Some examples of award documents will be shown, as well as a few period photographs. At the end of the chapter, some general information will be presented on awards of the Third Reich.

The 1939 Iron Cross Second Class was Germany's primary valor decoration during World War II. It was awarded for a single act of bravery in combat. Having the highest order of precedence, the Iron Cross Second Class was the decoration that was worn first on the medal bar. The Iron Cross was first instituted in March of 1813, when Prussia declared war on France.[2] It was in this year that Napoleon's Army was in retreat after an

*A single-place medal bar of the 1939 Iron Cross Second Class. The medal has an iron core and nickel-silver frames. It is 44.24mm square. $80-100.*

*Reverse of the Iron Cross medal bar. Steel mounting plates with copper finish. Integral hinge and catch. Brass pin.*

*Opposite: Example of an award document for the Iron Cross Second Class. This document was awarded on May 3, 1942 to an NCO of Artillery Regiment 120. The document is signed by the Commander of the 1st. Panzer Division, Generalmajor Walter Krüger.[1] 140mm x 200mm. $55-75.*

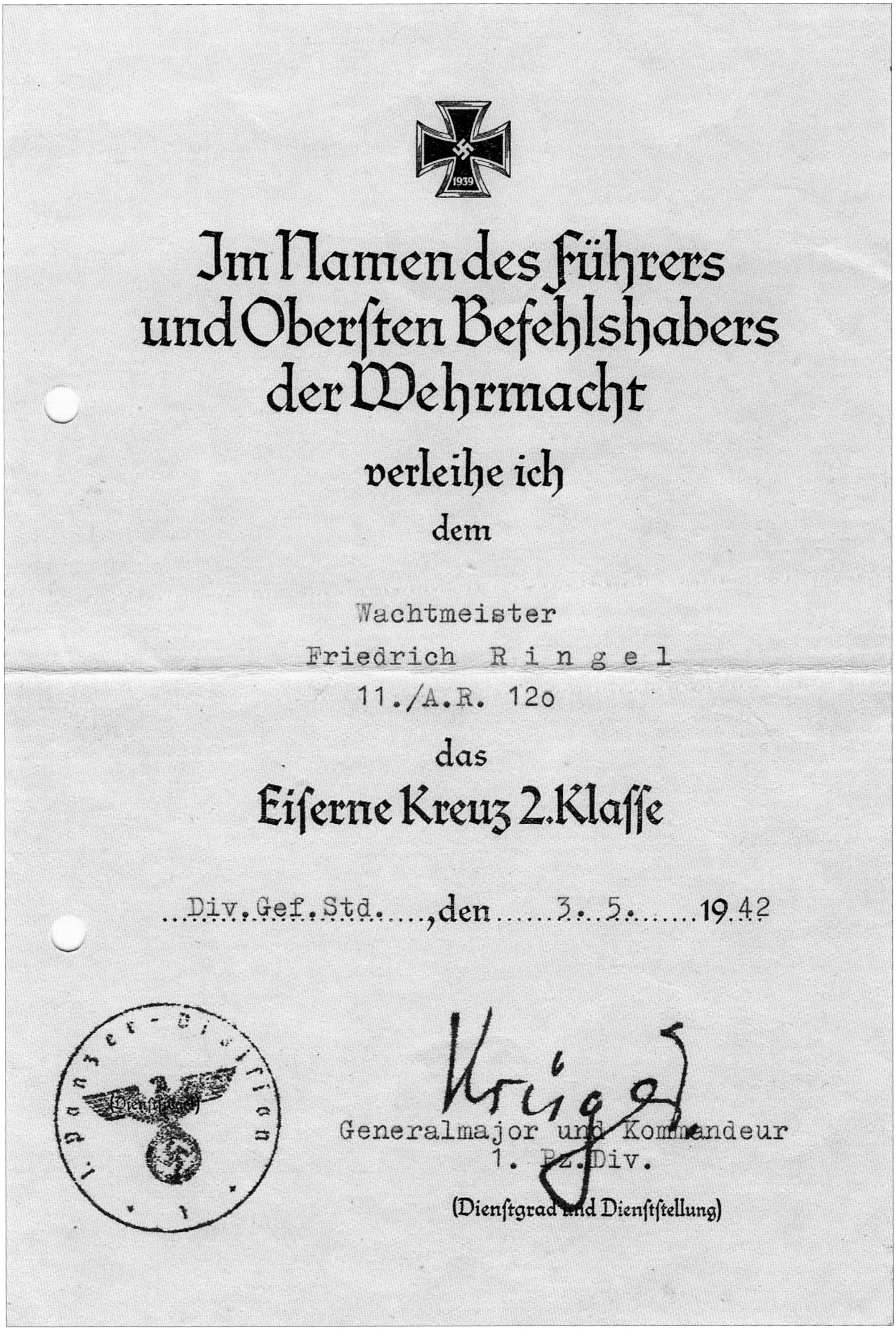

Im Namen des Führers
und Obersten Befehlshabers
der Wehrmacht

verleihe ich

dem

Wachtmeister
Friedrich R i n g e l
11./A.R. 12o

das

Eiserne Kreuz 2. Klasse

Div.Gef.Std., den 3. 5. 1942

Generalmajor und Kommandeur
1. Pz.Div.

(Dienstgrad und Dienststellung)

unsuccessful campaign in Russia. Since the French Army was severely weakened, Prussia saw this as an opportune time to declare war and free itself from French domination. The Iron Cross was only to be awarded during time of war. It was reinstituted in 1870 during the Franco-Prussian War, in 1914 during World War I, and lastly, in 1939 during World War II. Although it originated as a valor decoration solely for the Kingdom of Prussia, it eventually became the most recognized symbol of bravery throughout all of Germany.

The 1939 Iron Cross Second Class was made of three main parts, excluding the suspension ring and eyelet. There was a center core that was either chemically-darkened or painted, an obverse frame, and a reverse frame. The center core was sandwiched between the obverse and reverse frames, which were soldered together. Most of the cores were made from iron and are magnetic. However, some original crosses were made with non-magnetic cores of brass or zinc. **Remember that an Iron Cross is not necessarily a fake just because it does not attract a magnet.** On most 1939 Iron Crosses, the frames were made of nickel-silver rather than real silver. The obverse of the cross has a swastika at the center and the "1939" date on the lower cross arm. The reverse of the cross is plain, except for the original institution date of "1813" shown on the lower cross arm. Maker markings can sometimes be found on the suspension ring, but many had no markings at all.

With regard to measurements, collectors find this type of information very helpful in trying to determine authenticity. Measurements are in fact very useful, so long as you realize that measurements can vary amongst original medals. This is because many different manufacturers produced the medals using different sets of tooling. There were at least fifty different companies that produced the 1939 Iron Cross Second Class. Even two of the same medals produced by the same manufacturer with the same tooling can vary to a small degree. The manufacturing tolerances on a medal were not tight because there was no need for exact precision. The only function of a medal was to look good and be worn on a uniform. So don't expect a medal to have the precise specifications of something like compressor blades on a jet aircraft engine. According to one author, the 1939 Iron Cross Second Class measured anywhere from 43.8 to 45mm.[3] Just to check for myself, I selected four original 1939 Iron Crosses Second Class and measured them with dial calipers. The crosses measured from smallest to largest: 43.94mm, 44.19mm, 44.24mm, and 44.72mm. Weight of the medals can vary as well, not only because of slight size differences, but also due to the type and composition of the base metals and the finishes.

The 1939 War Merit Cross Second Class was a decoration that could be awarded for either bravery or outstanding service. It ranked below the 1939 Iron Cross, and it was usually awarded when the act of bravery or service was in a support role rather than actual combat. The decoration could be either with or without swords. The swords signified bravery while the award without swords signified service to the war effort. Members of the military as well as civilians were eligible to receive the War Merit Cross. In most cases, awards to the military were with swords, while civilians received the cross without swords. These decorations were awarded in large numbers. It is estimated that over 6 million with swords and almost 1.6 million without swords were awarded during World War II.[5] In addition to the number awarded, many more were produced. Because these decorations are so common, original specimens can still be obtained for inexpensive prices.

War Merit Crosses are made from either bronze or zinc. The bronze ones are considered early-war production pieces, while the zinc ones were made in the mid to late-war period. The zinc examples were either bronze-plated or given a bronze color wash. Many zinc examples will look gray because the bronze color has faded over time. On bronze examples,

*Single-place medal bar of the 1939 War Merit Cross Second Class with Swords. This example is made of zinc and is 48.48mm square. $40-50.*

*Reverse of the War Merit Cross medal bar. Zinc mounting plates, brass pin and catch. Blue-gray wool backing.*

*Opposite: Example of an award document for the 1939 War Merit Cross Second Class with Swords. The document was awarded to a medical NCO on January 30, 1942 at the Headquarters of the Army High Command. The document is signed by General der Flieger Rudolf Bogatsch as General of the Air Force at the Army High Command.[4] 140mm x 200mm. $50-75.*

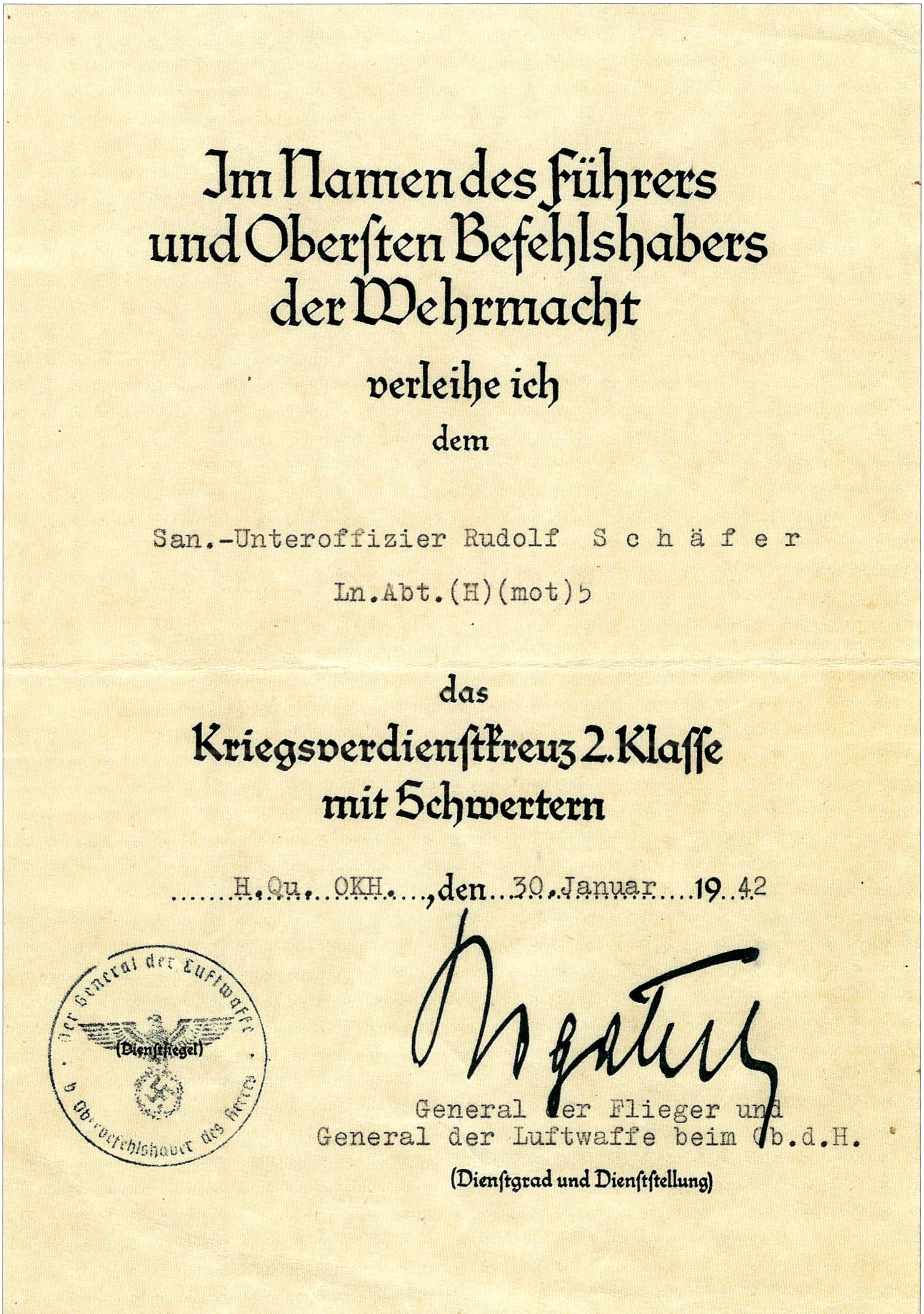

Im Namen des Führers
und Obersten Befehlshabers
der Wehrmacht

verleihe ich

dem

San.-Unteroffizier Rudolf Schäfer

Ln.Abt.(H)(mot)5

das

Kriegsverdienstkreuz 2. Klasse
mit Schwertern

H.Qu. OKH. , den 30.Januar 1942

Der General der Luftwaffe b. Oberbefehlshaber des Heeres

(Dienstsiegel)

General der Flieger und
General der Luftwaffe beim Ob.d.H.

(Dienstgrad und Dienststellung)

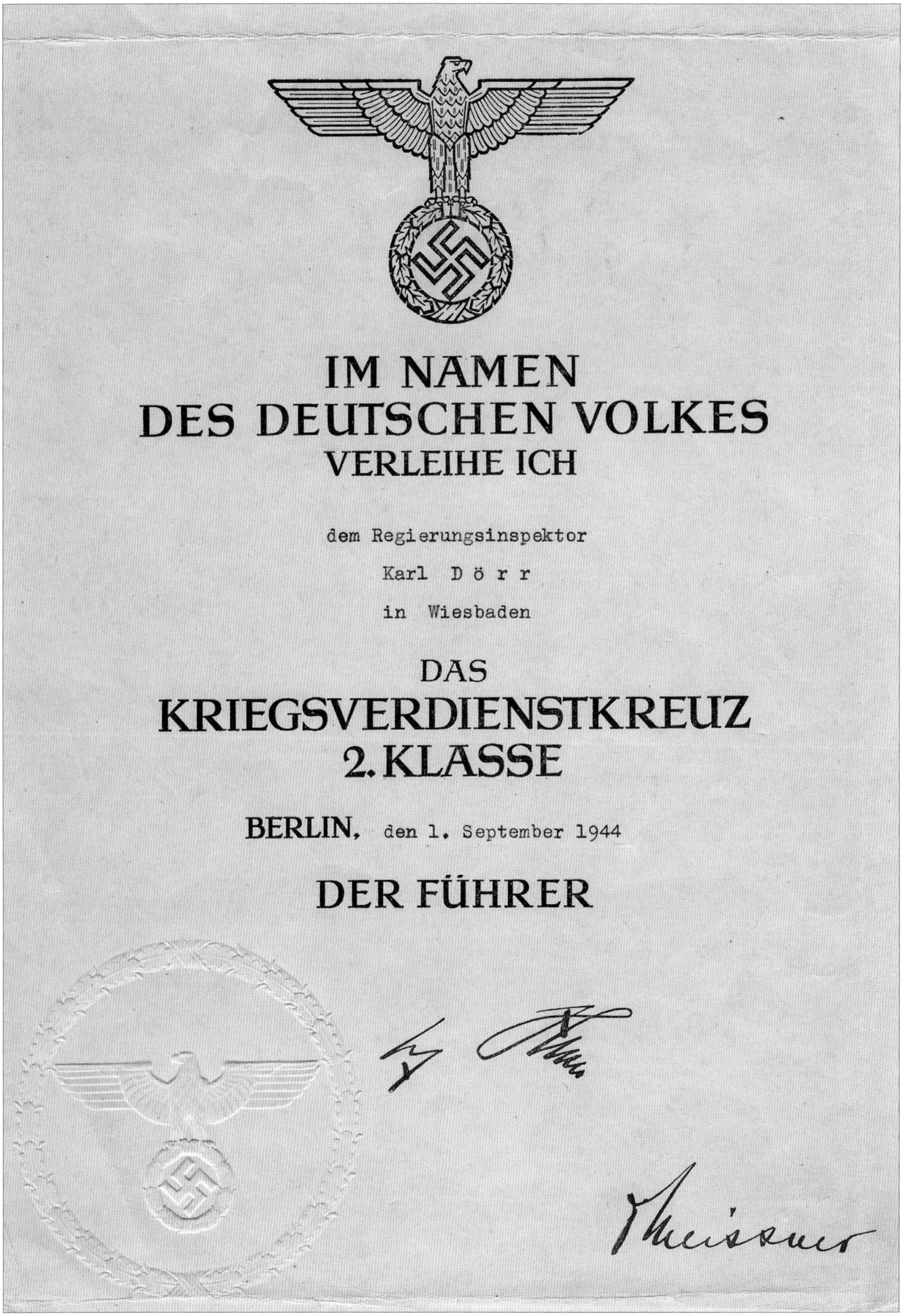

IM NAMEN
DES DEUTSCHEN VOLKES
VERLEIHE ICH

dem Regierungsinspektor
Karl Dörr
in Wiesbaden

DAS
KRIEGSVERDIENSTKREUZ
2. KLASSE

BERLIN, den 1. September 1944

DER FÜHRER

*Example of an award document for the 1939 War Merit Cross Second Class without Swords. It was awarded to a government inspector from Wiesbaden on September 1, 1944. The document has a large, embossed seal of the Führer at the lower left. It bears a facsimile signature of Adolf Hitler, and a counter-signature of Otto Meissner. 209mm x 298 mm. $50-75.*

the small suspension eyelet, holding the suspension ring, is a separate attachment that is soldered in place. On zinc examples, the suspension eyelet is an integral part of the cross itself. This not only saved production time, but was a matter of necessity as it is almost impossible to solder a small eyelet to zinc and get it to hold. The ribbon of the War Merit Cross has the same colors as the ribbon of the 1939 Iron Cross, but the red and black are reversed. There were many manufacturers that produced War Merit Crosses. The cross will sometimes have a one, two, or three-digit manufacturer code number stamped into the suspension ring. Many though, had no markings at all. I have noticed that manufacturer markings seem to be more prevalent on the zinc examples than on the bronze ones. Since numerous manufacturers produced these decorations, you should expect to see some variance in the measurements. In general though, the crosses should measure about 48 to 49mm square at the widest point. I measured four original examples and they are from smallest to largest: 48.03mm, 48.05mm, 48.49mm, and 48.89mm. A few of the many manufacturers of War Merit Crosses are listed in the table below:

| Manufacturer | Town or City |
|---|---|
| Jakob Bengel | Oberstein |
| Franz Breuning | Pforzheim |
| Deschler & Sohn | Munich |
| Wilhelm Deumer | Lüdenscheid |
| Erhard & Söhne | Schwäbisch Gmünd |
| Gebrüder Gengenbach & Co. | Pforzheim |
| Gebrüder Godet & Co. | Berlin |
| Franz Jungwirth | Vienna |
| Klein & Quenzer | Idar-Oberstein |
| Rudolf Leukert | Gablonz an der Neiße |
| Franz Mänert | Gablonz an der Neiße |
| Werner Redo | Saarlautern |
| Eugen Schmidthäussler | Pforzheim |
| Rudolf Souval | Vienna |
| Steinhauer & Lück | Lüdenscheid |
| Rudolf Wächtler & Lange | Mittweida/Sa. |

The 1939 War Merit Medal was instituted in August of 1940.[6] This medal was only awarded to civilians, and was given to recognize hard work in the furtherance of the war effort. The majority of recipients were those who worked in the factories that produced war materials. Germans as well as foreigners, both male and female, were eligible for the medal. However, in mid 1943, award to foreigners ceased with the institution of the 1943 Merit Medal of the German Eagle Order.[7] From this time onward, foreigners received this medal rather than the 1939 War Merit Medal.

War Merit Medals were die-struck from either bronze or a similar non-magnetic alloy. I have never seen any made from iron or zinc. The medals are about 32mm in diameter. I measured the diameter of seven original examples. From smallest to largest they are: 32.05mm, 32.13mm, 32.20mm, 32.20mm, 32.23mm, 32.35mm, and 32.51mm. The ribbon is the same as on the War Merit Cross, except for the addition of a narrow red stripe that runs down the center of the black field. Several million of these were awarded during World War II, so they are easy to find and inexpensive. Although the medal is common by itself, War Merit Medals are seldom seen on a medal bar. This is probably because most were awarded to factory workers. A civilian working in a factory had no need to have the medal mounted. Most probably gave it no thought other than taking it home and putting it away in a drawer. Many different manufacturers produced War Merit Medals, but it is almost impossible to find one that is maker marked. If present, the marking would be on the suspension ring. In the years that I have been collecting, I recall seeing only two examples that were marked. I have confirmed several manufacturers of the War Merit Medal from original issue packets. They are shown in the table below:

| Manufacturer | Town or City |
|---|---|
| Wilhelm Deumer | Lüdenscheid |
| Robert Hauschild | Pforzheim |
| Friedrich Keller | Oberstein |
| Franz Klamt & Söhne | Gablonz an der Neiße |
| Klein & Quenzer | Idar-Oberstein |
| L. Chr. Lauer | Nürnberg-Berlin |

*A single-place medal bar of the 1939 War Merit Medal in traditional style. 32.13mm in diameter. Steel suspension hook. $35-45.*

*Reverse of the War Merit Medal, single-place bar. Zinc mounting plates, zinc catch, and a brass pin. Blue-green wool felt backing.*

*A single-place medal bar of the 1939 War Merit Medal in Bavarian style. $35-45.*

*Reverse of War Merit Medal, single-place bar. Zinc mounting plates, zinc catch, and brass pin. Light gray cotton broadcloth backing.*

| | |
|---|---|
| Richard Simm & Söhne | Gablonz an der Neiße |
| Arno Wallpach | Salzburg |
| Walter & Henlein | Gablonz an der Neiße |

The Defense Wall Honor Award or Westwall Medal, as it is more commonly known, was instituted in August of 1939.[8] It was awarded to those that aided in the planning, construction, or defense of Germany's western fortifications. Civilians, as well as members of the military were eligible to receive the award. Civilian workers were required to be in the area for a minimum of ten weeks in order to be considered. Members of the military were only required to be stationed in the area for three weeks.[9] From the date of institution until January of 1941, about 600,000 were awarded. No further awards were made until late 1944. In response to the Allied invasion of Europe in June of 1944, Hitler sent additional troops and workers to refortify Germany's western defenses. To recognize their efforts, the Defense Wall Honor Award was reinstituted in October of 1944, and an additional 200,000 were awarded.

The Defense Wall Honor Award was made from either bronze or zinc. Early issues were bronze, and the later issues were zinc with a bronze color wash. Over time, many of the zinc examples have lost their finish and now appear dull and gray. The medal by itself is common, so originals are easy to find. However, it seems that the ribbons are an entirely different matter.

*A single-place medal bar of the Defense Wall Honor Award in traditional style. The medal is an early-issue, made of solid bronze. Medal is 32.86mm x 40.76mm. $35-40.*

*Reverse of the Defense Wall Honor Award medal bar. Note that this example is missing the back plate, allowing a good view of how the ribbon was secured to the front plate.*

*Opposite: Example of an award document for the Defense Wall Honor Award. This award was given to an NCO in Wiesbaden on March 20, 1940. The award was given under the authority of the Commanding General of Wehrkreis XII, General der Infanterie Albrecht Steppuhn. The document is signed by the Colonel and Commander of Artillery Regiment 33. 149mm x 209mm. $35-40.*

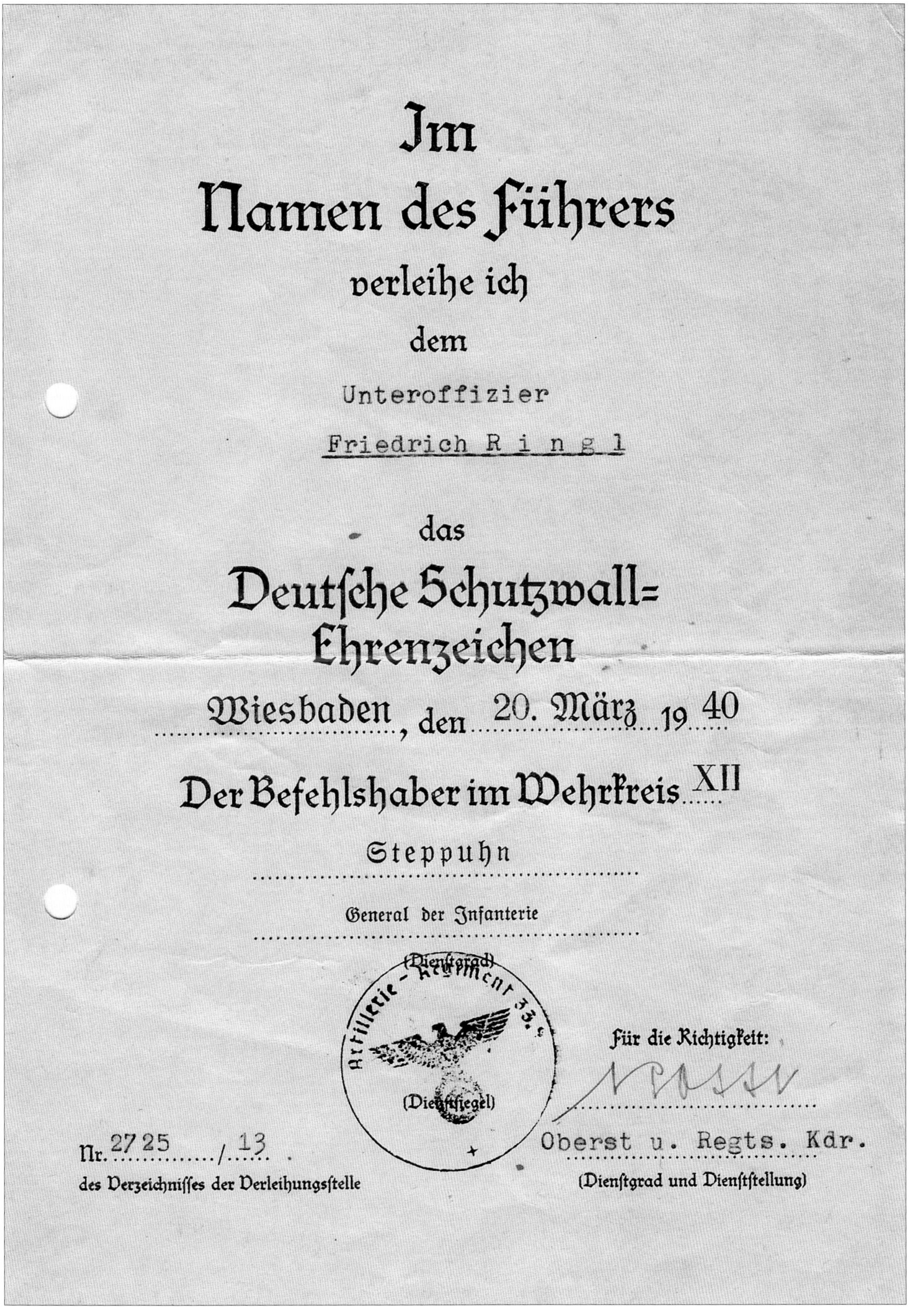

Im
Namen des Führers
verleihe ich
dem
Unteroffizier
Friedrich R i n g l
das
Deutsche Schutzwall=
Ehrenzeichen

Wiesbaden, den 20. März 1940

Der Befehlshaber im Wehrkreis XII

Steppuhn

General der Infanterie
(Dienstgrad)

Artillerie - Regiment 33 .
(Dienstsiegel)

Für die Richtigkeit:

Oberst u. Regts. Kdr.
(Dienstgrad und Dienststellung)

Nr. 2725 / 13
des Verzeichnisses der Verleihungsstelle

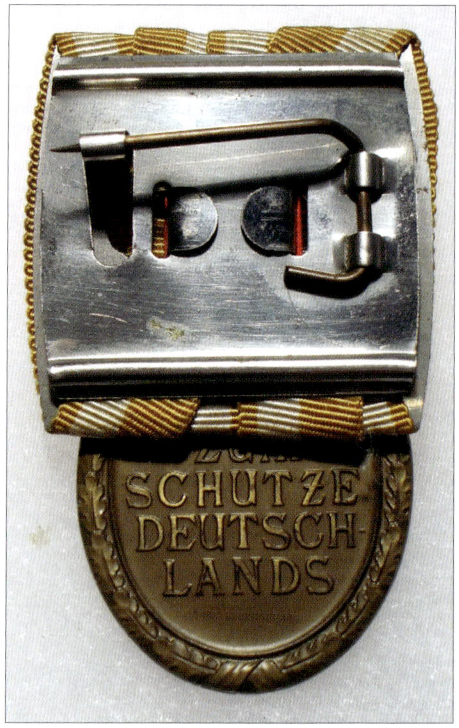


*Single-place medal bar of the Defense Wall Honor Award in Bavarian style. Also a solid bronze issue. About 33mm x 41mm. $40-50.*

*Reverse of the Defense Wall Honor Award. Steel mounting plates with nickel-plated finish. Integral catch and hinge. Brass pin.*

For whatever the reason, original ribbons seem to be scarce in today's collector market. Many of the original Westwall Medals I see at militaria shows are paired with reproduction ribbons. The medals are about 33mm wide x 40mm high. Three original examples that I measured are 32.86mm x 40.76mm, 33.07mm x 40.41mm, and 33.12mm x 40.91mm. Both the bronze and zinc types have suspension eyelets that are an integral part of the medal. The reverse of the medal has the inscription, "for work on Germany's defenses." Defense Wall Honor Awards were produced by many different manufacturers, but it seems that they were never marked by the manufacturer. I have never seen one with a maker marking on the suspension ring. A few of the manufacturers, confirmed by original issue packets, are listed below:

| Manufacturer | Town or City |
|---|---|
| F. W. Assmann & Söhne | Lüdenscheid |
| Wilhelm Deumer | Lüdenscheid |
| Friedrich Orth | Vienna |
| Karl Pichl | Innsbruck |
| Carl Poellath | Schrobenhausen |
| Josef Rössler & Co. | Gablonz an der Neiße |

The Medal for the 1941/42 Winter Battle in the East was instituted in May of 1942.[11] It was a campaign medal, and was awarded to those serving on the eastern front between the period of November 1941 and April of 1942. Initially, the medal was only awarded to members of the military. It could

*Single-place medal bar of the Medal for the 1941/42 Winter Battle in the East. (Modified-traditional style) The medal is maker marked "88" on the suspension ring. This code number was used by Werner Redo of Saarlautern. Made of die-forged zinc and measuring 36.50mm in diameter. $50-55.*

*Reverse of the medal bar. Zinc mounting plates, brass pin and catch. Red wool felt backing.*

*Opposite: An award document for the 1941/42 Winter Battle in the East Medal. This was awarded to a Luftwaffe NCO on August 30, 1942. The document is signed by the Major and Commander of Close Reconnaissance Group 8. 140mm x 200mm. $35-40.*

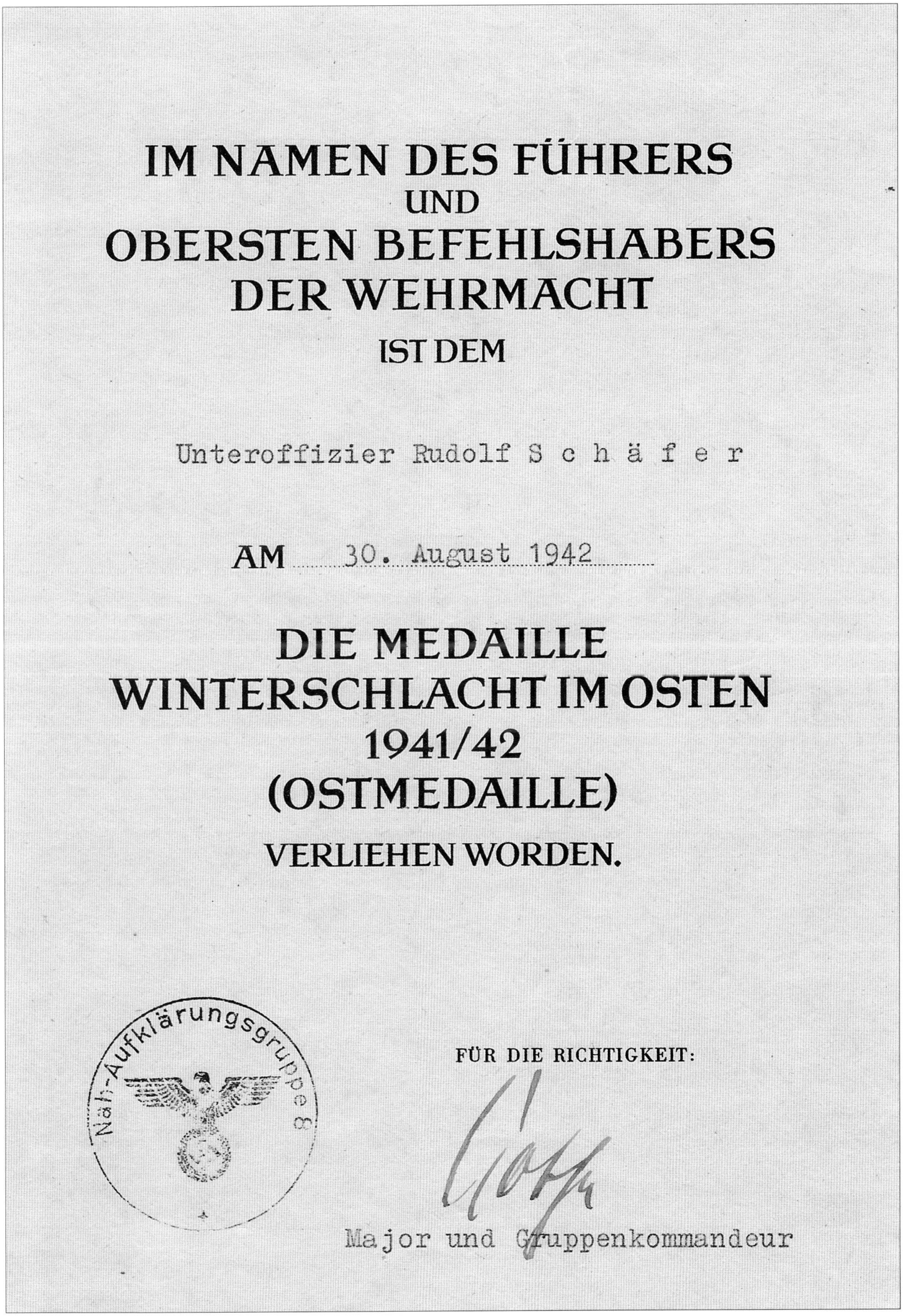

IM NAMEN DES FÜHRERS
UND
OBERSTEN BEFEHLSHABERS
DER WEHRMACHT
IST DEM

Unteroffizier Rudolf S c h ä f e r

AM 30. August 1942

DIE MEDAILLE
WINTERSCHLACHT IM OSTEN
1941/42
(OSTMEDAILLE)
VERLIEHEN WORDEN.

Nah-Aufklärungsgruppe 8

FÜR DIE RICHTIGKEIT:

Major und Gruppenkommandeur

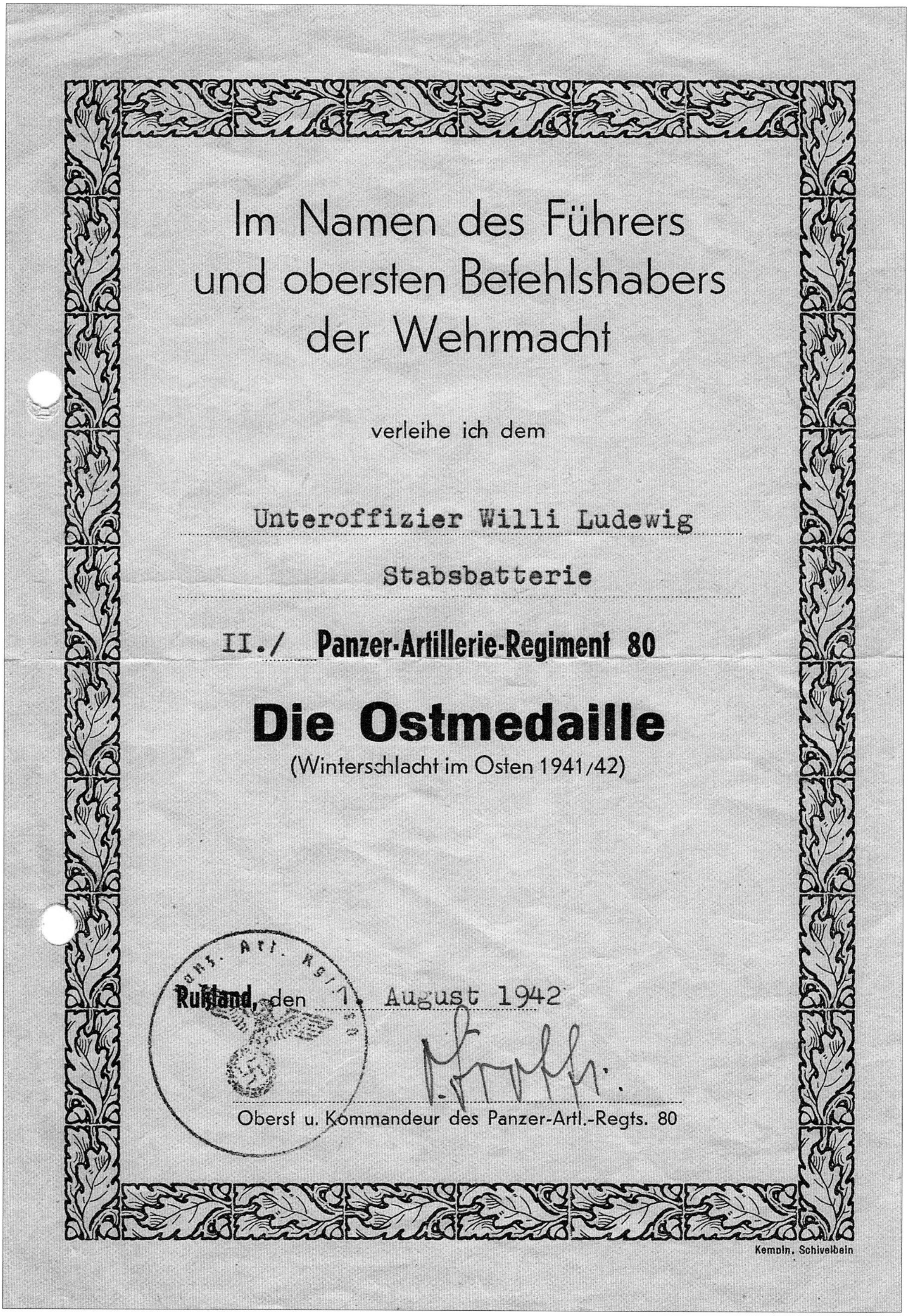

Im Namen des Führers
und obersten Befehlshabers
der Wehrmacht

verleihe ich dem

Unteroffizier Willi Ludewig

Stabsbatterie

II./ Panzer-Artillerie-Regiment 80

**Die Ostmedaille**

(Winterschlacht im Osten 1941/42)

Rußland, den 1. August 1942

Oberst u. Kommandeur des Panzer-Artl.-Regts. 80

Kempin, Schivelbein

*This is another example of an award document for the 1941/42 Winter Battle in the East Medal. This is a very scarce variation as it was awarded only to members of Panzer Artillery Regiment 80. It was awarded to an NCO of the Staff Battery of the Second Battalion on August 1, 1942. The document is signed by the Regimental Commander, Oberst Helmut von Scotti.[10] 150mm x 213mm. $75.*

be awarded after a minimum of two months unbroken service at the front, or after two weeks of actual combat. Air Force flying personnel were required to have thirty days of sorties over enemy territory. These time requirements could be waived in the event of being wounded or receiving a frozen limb. The Chief Staff Doctor of a field hospital was vested with the authority to award the medal, so some received it at the same time they received their Wound Badge. In January of 1943, the award criteria was modified to include civilians in the service of the Armed Forces, civilians working in area factories, foreign volunteers, administrative personnel, and those that were killed or missing in action. Awarding of this medal ceased in late 1944. In addition to the formal name, the award is more commonly called the Russian Front Medal or the East Medal. German soldiers on the eastern front gave it the harsh but realistic nickname of "Frozen Flesh Medal."

The Russian Front Medal was die-forged from either fine zinc or a cruder, zinc alloy known as kriegsmetall. Early examples of the medal were either chemically darkened or plated in altsilber (darkened silver). The rim of the medal and the helmet at the top were silver-plated. Later examples were usually bare kriegsmetall with only a silver wash to the rim and helmet. On many of these medals, the silver wash will appear faded or even totally absent due to the passage of time. The medals were produced with an integral suspension eyelet, to which the suspension ring was attached. On the reverse, the inscription reads, "winter battle in the east 1941/42." The medals are about 36mm in diameter, but expect to see some variance in the actual size since many different manufacturers produced them. I measured the diameters of three original examples. They measured: 35.81mm, 36.11mm, and 36.50mm. Russian Front Medals are frequently found with maker markings on the suspension ring. It is always interesting to look for these markings and to see how many different manufacturers you can find. Some collectors enjoy the challenge of trying to find every maker of a particular medal. If you plan on looking for maker markings, do not forget to bring along a 10x magnification loupe as it is sometimes impossible to make out the marking unaided. The marking will be either what is referred to as a Lieferant code number, or an LDO code number. A Lieferant code was a one, two, or three-digit number that was assigned to a manufacturer by the presidential chancellery. These manufacturers were official suppliers to the chancellery. An LDO code was a number assigned to manufacturers that were licensed to sell awards on the commercial market. An LDO code began with the letter "L" followed by a "/" and then a two-digit number. Some manufacturers had both a Lieferant number and an LDO number. (Appendices at the end of the book list the Lieferant and LDO numbers assigned to the various manufacturers.) A few of the firms that produced the Russian Front Medal are shown in the following table. These manufacturers have been confirmed from original issue packets and/or suspension ring markings. The list is by no means complete:

| **Manufacturer** | **Town or City** |
|---|---|
| Gustav Brehmer | Markneukirchen |
| Klein & Quenzer | Idar-Oberstein |
| Carl Poellath | Schrobenhausen |
| Werner Redo | Saarlautern |
| Rudolf Souval | Vienna |
| Steinhauer & Lück | Lüdenscheid |
| Rudolf Wächtler & Lange | Mittweida/Sa. |
| Walter & Henlein | Gablonz an der Neiße |
| E. Ferd. Wiedmann | Frankfurt am Main |
| Carl Wild | Hamburg |
| Work group of engraver/ smith guilds | Hanau am Main |
| C. F. Zimmermann | Pforzheim |
| Fritz Zimmermann | Stuttgart |

In a period of just over a year, Germany was able to expand its empire with a series of three bloodless conquests. These conquests involved the annexation of Austria, Czechoslovakia, and a part of East Prussia known as the Memel District. Austria became part of the German Empire in March of 1938. In October of 1938, the western part of Czechoslovakia, known as the Sudetenland, was annexed. Then by early 1939, all of Czechoslovakia was part of the German Empire. In March of 1939, the Memel District was surrendered by Lithuania, without incident, when Hitler demanded that it be returned to Germany. (As one of the many consequences of defeat in World War I, the Memel District had been taken from Germany and turned over to Lithuania.) The return of the Memel District marked the end of Germany's territorial expansion in peacetime. Hitler's next reach for empire, the invasion of Poland, was met with armed resistance and started the Second World War.

Medals were instituted to commemorate these three annexations. The Austrian Annexation Medal was instituted in May of 1938, the Czech Annexation Medal in October of 1938, and the Memel Medal in May of 1939. All three medals were designed by Professor Richard Klein of Munich.[12] Each medal has the same obverse design so only the reverses are different. The reverse of the Austrian Annexation Medal has the inscription, "one people, one empire, one leader" and the date, "13 March 1938." The Czech Medal has the same inscription, but with the date, "1 October 1938." The reverse of the Memel Medal has the inscription, "to commemorate the return of the Memel District" and the date, "22 March 1939." The three medals were die-struck, primarily from tombak or a similar alloy, and are of excellent quality. The suspension eyelet is a separate piece that was soldered in place. These medals were never made with an integral suspension eyelet. Also insure that there are no seams on the rim of the medal as this would indicate a cast reproduction. The Austrian Annexation Medal is finished in silver, while both the Czech and Memel Medals have a bronze finish. On some of the Austrian Annexation Medals, the finish will be almost black with tarnish, but others seem to stay fairly bright over the years. Czech Annexation and Memel Medals can have either a dark bronze finish, or a golden bronze coloration that holds up well. Since they were made from bronze alloys, most annexation medals will be non-magnetic. I have yet to see an Austrian or Memel Medal that will attract a magnet. However, there are original magnetic examples of the Czech Annexation Medal that are made of die-struck iron. They are very scarce though, and probably limited to a single production run by a single manufacturer. Dimensions seem to be fairly consistent with annexation medals. They do not vary to the degree of some other awards. I measured the diameter of three Austrian Annexation Medals and they were: 32.13mm, 32.25mm, and 32.35mm. Five examples of Czech Annexation Medals were: 32.13mm, 32.18mm, 32.20mm, 32.33mm, and 32.38mm. On four examples of the Memel Medal, the diameters were: 32.17mm, 32.20mm, 32.21mm, and 32.25mm. Of the three annexation medals, the Czech is the most common with over 1.1 million awarded. The Austrian Annexation Medal is also common with over 300,000 awarded. The Memel Medal is very scarce as just over 31,000 were awarded. In addition to the numbers awarded, many more were produced. Because of the large number of Austrian and Czech Annexation Medals awarded, they were undoubtedly produced by many different manufacturers. Memel

Medals, on the other hand, were probably produced by only a few firms due to the limited number of awards.

Trying to identify the actual manufacturers of annexation medals is difficult because these awards were almost never marked. I cannot ever recall seeing one with a marking on the suspension ring. I do own an example of the Austrian Annexation Medal that has the LDO code number "L/11" stamped into the rim of the medal, at the six o'clock position. This is the commercial production code used by Wilhelm Deumer of Lüdenscheid. I have also seen one other example like this in the possession of another collector. Check the rims of your annexation medals, and you might be surprised to find one with this marking. They are either very scarce, or have just gone unnoticed for all these years. Annexation Medals were usually issued in a case rather than a paper packet. Unfortunately, the cases for these medals are almost never marked. I do have a case for the Austrian Annexation Medal that has a label for the Central Mint of Vienna. I also have a paper packet for a Czech Annexation Medal by E. Ferd. Wiedmann of Frankfurt am Main. In *Military Awards of the Third Reich,* Angolia shows an identical packet pictured on page 62. It appears that F.W. Assmann & Söhne of Lüdenscheid also produced Austrian and Czech Annexation Medals, as they are shown in the manufacturer's sales catalog. I have yet to confirm a manufacturer for the Memel Medal.

*Single-place medal bar of the Medal for the Annexation of Austria. Die-struck tombak with a silver-plated finish. 32.25mm in diameter. $45-55.*

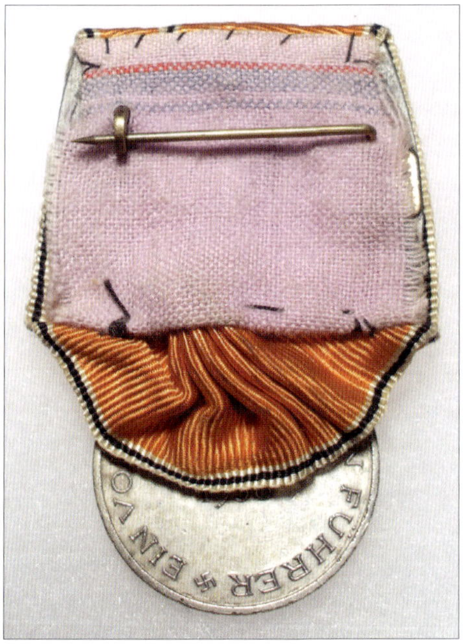

*Reverse of the Annexation of Austria medal bar. Zinc mounting plates, brass pin and catch. Violet-colored, cotton broadcloth backing.*

*Single-place medal bar of the Medal for the Annexation of Czechoslovakia. Die-struck bronze. 32.20mm in diameter. $35-45.*

*Reverse of the Annexation of Czechoslovakia medal bar. Steel mounting plates, steel catch, and brass pin. Green wool backing.*

*Opposite: An award document for the Annexation of Austria Medal. This was awarded to a rural district police official on January 23, 1939. The document bears the embossed seal of the State Minister at the lower left. The signature is that of Otto Meissner as the State Minister and Chief of the Presidential Chancellery. 209mm x 296mm. $50-60.*

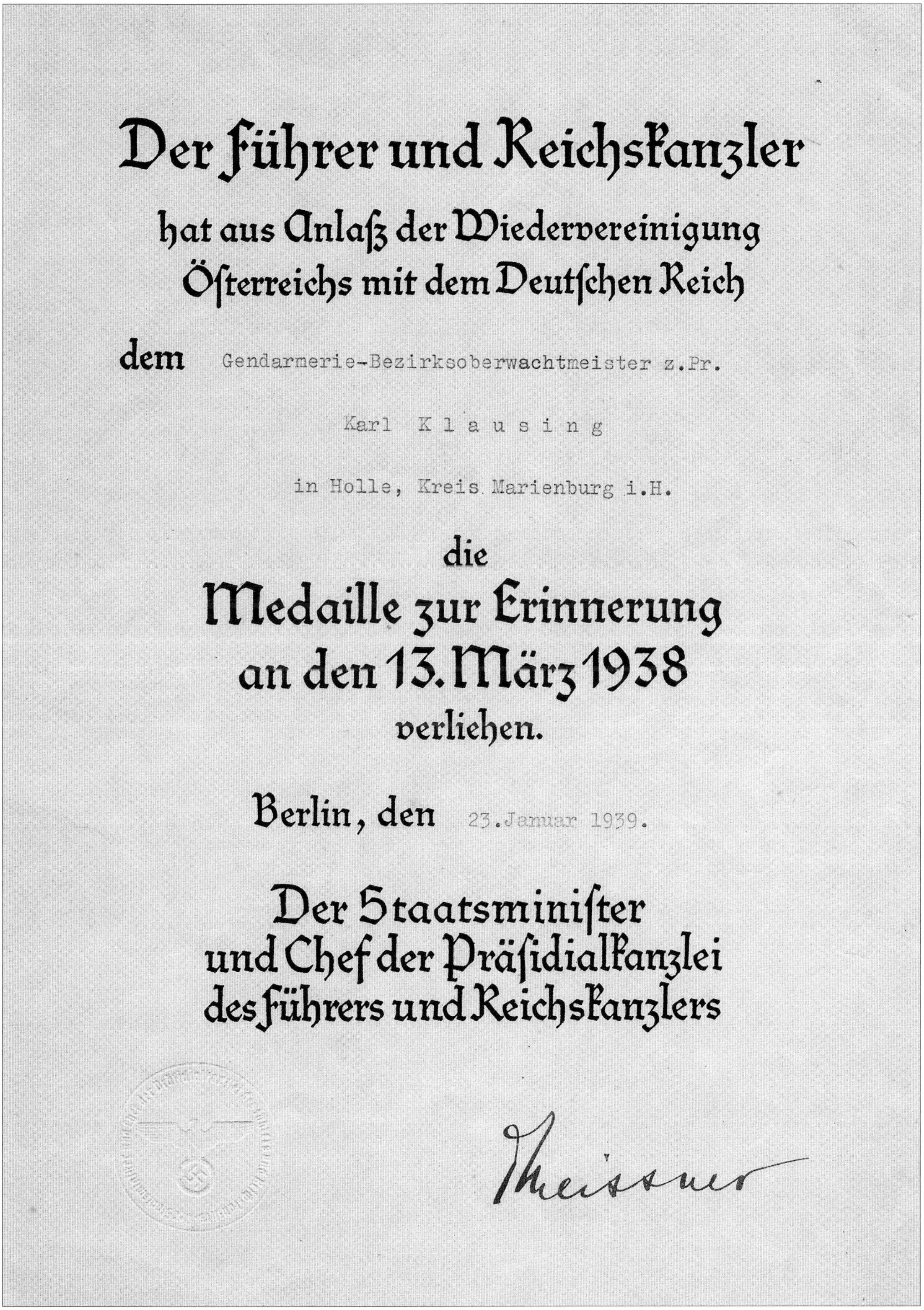

Der Führer und Reichskanzler

hat aus Anlaß der Wiedervereinigung
Österreichs mit dem Deutschen Reich

dem Gendarmerie-Bezirksoberwachtmeister z.Pr.

Karl Klausing

in Holle, Kreis Marienburg i.H.

die

Medaille zur Erinnerung
an den 13. März 1938

verliehen.

Berlin, den 23.Januar 1939.

Der Staatsminister
und Chef der Präsidialkanzlei
des Führers und Reichskanzlers

Meissner

# Im Namen des Führers
und
# Obersten Befehlshabers der Wehrmacht

verleihe ich

dem Unteroffizier Karl Tutzschky
(Dienstgrad, Vor- und Zuname)

3. Batterie Art. Regt. 60
(Truppenteil)

## die Medaille zur Erinnerung an den 1. Oktober 1938

O.U., den 12. Dezember 1939

Für die Richtigkeit

Hoffmann

Major u. Abteilungskommandeur
(Dienstgrad und Dienststellung)

(Stempel)

Der Kommandierende General
des IV. Armeekorps
und Befehlshaber im Wehrkreis IV

v. Schwedler

General der Infanterie

Nr. 9171/3
(des Verzeichnisses der Verleihungsbehörde)

*Opposite: An award document for the Annexation of Czechoslovakia Medal. This document was awarded on December 12, 1939 to an NCO in the 3rd. Battery of Artillery Regiment 60. The issuing authority was the Commanding General of the Fourth Army Corps, General der Infanterie Viktor von Schwedler. The document is signed by the Commander of the 1st. Battalion of Artillery Regiment 60, Major Hoffmann. 209mm x 296mm. $40-50.*

*Two examples of the Medal for the Return of the Memel District in single-place parade form. Both are mounted in traditional style. The medals are bronze. The example on the left measures 32.21mm in diameter and the example on the right is 32.17mm. Courtesy of George Robinson. $150-175 each.*

*Reverse of the two Memel Medals. The example on the left has steel mounting plates with an integral hinge/catch setup and steel pin. The example on the right has a zinc mounting plate with an integral hinge/catch setup and brass pin. Gray-green wool backing. Courtesy of George Robinson.*

The Medal of the German Red Cross was a medal with a very short history. Although there were German Red Cross Decorations as far back as 1922, the Medal of the German Red Cross did not exist until 1937. It was instituted in April of 1937, when the existing Red Cross Decorations were being redesigned for a third and final time. The last design change involved the addition of the swastika, which was not featured on Red Cross Decorations prior to 1937. Then in May of 1939, all awards of the German Red Cross were superseded by the Social Welfare Decorations. Red Cross Decorations were no longer to be awarded, but they could still be worn by those that already had one. And if a recipient was subsequently awarded with a Social Welfare Decoration of the same class, the Social Welfare Decoration was to be worn in lieu of the Red Cross Decoration.

The Medal of the German Red Cross is an attractive award. They should be considered scarce since they were only manufactured and awarded over a period of two years. The medal is not seen often on a medal bar, and they are even hard to find un-mounted. Originals of this medal should be well made. As far as I know, they were all die-struck from tombak bronze. The medal was finished in darkened silver, and features white and red enamel work. The white enamel should be opaque, while the red is translucent. There is an eagle clutching a wreathed-swastika applied to the center of the medal. The eagle and swastika feature black enamel work with gilt-finished highlights. The reverse of the medal has the inscription, "for service in the Red Cross." Every original example I have seen has a ball-type suspension eyelet that is an integral part of the medal. The suspension ring is usually very small on these medals. I have never seen one with a marking, so identifying manufacturers is practically impossible. I do know that Godet of Berlin manufactured some of the higher classes of Red Cross Decorations, so in all likelihood they made the Red Cross Medal as well. There were probably only a few firms that manufactured Red Cross Decorations. I measured the diameters of two original medals. One was 38.10mm and the other was 38.15mm. I would not expect to see much size variance on these medals, especially if only made by a few manufacturers.

The Medal for German Social Welfare was the replacement for the short-lived Red Cross Medal. It was instituted in May of 1939 and remained in use until Germany's defeat in 1945. The Social Welfare Medal was nowhere near as attractive as the medal it replaced. It was a simple round medal with no enameling. On the front, an eagle and swastika is superimposed over a large Red Cross symbol. The reverse bears the inscription, "Medal for German Social Welfare." Social Welfare Medals were finished in darkened silver. Early production pieces were struck from tombak, then zinc and *kriegsmetall* became the standard from about 1942 onwards. The medals made from zinc and *kriegsmetall* usually have an unattractive, dark gray appearance. Examples made from tombak have a separately applied suspension eyelet, while the zinc examples have an integral eyelet. Occasionally, a marking might be found on the suspension ring. The only marking I have noted has been the Lieferant code number "3" of Wilhelm Deumer, seen on two zinc examples. From an original issue packet, I can also confirm that the Bavarian Central Mint in Munich also produced Social Welfare Medals. Tombak examples seem to be consistent in size. The diameters of three that I measured were 38.02mm, 38.02mm, and 38.07mm. A die-forged, zinc example by Deumer measured 38.43mm.

*Single-place bar of the Medal of the German Red Cross. 38.10mm in diameter. $200-225.*

*Reverse of the Medal of the German Red Cross medal bar. Brass pin and catch, zinc mounting plate, and red wool felt backing.*

*Single-place bar of the Medal for German Social Welfare. 38.02mm in diameter. $50-60.*

*Reverse of the Medal for German Social Welfare medal bar. Sheet steel mounting plates with integral hinge and catch mounts. Steel pin and catch.*

*Opposite: Example of an award document for the Social Welfare Medal. The document was awarded to a German Red Cross helper on March 7, 1941. The document has a large, embossed seal of "der Führer." It bears the facsimile signature of Adolf Hitler, and the counter-signature of the State Minister, Otto Meissner. 209mm x 296mm. $45-55.*

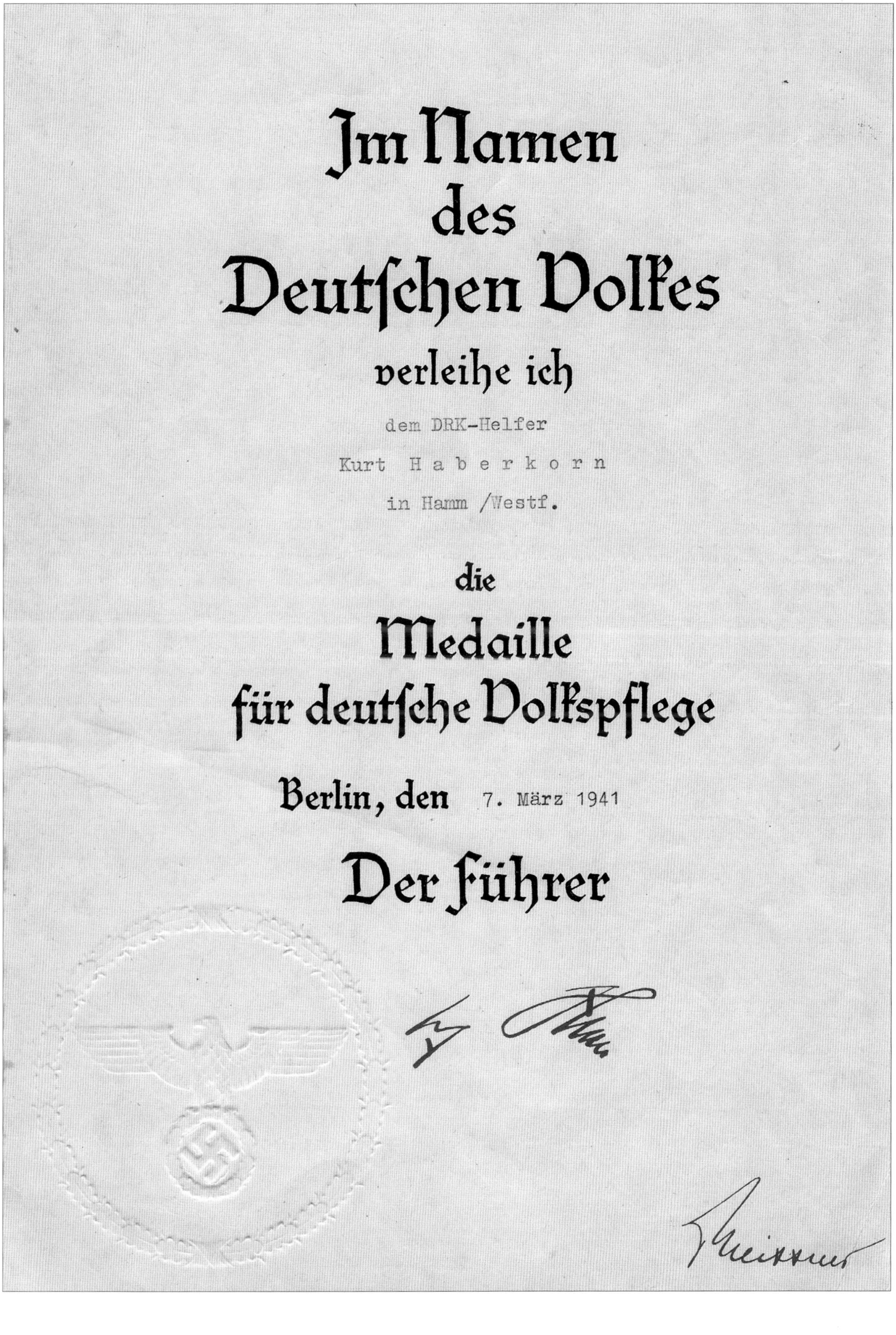

Im Namen
des
Deutschen Volkes
verleihe ich

dem DRK-Helfer

Kurt H a b e r k o r n

in Hamm /Westf.

die
Medaille
für deutsche Volkspflege

Berlin, den 7. März 1941

Der Führer

Long Service Awards will be covered in more detail as they appear in the appropriate chapters. In general though, they were worn on a cornflower blue ribbon. The only exception to this was the NSDAP Long Service Awards, which had their own characteristic ribbon. Anytime you see a cornflower blue ribbon on a German medal bar, you should immediately recognize that the particular medal was awarded for a period of long and faithful service. On the medal bar, long service awards should be placed after bravery and merit decorations and before annexation, commemorative, and foreign awards. The different long service awards were instituted in the mid to late 1930s, prior to the start of World War II. The quality and finish of most were excellent. Long service awards were not produced from zinc, except for some of the 10-Year NSDAP Long Service Crosses. Long service awards of the German Armed Forces were made from iron and tombak. Long service awards of the German Police, as well as the civilian Faithful Service Decorations, were made from tombak. Awards for the National Labor Service were aluminum or tombak. NSDAP Long Service Awards were made of tombak or aluminum for the 15- and 25-year, and aluminum or zinc for the 10-year.

*Single-place medal bar of the Armed Forces 4-Year Long Service Medal. This example is mounted in Bavarian style. Iron medal and eagle device. 30.07mm in diameter. $45-50.*

*Medal bar reverse. Steel mounting plate with integral catch and a brass pin. Green wool backing material.*

*Single-place medal bar of the Armed Forces 4-Year Long Service Medal. Another example of a Bavarian style mounting. Iron medal and a non-magnetic eagle device. 29.79mm in diameter. $45-50.*

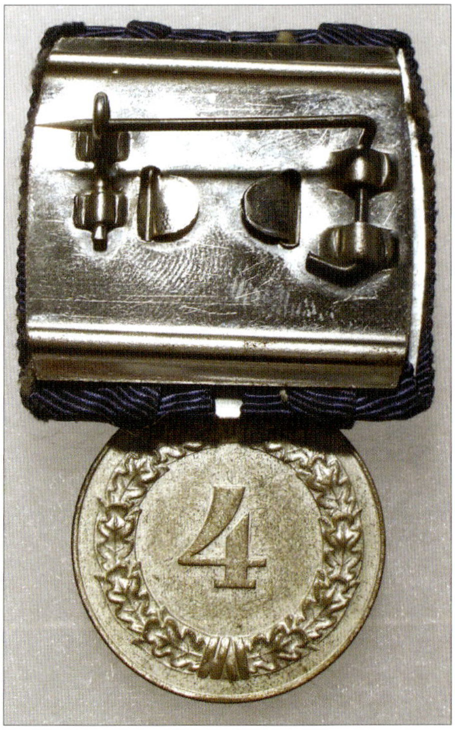

*Medal bar reverse. Nickel-plated, steel plates with a steel pin and catch.*

*Armed Forces 4-Year Long Service Medal mounted in tradition style. Iron medal and eagle device. 30.02mm in diameter. $45-50.*

*Medal bar reverse. Steel mounting plate with a brass, "tinnie" style pin. Black wool backing cloth.*

*Another example of the 4-Year Long Service Medal mounted in traditional style. $45-50.*

*Medal bar reverse. Sheet steel mounting plates (nickel-plated), with a steel pin and catch.*

*Single-place medal bar of the Luftwaffe 4-Year Long Service Medal, mounted in modified traditional style. Both the medal and Luftwaffe eagle device are made of iron. $50-60.*

*Medal bar reverse. Zinc mounting plate with applied, brass hinge and catch. Brass pin. White cotton batting and green wool backing.*

*This German Army NCO wears the 4-Year Long Service Medal in parade form.*

*Single-place medal bar of the Armed Forces 12-Year Long Service Medal, mounted in traditional style. It is unusual to find the 12-Year Medal mounted singly. Anyone rating the 12-Year Medal would also have the 4-Year Medal, and regulations allowed for both medals to be worn on the medal bar. Iron with matt gold finish. Eagle device is also struck in iron. 30.27mm in diameter. $60-70.*

*Medal bar reverse. Nickel-plated, steel mounting plates with integral hinge/catch setup. Brass pin. Charcoal gray, cotton broadcloth backing.*

*This Luftwaffe NCO wears the Luftwaffe 4-Year Long Service Medal in parade form. Photo was taken in December of 1938.*

Single-place medal bar of the 10-Year NSDAP Long Service Cross. This example is a one-piece, lightweight version, made of aluminum. $150-175.

Reverse of the 10-Year NSDAP medal bar. Zinc mounting plates with integral catch, copper pin, and gray-green wool backing.

Single-place medal bar of the 8-Year Police Long Service Medal. Tombak with a matt silver finish. 38.15mm in diameter. Courtesy of George Robinson. $125-140.

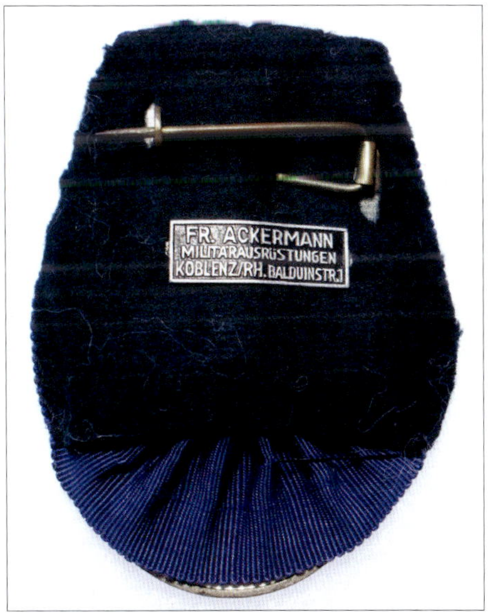


Reverse of the 8-Year Police medal bar. Note the metal assembler tag. Zinc mounting plates, brass pin, hinge, and catch. Dark blue, wool backing cloth. Courtesy of George Robinson.

Ribboned awards of the Third Reich were issued in a case, box, or paper packet. Some of the medals, usually those in a case or box, had the medal pre-mounted with a brooch pin attachment for individual wear. This was common for awards such as the Annexation Medals, Faithful Service Decorations, Labor Service Awards, Luftschutz Honor Awards, and the 8-Year Police Medals. The vast majority of other ribboned awards were issued in paper packets. The medal was wrapped in tissue paper and came with an un-mounted length of ribbon. Once awarded, it was then up to the recipient to have the medal properly mounted for wear. Awards such as the Iron Cross Second Class, War Merit Cross Second Class, War Merit Medal, Russian Front Medal, and Defense Wall Medal were typically issued in this manner.

*Above: Medals such as these were usually awarded in a case or box. (L-R): 40-Year Faithful Service Decoration, with case. $110. 25-Year Faithful Service Decoration, with box. $70. Austrian Annexation Medal, with case. $90. Czech Annexation Medal and Prague Castle Bar, with case. $140. 25-Year Police Long Service Cross, with case. $250.*

*Opposite*

*Top: Some ribboned medals, like the ones shown here, were usually issued with pre-mounted ribbons and brooch pin attachments. An obverse and reverse view is shown for each. Top row (L-R): Bravery and Merit Decoration for the Eastern Volunteers Second Class in Gold. $75. Bravery and Merit Decoration for the Eastern Volunteers Second Class in Silver. $65. Czech Annexation Medal with Prague Castle Bar. $90. Austrian Annexation Medal. $50. Bottom row (L-R): 40-Year Faithful Service Decoration. $60. 25-Year Faithful Service Decoration. $40. 8-Year Police Long Service Medal. $100. 4-Year Long Service Award of the National Labor Service. $90.*

*Bottom: Here is a selection of ribboned medals that were usually awarded in paper packets. These medals were issued with a length of un-mounted ribbon. From (L-R): 1939 War Merit Cross Second Class with Swords, by Franz Jungwirth. $45. Medal for the 1941/42 Winter Battle in the East, by Rudolf Souval. $55. 1939 War Merit Medal, by Richard Simm & Söhne. $35. 1939 Iron Cross Second Class, by Richard Simm & Söhne. $125. 1939 War Merit Cross Second Class with Swords, by Rudolf Leukert. $50. 1939 War Merit Cross Second Class without Swords, by Friedrich Keller. $45.*

EIN VOLK EIN REICH EIN FÜHRER
1. OKTOBER 1938
Für treue Dienste

Kriegs-
Verdienstkreuz
2. Klasse
Medaille
„Winterschlacht im Osten
1941/42"
(Ostmedaille)
Kriegs-
Verdienstmedaille
1939
Eisernes Kreuz
2. Klasse
1939
Kriegs-
Verdienstkreuz
2. Klasse
mit Schwertern
Kriegs-
Verdienstkreuz
2. Klasse
ohne Schwerter

*This is an original sample board from the manufacturing firm, Wilhelm Deumer of Lüdenscheid. It features an assortment of ribboned medals, pin back decorations, badges, and campaign shields. All of the awards displayed on this board were produced by Deumer. They were one of the largest producers of awards during the Third Reich Period. $1000.*

In addition to ribboned awards that were worn on the medal bar, Germany awarded many different kinds of pin-back decorations, qualification badges, and combat badges. With but a few exceptions, these awards were worn below the medal or ribbon bar, on the wearer's left side. Unlike ribboned awards, these badges and decorations were worn on service and combat tunics as well as the formal dress uniform. Ribboned medals were not worn on the service and combat uniforms, except in the form of a ribbon bar or buttonhole ribbon. The medal bar was only worn on the dress uniform for special occasions.

Some of the badges and decorations, such as the Iron Cross First Class, German Cross, and Wound Badges, could be awarded to all three branches of the Armed Forces. Additionally, the Army, Navy, and Air Force all had qualification and combat badges that were exclusive to their branch. The pictures show a selection of some of these types of awards. The photo captions will identify the award and the manufacturer. A value is also shown for the items illustrated. Bear in mind that values can vary significantly depending on condition, rarity, maker, and whether the badge is made of buntmetall or zinc. As with ribboned awards, qualification and combat badges could be issued in cases, boxes, or paper packets. Other than this basic information, badges and pin back decorations will not be examined further as that is beyond the scope of this book.

*A selection of decorations and badges that were used by all branches of the German Armed Forces. Top row (L-R): 1939 Wound Badge in Gold, by Carl Wild of Hamburg. $200. 1939 Wound Badge in Silver, made by the Vienna State Mint. $80. 1939 Wound Badge in Black, by Wilhelm Deumer of Lüdenscheid. $30. Middle row (L-R): 1939 Clasp to the 1914 Iron Cross First Class, paired with a 1914 Iron Cross by Wagner & Sohn. $425 and $225 respectively. 1941 German Cross in Gold, by C. F. Zimmermann of Pforzheim. $2000. At the lower right is a 1939 Iron Cross First Class, by Paul Meybauer. $250.*

*Above: A selection of combat badges that were awarded by the German Army. Clockwise from top: Close Combat Clasp in Silver, by Funcke & Brüninghaus. $300. Infantry Assault Badge in Bronze, by Josef Feix Söhne. $175. Army Flak Badge, by Hermann Aurich of Dresden. $550. Panzer Assault Badge in Bronze, possibly made by Schwerdt or Scholze. $275. Panzer Assault Badge in Silver, made by Schwerdt or Scholze. $275. General Assault Badge, by Rudolf Karneth of Gablonz. $140. Infantry Assault Badge in Silver, made by Schwerdt or Scholze. $150.*

*Opposite: A selection of original combat badges awarded by the German Navy. Top row (L-R): Minesweeper Badge, probably made by Juncker. $200. Auxiliary Cruiser Badge, by Schwerin of Berlin. $750. High Seas Fleet Badge by Schwerin of Berlin. $275. Middle row (L-R): S-Boat Badge 1st. type, by Steinhauer & Lück of Lüdenscheid. $650. S-Boat Badge 2nd. type, by Rudolf Souval of Vienna. $375. Blockade Runner Badge, by Schwerin of Berlin. $325. Bottom row (L-R): Destroyer Badge, by Steinhauer & Lück. $350. U-Boat Badge, by Funcke & Brüninghaus of Lüdenscheid. $325. Coastal Artillery Badge, by Juncker of Berlin. $275.*

*A selection of German Air Force qualification and combat badges. Top row (L-R): Combined Pilot/Observer Badge, probably made by Friedrich Linden of Lüdenscheid. $500. Air Gunner/Radio Operator Badge, by Brüder Schneider of Vienna. $400. Paratrooper Badge, by Paul Meybauer of Berlin. $475. Middle row (L-R): Pilot Badge, probably made by Friedrich Linden. $350. Air Gunner/Flight Engineer Badge, by Juncker of Berlin. $475. Ground Assault Badge, by Gustav Brehmer of Markneukirchen. $275. Bottom row (L-R): Bomber Clasp in Gold, by Richard Simm & Söhne (above) and Reconnaissance Clasp in Bronze, by Brüder Schneider (below) $325 and $275 respectively. Flak Badge, by Juncker of Berlin. $250.*

# MEDAL BARS OF THE GERMAN POLICE

Collecting German Police medal bars has always been an area of special interest for me. Whenever I go to a militaria show and find a police medal bar for sale, it is hard to resist buying it. I especially like the medal bars that have a Police Long Service Cross in combination with a 1936 Olympic Games Commemorative Medal. German Police medal bars are somewhat common in the collector market. This is probably because there were a large number of policemen utilized during the Third Reich Period. Since most were on the home front, maintaining order in the towns and cities, they had more time for things such as having their medals mounted. They also had more opportunities to wear their medals. A soldier fighting on the front had little time to even think of such formalities.

This is a beautifully made, four-place *Ordensschnalle* (medal bar) of a German policeman (**page 48**). The Iron Cross has a magnetic iron core and obverse and reverse frames of .800 silver. Several areas of rust are visible on the iron core, where the black finish has come off, leaving the bare iron exposed to the effects of air and humidity. The silver frames appear very dull and even black in places. This effect is unavoidable, and is the result of the silver's exposure to the air. It is usually referred to as oxidation or tarnish. The Cross of Honor is made of iron and has a bronze finish. On the reverse, it is maker marked with a stylized "JK" within a triangle. The Police Long Service Cross is of excellent quality. It is die-struck tombak bronze with a gold-plated finish, applied by a process known as fire gilding. The finish on these crosses holds up well over time so most of these awards look as nice today as when they were made. The ribbon of the Police Long Service Cross displays the police insignia, which is machine-embroidered in thread of golden yellow cotton. The 1936 Olympic Commemorative Medal is die-struck iron with a silver finish. The ribbon is reddish-orange, with black edges and five narrow white stripes in the center to represent the five Olympic rings. The Olympic rings are also depicted on the medal, above the eagle. This medal was awarded to persons who took part in the planning and/or running of the Olympic Games, held in Germany in 1936. The medal is scarce, as less than 55,000 were awarded.[1] It is however, somewhat common to find on a police medal bar. A large number of the recipients of this award were policemen, who worked at the Olympic Games in their official capacity.

This medal bar follows the regulations to the letter, and the arrangement of the medals is completely correct. The Iron Cross is worn first, being a valor decoration. Next is the Cross of Honor, which was Nazi Germany's only award given to recognize service in World War I. When this award was instituted in 1934, it was intended to replace many of the unofficial state awards that were issued to veterans by the different states of Imperial Germany.[2] This was to show that the new Germany was no longer a number of divided states, but one united nation. Some veterans however, chose to ignore this regulation and continued to wear their unofficial state awards. Police long service awards were given for 8, 18, and 25 years of service, and military service time was counted towards years of police service. The owner of this bar earned the 25-Year Long Service Cross, so obviously he rated the 8-Year Medal and the 18-Year Cross as well. The regulations stipulated though, that only one police long service award could be worn, and the recipient would wear the highest one that he rated. Since the 1936 Olympic Medal is a commemorative medal, it is worn last on this bar, after the long service award.

The reverse of this bar shows the same superb workmanship. The bar has a backing of fine quality, mouse gray wool. The pin and catch are steel. The mounting plate is magnetic, and has a nickel-silver finish to it. This bar also has the nice custom touch of a maker's label, which is sewn to the backing cloth. Labels are not seen too often on medal bars. I would estimate that only about five to ten percent of medal bars will have a maker label on them. This label is of the medals and decorations shop of Bruno Görlich. This label represents the shop that assembled the medal bar, not the manufacturer of the actual medals. On the lower right part of the label is the street address for the shop, which was located in Berlin. I wonder if the shop is still in business.

This five-place medal bar (**page 49**) belonged to a World War I veteran and long-time policeman. It is another example of a well made bar, worn with pride and taken care of over the years. The ribbons on this bar are nicely wrapped, and they are padded underneath to give them a fuller appearance. The medals' suspension rings are sewn down inside. In addition, string secures each medal at the suspension eyelets, and even on the lower cross arms on a couple of the medals. If you look closely, you can see the string on the Lippe-Detmold War Merit Cross, immediately below the center blossom. The Cross of Honor is tied down just above each of the sword hilts. String once secured the lower arm of the Iron Cross as well, but it has broken away. The Iron Cross is the usual three-part construction with a magnetic center. Tarnish is very evident on the frames. The War Merit Cross of Lippe-Detmold is die-struck bronze, with

*A four-place German Police medal bar. The medals are from (L-R): 1914 Iron Cross Second Class, 1914-1918 Cross of Honor with Swords, 25-Year Police Long Service Cross, and the 1936 Olympic Games Commemorative Medal. $350-400.*

*Medal bar reverse. Note the assembler label from the shop of Bruno Görlich of Berlin.*

*A five-place German Police medal bar. The medals are from (L-R): 1914 Iron Cross Second Class, 1914 Lippe-Detmold War Merit Cross Second Class, 1914-1918 Cross of Honor with Swords, Prussian Military Long Service Medal Third Class (for 9 years of service), and the 25 Year Police Long Service Cross. $325-375.*

*Medal bar reverse.*

a beautiful gilded finish. It is a scarce decoration as only about 18,000 of these were awarded.[3] This was Lippe-Detmold's primary valor decoration, comparable to the Prussian Iron Cross. Both the Kingdom of Prussia and the Principality of Lippe-Detmold decorated this man for bravery in World War I, and both of these decorations are worn on combatant ribbons. For non-combatant versions of these awards, the ribbon colors would be reversed. (The black and white would swap places on the Iron Cross ribbon, and the yellow and white would swap positions on the Lippe-Detmold War Merit Cross ribbon.) The Cross of Honor is bronze finished iron. The maker marking cannot be seen because the cross is securely tied down. The Prussian Long Service Medal is die-struck and made of solid nickel-silver. The Police Long Service Cross is the typical fire gilded finish over tombak.

On the reverse of this bar, we see nicely gathered, semi-circular rosettes. There are some knotted string ends visible for where the lower cross arms are tied down. All of the mounting and attachment hardware on this medal bar is made of steel and magnetic. Both the pin and catch are made of round wire stock. The mounting plate has a nickel finish. The protective cloth, covering the mounting plate, is ribbed cotton twill. The color of the backing material is a close match to the cornflower blue of the long service ribbons. The hand stitching with heavy thread is very evident along the top edge of the backing material. The raw cut edges of the cloth show quite a bit of fraying, especially along the bottom.

*A close up of the 1914 War Merit Cross Second Class of the Principality of Lippe-Detmold. This decoration is not seen often on a medal bar. Notice how string secures the lower cross arm, directly below the center blossom.*

With medal bars, bigger is not necessarily better. Here is an attractive two-place medal bar (**below**) that shows much character. The recipient had no World War I service, as he was probably too young at the time. In the years between the wars, he accumulated service time as a policeman, and his police service probably continued through World War II. The War Merit Cross without Swords was awarded for outstanding service that was not directly related to combat in the field. This example is early quality, die-struck solid bronze. The cross displays beautiful age toning that only time can achieve. It would be very difficult to duplicate this natural aging by chemical/artificial means. The Police 18-Year Cross is also of excellent quality. It is made of die-struck tombak bronze, with a frosted silver finish and burnished highlights. On the ribbon of the long service award, the police insignia is machine-embroidered with light gray cotton thread. At

*Two-place German Police Medal Bar. The medals are from (L-R): 1939 War Merit Cross Second Class without Swords, and the 18-Year Police Long Service Cross. Right: Medal bar reverse. $200-225.*

the time this bar was assembled, the owner had at least 18, but less than 25 years of service. The owner of this bar would have also rated the Police 8-Year medal, but per regulations, he only wore his highest service award. I would estimate that this bar was assembled in 1940 or 1941. The ribbons on this bar display a nice, but more simplified type of wrap. There are no rosettes formed at the bottom. This type of mounting is usually referred to as the "Bavarian style." The ribbons are padded underneath to enhance the overall appearance of the bar.

On the reverse of this two-place bar, the quality is still very evident. The pin is brass wire, and the catch was stamped out from brass sheet. The bar has a zinc mounting plate, which is covered by a protective backing of dark gray, cotton broadcloth. The cloth is hand-sewn on all four sides. I like this style of mounting because the reverse of each medal is completely visible. On the reverse of this long service cross, you can see some of the tombak base metal showing through in places where the silver finish is worn. The wording on the reverse reads, "For faithful service in the Police." The "1939" on the reverse of the War Merit Cross represents the year the award was instituted, not the date of award to the individual.

Here is another medal bar to a World War I veteran and career policeman (**below**). This "modified traditional style" three-place medal bar is another fine example of the quality of workmanship that went into the mounting of medals. The Cross of Honor is die-struck iron with a

*Three-place German Police medal bar. Medals are from (L-R): 1914-1918 Cross of Honor with Swords, 25-Year Police Long Service Cross, and the 1936 Olympic Games Commemorative Medal. $300-325.*

*Medal bar reverse.*

bronze finish. It is maker marked on the reverse with a stylized "JK" within a triangle. The Police Long Service Cross is tombak bronze with a matt gold finish and polished highlights. The police insignia on the ribbon is a separate attachment. The ribbon with the insignia was mounted to a metal plate, having two metal prongs on the reverse. This plate was then attached to the plain, cornflower blue ribbon below. The Olympic Medal is die-struck iron and is magnetic. The silver finish on this example has darkened with time, and the finish on the front now appears speckled and somewhat rough in texture. Most of the original Olympic Medals that I have seen over the years have been magnetic. However, there are also non-magnetic originals that were made from tombak bronze. Another point of interest on this bar can be seen at the top of the Cross of Honor and the Olympic Medal. You will notice that ribbon was used to cover the suspension eyelets of the medals and secure them to the mounting. These little extra touches really add character to a medal bar. Other than a little bit of natural age, this medal bar looks almost as good as the day it was made.

This is a well made medal bar on both the front and back. Even though the reverse of the medal bar was hidden from view, the assembler put as much care into the back of the bar as the front. On this example, "police" gray-green wool felt was used as a backing material. This color was used in making many of the police uniforms. Not all medal bars had cloth backings on the reverse, but this was pretty much the standard for pre-World War II and early wartime assemblies, especially if the work was done by a uniform or decorations shop. The backing was sewn into place with cotton thread of the same color. The bottom edge of the backing was cut with pinking shears. When the medal bar was worn, this backing cloth would protect the tunic from being damaged by the metal mounting plate. These thick, wire attachment pins were never pinned through the tunic either. They would have left large holes in the uniform, ruining its appearance. Instead, loops were sewn on the uniform at the place were the ribbon/medal bar would be worn. Loops were also sewn lower on the tunic at the places where other awards were worn, such as the Iron Cross First Class, assault/qualification badges, and wound badges. In this manner, the pins would pass through the loops, not the uniform. The pin and catch on this example are brass. The mounting plate, below the backing cloth, is zinc. Cotton batting was used to pad the ribbons, enhancing their appearance. Notice that the finish on the reverse of the Olympic Medal looks much brighter than on the front. This effect will be seen from time to time on medal bars. I think it happens because bars are usually stored right side up and therefore the front gets more exposure to air, lighting, etc. The reverse is more protected from air and light, and even the ribbons that cover some or all of the medal's reverse offer some protective effect. On silver, or silver-plated medals, it is common to see tarnish to a lesser degree on the reverse.

This "Bavarian style" two-place grouping (**below**) is almost in mint condition. The ribbon colors are still nice and bright, and the medals show only a minimal amount of wear. Undoubtedly, this bar was hardly, if ever worn. Over the years, it was stored well and cared for. This is another example of a medal bar belonging to a World War I veteran and career policeman. The medals are made of the usual base materials, and have the typical finishes. This particular Cross of Honor is a bit unusual, as it has no maker marking on the reverse. The majority of these are found with maker markings. As with most other medals to be found on a medal bar, the Police Long Service Cross would be marked on the suspension ring if even marked at all. The medals' suspension rings are usually covered over by the ribbons on parade mounts, so the markings cannot be seen if present. I do not recommend trying to poke around underneath the ribbons in hope of finding a maker marking on the suspension ring of a medal. Chances are that you will not find one anyway. The desire to locate a hidden marking is not worth taking the chance of damaging something, hence ruining the integrity of the medal bar. Long service awards, annexation medals, and commemorative medals were seldom maker marked, on the suspension ring or anywhere else for that matter. Other awards, such as the Iron Cross Second Class, 1939 War Merit Cross, and Russian Front Medal are frequently found with maker markings on the suspension ring. Even so, if the ring is not visible or easily accessible, it is better left alone.

*German Police two-place medal bar. The medals are from (L-R): 1914-1918 Cross of Honor with Swords, and the 25-Year Police Long Service Cross. Right: Medal bar reverse. $200-225.*

The reverse of this well made bar has tan colored, cotton broadcloth sewn in place over the zinc mounting plate. The catch on this bar is zinc, and the attachment pin is steel. The wording on the reverse of the Police 25-Year Long Service Cross is the same as on the 18-Year Cross. In fact, except for the color of finish, the 18 and 25-Year Police Long Service Crosses are identical, front and back.

This is without a doubt my favorite police medal bar (**below**). It is a very interesting bar because all of the awards are from the Third Reich Period. The majority of original police medal bars usually display a combination of Imperial and Third Reich awards. The owner of the bar was undoubtedly too young for military service in the First World War. He became a policeman, and accumulated at least 18 years of unbroken

*German Police medal bar consisting of all-Third Reich awards. The medals are from (L-R): 1939 War Merit Cross Second Class without Swords, 18-Year Police Long Service Cross, Medal for the Annexation of Czechoslovakia with attached Prague Castle Bar, Luftschutz Honor Award Second Class, and the 1936 Olympic Games Commemorative Medal. Below: Medal bar reverse. $450-475.*

service by the time this bar was assembled. The bar is definitely a wartime construction, not a pre-war assembly. The 1939 War Merit Cross confirms this as it was not instituted until October of 1939.[4] This bar was probably made sometime between 1940 and 1942, although it could have been even later in the war. Although there are five medals on this mounting, this is actually considered a six-place medal bar because of the clasp attached to the ribbon of the Czech Annexation Medal. This clasp, known as the Prague Castle Bar, is a separate award. When attached to the ribbon of the Czech Annexation Medal, it signifies that the recipient was involved in both the occupation of the Sudetenland of western Czechoslovakia, and the occupation of Bohemia and Moravia. While there were over a million Czech Annexation Medals awarded, there were less than 135,000 awards of the Prague Castle Bar.[5]

Despite some fading to the colors of the ribbons and darkening to the finishes on the medals, this bar still has a nice look to it. It is actually in very good condition, considering its age. The War Merit Cross is an early-war, solid bronze type. It shows uniform age darkening. The Police Long Service Cross shows some dulling and wear to the silver finish. Some of the tombak base metal is visible where the finish is worn. Both the Czech Annexation Medal and the Prague Castle Bar are non-magnetic. The bronze shows only light age and no darkening. The Luftschutz Honor Award is made of aluminum. This medal was instituted in January of 1938, to recognize those that served honorably in the civil defense of Germany, usually as a civil defense volunteer or as a member of the air raid protection service.[6] The inscription on the front of the medal reads, "For merit in the air defense." In addition to aluminum, Luftschutz Medals were also produced from zinc. The early-made ones were usually aluminum, and the later ones were typically in zinc. The 1936 Olympic Games Commemorative Medal on this bar has tarnished to an almost black appearance. The medal is die-struck iron with a silver-plated finish. The silver content of the finish must be quite high for it to tarnish to this degree.

The reverse of the medal bar is covered with medium gray wool that is hand-stitched in place. The lower edge of the backing has a deep, zigzag cut to it. The pin and catch are brass. The mounting plate is non-magnetic, and appears to be made of zinc. Only a small portion of the plate is visible at the lower-left corner of the bar. Notice that the reverse of the Olympic Medal has not tarnished to the extent that the front has. The degree of fading to the ribbons is about the same on the reverse as it is on the front.

*Both of these Luftschutz Honor Awards were produced by the same manufacturer. Each is marked with the number "60" on the suspension ring. This code number was used by the firm of Katz & Deyhle of Pforzheim. The example on the left is made of die-cast aluminum. It measures 40.33mm in diameter and weighs 14.3 grams. $55-75. The example to the right is die-forged zinc with a silvered finish. It measures 38.81mm in diameter and weighs 27.2 grams. $55-65.*

*The reverse of the aluminum (left) and zinc (right) versions of the Luftschutz Honor Award Second Class. The "1938" represents the year that the medal was instituted.*

### The Elusive 8-Year Police Long Service Medal

The 8-Year Medals are the most common of the Police Long Service Decorations. Obviously, more policemen would have received the 8-Year Medal as opposed to the 18 or 25-Year Crosses. The 8-Year Medal can be frequently found for sale by itself, but it is very seldom seen on a medal bar. In all the years that I have been collecting, I have only seen a couple of them on medal bars. So why are they so difficult to find on a medal bar? The answer to this question rests partly with the regulations for the wearing of Police Long Service Decorations. Regulations specified that only one Police Long Service Award could be worn, and the recipient would wear the highest service award that he was entitled to. The other part of the answer is a matter of age. Many of the policemen who served during the Third Reich Period were veterans of the First World War. They accumulated their years of police service between the wars. By the time the Second World War began, these men were generally too old to be conscripted into the armed forces, so they continued to perform their duties as policemen. For the younger policemen though, it was an entirely different story. Once the war began, they were probably needed more as soldiers, sailors, and airmen rather than as policemen. So as unusual as it may seem, it is the 25-Year Cross that is encountered most often on a police medal bar. How strange it is when the common becomes scarce and the scarce, common.

This six-place medal bar (**page 56**) belonged to another career policeman. He served during World War I in some non-combatant role. This large grouping of awards looks impressive; but the bar consists mostly of commemorative medals for service in World War I. There are no valor decorations on this bar. The scarcest awards are the medals in the second and third positions. The other medals are very common. Still, it is an attractive looking medal bar that was assembled with skill and care. The Cross of Honor is correctly placed first on the bar, but the 1936 Olympic Medal should not be in the second position. The Police Long Service Cross should actually be second on this bar, and the Olympic Medal should be in the third position. Errors such as this will be seen from time to time on original medal bars. **Remember that a bar is not necessarily a fake just because it is assembled somewhat contrary to**

*Obverse (left) and reverse (right) of the 8-Year Police Long Service Medal. The medal was die-struck from tombak bronze and finished in frosted silver. It measures 38.15mm in diameter. The medal was worn on a plain, cornflower blue ribbon. Most original 8-Year Medals are found with a brooch pin, attached to the top reverse of the ribbon. The inscription on the reverse reads, "For faithful service in the police." $75-100.*

*The 25-Year Cross was the highest of the Police Long Service Decorations. This example is in mint condition, and is shown alongside the original issue case. The 18-Year Cross was usually issued in a similar style case, but having the number "18" and the oak leaves embossed in silver rather than gold. The 8-Year Medal was issued in a simpler, green colored box. The box lid would have the number "8" within a circle, embossed in silver. $250-275.*

**the regulations.** However, no original medal bar should show a total and blatant disregard for all the regulations. After examining this bar in-hand, there is no doubt in my mind that this is entirely genuine. Even the pictures alone send out strong indications of originality. So why does it not follow the regulations to the letter? There are a number of possible reasons for this. In the first place, it may have been a simple mistake and nothing more. The medal bars were assembled by human beings so mistakes were bound to occur. Another explanation could be a matter of ignorance. Just because a person is handy with a needle and thread and has the other skills necessary to assemble a medal bar, it does not make them an expert on military regulations. In addition, the regulations were complicated and even changed from time to time as more awards were instituted. The very nature of regulations can lead to all sorts of misinterpretations. Regulations can be confusing enough for those in the military, let alone a civilian trying to assemble the bar. The civilian worker was more concerned with producing a nice looking piece of work rather than understanding all the written technicalities. I would think that a mistake like the one seen on this bar would simply be overlooked by higher authority. This kind of thing would not get you a date with the firing squad nor shipped off to the Russian Front. When I look at this particular medal bar, I also see one other possible explanation for the incorrect placement of the two medals. It may have been done intentionally to give the bar a more balanced look. With the 18-Year Police Cross placed nearer the center, the bar does have a more pleasing appearance. If the Police Long Service Cross was where it should be in the second position, the bar would not look as nice and all sense of balance would be lost.

The reverse of the medal bar has a cloth backing of what appears to be a loose-weave of gray woolen fibers. Several damaged areas on the backing are probably the work of some hungry moth. The mounting plate is zinc, and the pin and catch are brass. The label of the shop that assembled the medal bar is stitched to the backing material. In this case, the shop of Louis Kase, located in Stettin. The 1914-1918 Cross of Honor and the 1936 Olympic Medal are both magnetic and made of iron. All of the other medals on this bar are made of non-magnetic metals. The reverse of the Cross of Honor is marked, "O u C L" within a diamond. This logo was used by the manufacturer: Overhoff and Cie, located in Lüdenscheid.

On this five-place medal bar (**page 57**), we see a mostly common grouping of awards set off by the inclusion of a very scarce award at the center. This bar belonged to a veteran of World War I, who then served as either a volunteer or an active member of the Fire Police. The Iron Cross is the usual three-part construction, with a magnetic iron core. The silver framing has darkened with tarnish. The Cross of Honor is also magnetic, with a bronze finish over iron. The Fire Brigade Decoration is made of tombak bronze with a silver finish and enamel work of white, reddish-orange, and black. The center disc, with the swastika, is a separate piece that was soldered into place. The Fire Brigade Decoration was instituted in December of 1936.[7] It was awarded to both active and volunteer members in recognition of 25 years of service. This award is seldom found on a medal bar. Both the Hungarian and Bulgarian World War I Commemorative Medals are die-struck from some sort of non-magnetic alloys. The Hungarian Medal has an antiqued silver finish,

*A six-place German Police medal bar. The medals are from (L-R): 1914-1918 Cross of Honor without Swords, 1936 Olympic Games Commemorative Medal, 18-Year Police Long Service Cross, Hungarian World War I Commemorative Medal, World War I Commemorative Medal for Austria, and the Bulgarian World War I Commemorative Medal. $325-375.*

*Medal bar reverse. Note the assembler label from the shop of Louis Kase of Stettin.*

*A five-place Fire Police medal bar. The medals are from (L-R): 1914 Iron Cross Second Class, 1914-1918 Cross of Honor with Swords, Fire Brigade Decoration Second Class, Hungarian World War I Commemorative Medal, and the Bulgarian World War I Commemorative Medal. Below: Medal bar reverse. $300-325.*

while the Bulgarian Medal has a bright gilt finish. The Hungarian Medal was instituted in May of 1929.[8] It was awarded with swords and helmet for combatants and without swords and helmet for non-combatants. The Bulgarian Medal was instituted in December of 1933 and awards continued until the end of 1939.[9] All the medals on this bar have been secured with heavy thread across the suspension eyelets. In addition, the three crosses are all secured at some lower point. The Iron cross is secured across the lower cross arm, the Cross of Honor is secured just above the left sword hilt, and the Fire Brigade Decoration is secured directly below the left cross arm.

On the reverse, the medal bar is backed with gray-green wool. There is a deep, zigzag cut along the bottom edge of the backing. The pin is steel and the catch is brass. The front mounting plates are steel and the rear mounting plate is brass.

On this five-place medal bar (**opposite**), we see the same combination of medals that are on the Fire Police medal bar shown previously. The only difference being that this one has the 25-Year Police Long Service Cross in the third position, instead of the Fire Brigade Decoration. All of the medals on this bar are of the typical base materials, constructions, and finishes. The Cross of Honor is marked on the reverse, "F.L." for the manufacturer, Franz Lipp of Pforzheim. The reverse of the medal bar is backed with gray-green wool. The pin and catch are made of brass, and the mounting plates are steel with a brass finish.

While this four-place Fire Police medal bar (**page 60**) does have two nice enameled awards on it, the overall quality of the bar leaves much to be desired. In fact, it is quite an unattractive looking medal bar. The staggered mounting of the medals allows for less overlap, but the bar would look nicer if the medals were aligned on a single plane. The ribbons have a simple wrap around their mounting plates, and they have a very flat look to them, as there is no padding underneath to enhance their appearance. A mounting such as this may have been a homemade job, done by the recipient himself or a member of his family. It would not have been assembled by a shop that specialized in doing fine quality, custom work. Overall quality can vary considerably on medal bars. Much depended on where the work was done and who did the work. Another factor may have been what the customer was willing to pay to have the work done. The shops charged the customer for the work they did, so the more time and labor that went into the assembly, the more expensive the end product. I suppose that medal bars were in a way like an officer purchasing a custom-made uniform from a tailor shop. The more you paid, the finer the product. Despite the sub-par quality of this bar, it would still serve its purpose. The order of the medals on the bar is exactly per regulations. The Iron Cross has the usual three-part construction with an iron core. The Hamburg Hanseatic Cross is tombak bronze with a silver-plated finish and translucent red enamel. This attractive medal was instituted by the City of Hamburg in September of 1915.[10] It was awarded to those from the Hamburg area who served in World War I. The medal could be given for bravery or for war merit. There was only a single class of this medal, and both officer and enlisted ranks were eligible to receive the award. In addition to Hamburg, two other German port cities (Bremen and Lübeck) instituted their own Hanseatic Crosses. The three Hanseatic Crosses were all identical except for the round medallion on the front. The medallion depicted the coat-of-arms for the particular city. About 50,000 Hamburg Hanseatic Crosses were awarded.[11] The Bremen and Lübeck Crosses are scarcer. The Cross of Honor is iron with a bronze finish. It is maker marked on the reverse, "R.V.43. PFORZHEIM." The Fire Brigade decoration is tombak with a silver finish and opaque enamel of reddish-orange, white, and black.

*Obverse detail view of the Fire Brigade Decoration Second Class. These medals were well made. The base metal is usually tombak with a silver finish. The enamel portions should be opaque. The wording on the front reads, "For merit in the Fire Brigade." There are fairly good quality fakes of this medal in circulation. The majority of the fakes are completely flat-backed. Personally, I would not buy one of these unless the reverse is slightly concave. The central disc on these is a separate attachment.*

The reverse of this bar shows the same lack of custom touches. There is no cloth backing to this bar. All the mounting hardware is steel, except for the pin, which is brass. The steel plates are nickel-plated. Not having a cloth backing in place allows us to see how the bar was assembled. The back mounting plate has an integral catch and pin hinge that were stamped from the plate and bent out. The short end of the pin was fed through the hinge and bent up to keep it from falling out. Eight slots are cut into the mounting plate. On this mounting, each medal has its own front mounting plate. The front has a clip for attaching the medal, and the reverse has two locking tabs. The ribbon for the medal was wrapped around the front plate. The medals were then inserted into the bar one at a time. The two tabs of each medal's front plate would be inserted into the slots of the back plate and then bent over. This would lock the plates together and clamp the ribbons between them. Because of the overlap of the front plates, it is obvious that the medals were inserted into the back plate in reverse order. The Fire Brigade Decoration was inserted first, then the Cross of Honor, the Hamburg Hanseatic Cross, and lastly, the Iron Cross.

*A five-place German Police medal bar. The medals are from (L-R): 1914 Iron Cross Second Class, 1914-1918 Cross of Honor with Swords, 25-Year Police Long Service Cross, World War I Hungarian Commemorative Medal, and the World War I Bulgarian Commemorative Medal. Below: Medal bar reverse. $275-300.*

*Four-place Fire Police medal bar. The medals are from (L-R): 1914 Iron Cross Second Class, Hamburg Hanseatic Cross, 1914-1918 Cross of Honor with Swords, and the Fire Brigade Decoration Second Class. Below: Medal bar reverse. $300-325.*

This three-place medal bar (**page 62**) is another fine example of a German Police grouping, mounted in the modified traditional fashion. The owner of this bar was a combatant in World War I, but did not receive the Iron Cross Second Class. In World War II he was decorated for outstanding service by virtue of the 1939 War Merit Cross without Swords. The award placement on this bar is completely according to regulations. The War Merit Cross is an early-war example, made of solid bronze. There is no maker marking on the suspension ring. The Cross of Honor is iron with a bronze finish. In all my years of collecting, I have never seen a Cross of Honor made from anything other than iron. Every one that I have checked has been magnetic. The reverse of this example is marked, "G19." The Police Long Service Cross is tombak bronze with the usual fire gilded finish. It still looks bright, as this type of finish is quite durable. The first two medals on this bar are removable. You will notice that there are metal clips visible on the front of the bar. If you would push down on the uppermost part of the clip, the suspension ring can be lifted out, totally freeing the medal from the bar. In a way, this is a nice feature because it allows you to better study the medals individually if so desired. Even without removing the medals, it allows a clear view of the suspension ring if trying to locate a maker marking. In my opinion, it is best to leave the bar alone and to not try removing any of the medals, even on this type of setup. Given the age of these items, it is risky to play around with them too much. The clips are usually made of spring steel. Over time, and due to rusting, they can become brittle. It would certainly be upsetting to break a clip off just because curiosity gets the best of us. As a collector, I consider myself a custodian of these historical artifacts. They should be kept in the best condition possible so that future generations can own and study them. It is also important to care for these artifacts in order to protect the investment. By virtue of their age alone, these items should continue to increase in value. However, once they are broken or damaged, the value of the item drops significantly. Another downside to this type of setup is that it makes it easy for the unscrupulous individual to remove original medals from the bar, and replace them with reproductions. **Always remember to check every medal on the bar to insure authenticity.** The Police Long Service Cross on this bar is sewn in. It would be impossible to remove it without cutting stitching and damaging the ribbon.

The reverse of the medal bar has police gray-green wool backing in place over the zinc mounting plate. The pin and catch are made of brass wire. The mounting clips for the first two medals are steel, with a black painted finish.

*Hamburg Hanseatic Cross (obverse). Note the translucent red enamel & the City of Hamburg coat-of-arms at the center. The central disc is a separate attachment. The striations in the arms of the cross should be visible through the red enamel.*

*Hamburg Hanseatic Cross (reverse). The inscription reads, "For Merit in the War 1914."*

*Fire Brigade Decoration (obverse). Note that the enamel is opaque on this cross. The central disc is a separate piece, soldered into place.*

*Fire Brigade Decoration (reverse). The reverse is plain, but slightly concave. Note the ball-type suspension eyelet, which is typical for these crosses.*

Opposite bottom: Three-place police medal bar. The medals are from (L-R): 1939 War Merit Cross Second Class without Swords, 1914-1918 Cross of Honor with Swords, and the 25-Year Police Long Service Cross. Above: Medal bar reverse. $225-250.

This view shows the steel clips and the suspension rings of the War Merit Cross and 1914-1918 Cross of Honor. The medal bar was undoubtedly exposed to some damp weather. Notice how the rusting of the steel clips has caused rust stains to the ribbons, in the area immediately surrounding the clips. Only the two clips and the 1914-1918 Cross of Honor are iron/steel and prone to rust. All other metal parts on the bar are non-ferrous.

### Methods of Displaying the Police Insignia

Both of these medal bars have the same combination of awards, yet each one looks unique. (Example A) is in the best overall condition by far. (Example B) shows more age discoloration and wear. (A) has a standard three-piece Iron Cross, with silver frames and a magnetic core. On (B), the Iron Cross is also three-piece, but with nickel-silver frames and a non-magnetic core. Each 1914-1918 Cross of Honor is made of bronzed iron, and both just happen to have the same maker marking, "32 R.V. PFORZHEIM." The 18-Year Police Long Service Crosses are tombak with a silver finish. On medal bar (A), the police insignia is on a separate piece of ribbon that was sewn into place. On (B), the police insignia is mounted to a steel plate, which is attached to the medal bar by two metal prongs.

Both of these medal bars have the same style of mounting plates. (A) has no backing cloth while (B) has the mounting plate covered over with red wool. On medal bar (B), the integral catch and pin are broken off. Only a small portion of the pin remains at the hinge area, underneath the wool backing. All of the mounting and attachment hardware on both bars is made of nickel-plated steel. The only exception is the front mounting plate for the Police Long Service Cross on medal bar (A). This piece is non-magnetic and appears to be either copper or brass with a dark brown patina. Notice that the pin on (A) is of very thin gauge when compared to the pins found on most other medal bars. Medal bar (B) would have had this same style of pin. Thin steel pins such as these could break more easily as (B) clearly shows.

*Example 1: An extra wide ribbon width (50mm) was used with the embroidered insignia already in place. The ribbon was cut up the middle to just below the insignia, and then worked around the suspension ring of the medal. This method gives the best overall look, but it required the most skill to accomplish.*

*Example 2: A narrower width (30mm) of plain, cornflower blue ribbon was used to make the double wrap in the traditional manner. A separate piece of wider ribbon, with the police insignia on it was then cut to size, doubled over, and stitched into place.*

*Example 3: On this mounting, a piece of ribbon with the police insignia on it was placed over a slightly vaulted piece of sheet steel. The top & bottom ends of the ribbon are folded over the steel plate and the ends are sewn together on the backside. The finished insignia plate is attached to the ribbon below by two, flat metal prongs. Police bars that are missing their insignia probably had this type of attachment. They may have broken off, or been removed by someone. You will usually notice two prong holes in the ribbon.*

*Example 4: This example uses a smaller than usual police insignia. Plain cornflower blue ribbon was used for the traditional wrap on the medal bar. A separate piece of ribbon with the police insignia on it was then trimmed until only the eagle, wreath, and the little bit of blue in the middle remained. This small, embroidered insignia was then placed in the proper position and stitched into place. This method required meticulous effort, but the result is quite pleasing.*

*Example 5: This method is very similar to that shown in example 2, except that the piece of ribbon with the police insignia is folded into a triangular shape, and then sewn to the ribbon below. In addition to the examples shown, there were surely other methods as well. There were many ways to achieve a nice looking result. Details such as this make every bar unique. The medal bar was a hand-made product, reflecting the creativity and skill of the assembler.*

*Opposite*
*Top: A three-place police medal bar consisting of the 1914 Iron Cross Second Class, 1914-1918 Cross of Honor, and the 18-Year Police Long Service Cross. (Example A) $225-250.*

*Bottom: This medal bar has the exact combination of awards, yet it has a look all its own. (Example B) $150-175.*

1914
1918

1914
1918

*Reverse of medal bar. (Example A)*

*Reverse of medal bar. (Example B)*

This four-place medal bar (**below**) is nicely mounted, but in a more unusual manner. The majority of German medal bars were set up so that the bottoms of the medals were in alignment. On this bar however, the tops of the medals are aligned, giving the bottom a staggered effect. If you look at most of the other bars pictured in this book, you will see exactly what I am referring to.

The Iron Cross is the standard three-part, magnetic core type. The Cross of Honor is iron with a bronze finish. It is marked on the reverse with a stylized "JK" within a triangle. The Police Long Service Cross is tombak with a silver finish. Notice that the police insignia on the ribbon is smaller than usual. The 1936 Olympic Games Commemorative Medal is magnetic and made of silver-finished iron.

The reverse of this medal bar has no backing cloth, which is nice because it allows us to see the well-made mounting plate. The front and back plates are steel, as well as the pin and catch. All metal parts have a nickel-plated finish. The back mounting plate has an integral hinge and mounts for the catch. Both the pin and catch are round steel wire. The pin is held in place by a 90-degree bend, just below the hinge. The catch was

*A four-place German Police medal bar. The medals are from (L-R): 1914 Iron Cross Second Class, 1914-1918 Cross of Honor with Swords, 18-Year Police Long Service Cross, and the 1936 Olympic Games Commemorative Medal. $350-375.*

*Medal bar reverse.*

*Obverse of the 1936 Olympic Games Commemorative Medal. This example is made of die-struck iron and measures 37.33mm in diameter. $150.*

*Reverse of the 1936 Olympic Games Commemorative Medal.*

crimped into place. Also note the eight, bent over metal tabs which locked the front and back plates together. Once in a while, a maker marking can be found on a medal bar mounting plate. It is hard to see in the photo, but the lower, center part of the plate is marked, "Alfred Kochmann, Berlin-Friede..." The last few letters are not legible. This is the manufacturer of the mounting plate, not the assembler of the medal bar.

Most of the original 1936 Olympic Games Commemorative Medals were die-struck in iron and finished in silver. They are usually magnetic, but there are also non-magnetic originals made of tombak bronze. The example shown is made of iron. The inscription on the reverse of the medal reads, "For meritorious cooperation at the Olympic Games 1936." Good quality fakes of this medal abound. Insure that the medal is die-struck, not cast. The detail should be crisp. Study the details & lettering carefully.

Although only a two-place medal bar (**below**), this is one of my favorites. The bar consists of the 1939 Iron Cross Second Class and the 18-Year Police Long Service Cross. For a police medal bar, this combination of awards is quite rare. The owner of this bar did not serve in World War I. However, by the time of the Second World War, he had been a policeman for at least 18 years. While a decoration such as the 1939 War Merit Cross is commonplace on a police medal bar, the 1939 Iron Cross is almost never seen. In World War I, the 1914 Iron Cross could be awarded to both combatants and non-combatants. For the non-combatant version, the medal was the same but the ribbon colors were reversed. In Word War II, the 1939 Iron Cross was strictly a valor decoration, awarded for an act of bravery in combat. There was no non-combatant version of the 1939 Iron Cross as there was for the 1914 Iron Cross of World War I. In a way, the 1939 War Merit Cross was like a non-combatant version of the Iron Cross, even though an entirely different medal. If you look at the ribbon of a 1939 War Merit Cross, you will see that the ribbon colors are reversed from that of the 1939 Iron Cross. So how did this policeman earn a decoration for bravery in combat? Lacking provenance on this medal bar, it is purely a matter of conjecture. However, at some point, he may have been involved in actual combat with the enemy. Or perhaps he was responsible for single-handedly capturing escaped prisoners, a spy or saboteur. Whatever the act, it most surely involved bravery and danger to life and limb. The Iron Cross on this bar is the usual three-part construction. The frames are nickel-silver, and the core is iron with a black painted finish. The Police Long Service Cross is tombak with a frosted finish and polished highlights. The police insignia is on a separate piece of ribbon that was folded into a triangular shape and sewn in place.

All of the metal mounting and attachment hardware on this bar is non-magnetic. The pin and catch are brass, while the mounting plates are zinc. The pin has darkened to the point that it looks like copper. The hinge and small part of the back plate are visible. The white, speckled effect is some corrosion of the zinc, also referred to as zinc pest. The medal bar is backed with dark green wool felt, and it shows a small amount of moth damage. Just below the backing, on the left, some of the white fiber ribbon padding is visible. The string that holds the rosettes together is also visible below the backing material.

*Two-place German Police medal bar. The medals are from (L-R): 1939 Iron Cross Second Class and the 18-Year Police Long Service Cross. Right: Medal bar reverse. $250-275.*

*Opposite: Shown here is an original award document for the 18-Year Police Long Service Cross. This same style document was also used for the Police 8-Year Long Service Medal. The documents were printed on heavy parchment. On the lower left is the embossed seal of the State Minister. Both the 8 and 18-Year documents should have a facsimile signature of Otto Meissner, as State Minister and Chief of the Presidential Chancellery. 209mm x 296mm. $75-100.*

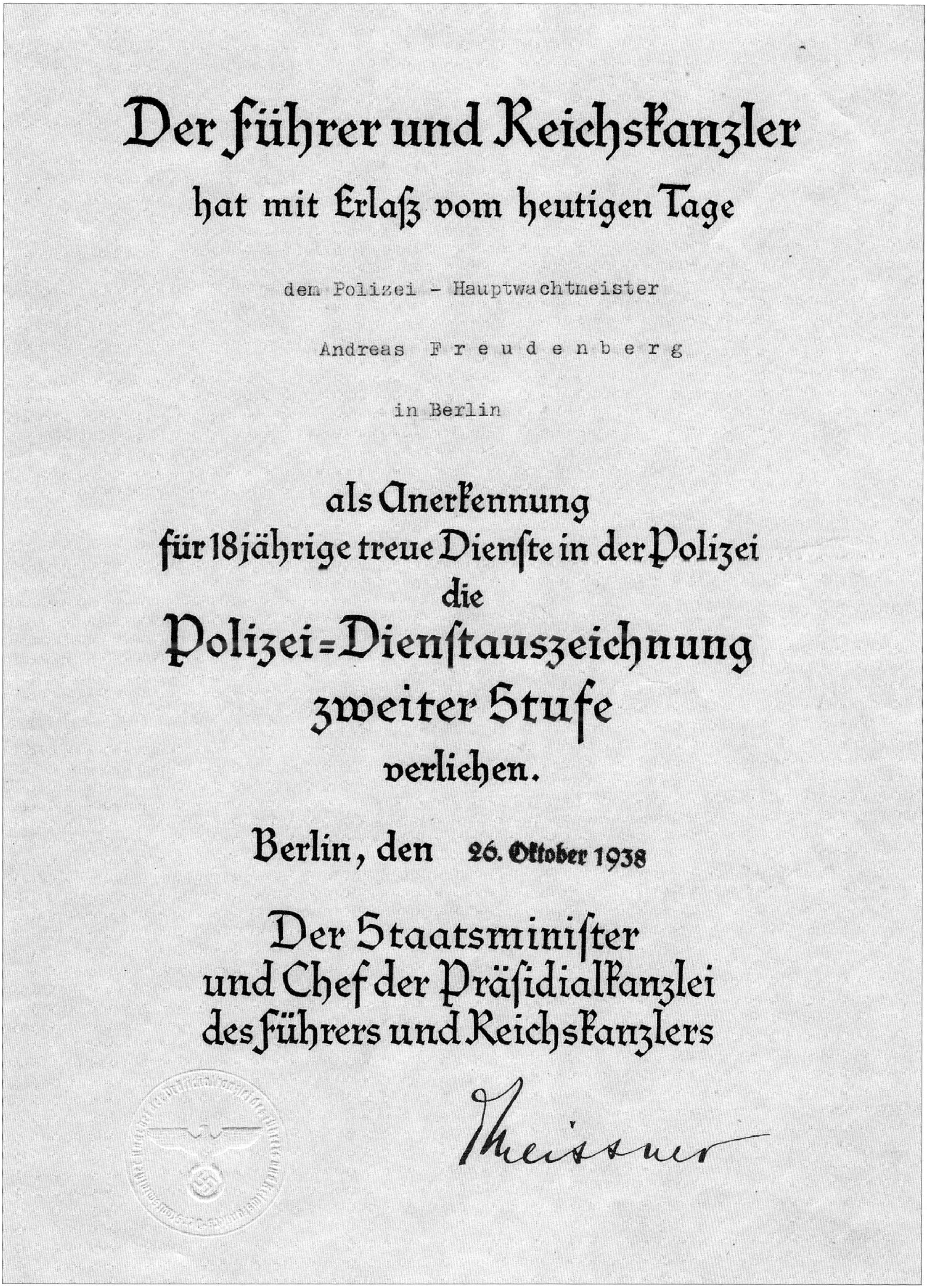

Der Führer und Reichskanzler

hat mit Erlaß vom heutigen Tage

dem Polizei - Hauptwachtmeister

Andreas F r e u d e n b e r g

in Berlin

als Anerkennung
für 18jährige treue Dienste in der Polizei
die
Polizei=Dienstauszeichnung
zweiter Stufe
verliehen.

Berlin, den 26. Oktober 1938

Der Staatsminister
und Chef der Präsidialkanzlei
des Führers und Reichskanzlers

Meissner

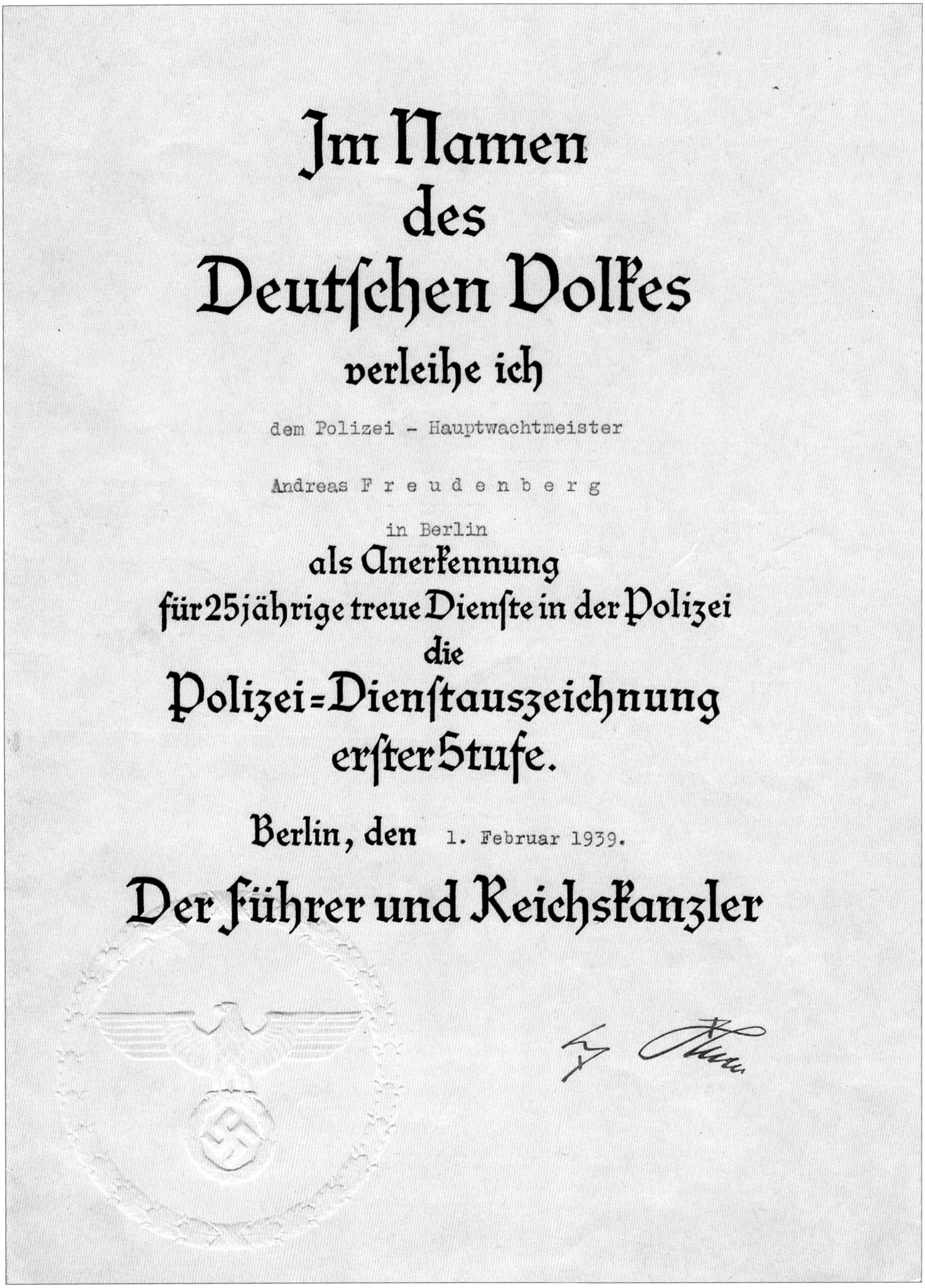

Im Namen
des
Deutschen Volkes
verleihe ich
dem Polizei - Hauptwachtmeister
Andreas F r e u d e n b e r g
in Berlin
als Anerkennung
für 25jährige treue Dienste in der Polizei
die
Polizei=Dienstauszeichnung
erster Stufe.

Berlin, den 1. Februar 1939.

Der Führer und Reichskanzler

*This is the 25-Year Police Long Service document to the same recipient, awarded just over three months later. When he was awarded the 18-Year Cross in October of 1938 (the year the Police Long Service awards were instituted) he was just short of 25 full years of service. Notice that the text on the 25-Year document is different. In addition the 25-Year document has a large, embossed seal of the Führer and Chancellor, and the facsimile signature of Adolf Hitler. 209mm x 296mm. $100-125.*

The ribbons and medals of this four-place police bar (**below**) are in excellent condition, showing only slight age and little if any wear. It is an attractive looking bar, although the medals are mounted in a staggered fashion. The tops of the Cross of Honor and the Police Long Service Cross are aligned, but the Iron Cross is mounted slightly higher and the Prussian Long service Medal is slightly lower. The Iron cross has a magnetic core and nickel-silver frames. The Cross of Honor is bronzed iron. It is maker marked on the reverse, "GBR.D.L." The marking is that of Gebrüder Dornbach of Lüdenscheid. It is an incuse-relief type marking, with the letters raised within an impressed circular area. The Prussian Long Service Medal is solid nickel-silver. The inscription on the front of the medal reads, "For faithful service alongside the flag." The Police Long Service Cross is tombak with a matt gold finish and polished highlights.

The pin and catch of the medal bar are brass. The mounting plates are zinc. The bar is backed with blue-green wool felt. The bottom edge of the backing was trimmed to follow the contours of the ribbon rosettes.

*Four-place German Police medal bar. The medals are from (L-R): 1914 Iron Cross Second Class, 1914-1918 Cross of Honor with Swords, Prussian 9-Year Long Service Medal, and the 25-Year Police Long Service Cross. Below: Medal bar reverse. $275-300.*

*Detail view of the 25-Year Police Long Service Cross. (Obverse) This example is 43.05mm square.*

*Detail view of the 25-Year Police Long Service Cross. (Reverse)*

The 25 and 18-Year Police Long Service Crosses are identical except for their finishes. All of the original examples I have seen over the years have been non-magnetic, and made of tombak bronze. If originals do exist made of iron or zinc, they have certainly eluded me. These crosses should have a high-quality, matt finish with polished highlights. Notice that the outer borders of the cross arms are smooth, while the inner areas of the arms have a lightly stippled effect. Notice also that the areas between the small, round wreath and the swastika have the stippled effect. However, the areas between the larger, oval wreath and the eagle have no stippling whatsoever. On the reverse, the oval area with the wording should be smooth as well. Some fairly convincing fakes abound that have stippling in areas that should not be stippled. As long as you know what to look for, these fakes will be easy to spot. Always remember to study each medal carefully.

This is a really nice looking, four-place police medal bar (**opposite**). It is even nicer because it has the matching ribbon bar. Only occasionally will you still be able to find a medal bar paired with its original ribbon bar. Over time, these items tend to be split up and sold off individually. Once that happens, the grouping is lost forever. Collectors realize the importance of keeping groupings intact. Dealers however, see the items from a business sense. They can usually sell the items for more individually, so they have no problem with breaking up a set. I have even seen dealers take original medal bars apart because they can get more money by selling the medals separately. This was especially true in the past. Nowadays, I think more people have an appreciation for what the medal bar is, and they realize that a mounted grouping is more valuable than individual medals. I was fortunate to obtain this medal bar and ribbon bar as a grouping. If I ever decide to sell these items, I will only sell them together.

The medals on this bar are in fine condition. The Cross of Honor and the Olympic Medal are magnetic, while the other two medals are non-magnetic.

The arrangement of the medals is a bit contrary to regulations. The Olympic Medal should be placed after the Long Service Cross, not before it. This may have been nothing more than a simple mistake, or it may have been done intentionally to give the bar a more balanced look. The Cross of Honor is marked on the reverse, "N. & H." The manufacturer logo is that of Noelle & Hueck, located in Lüdenscheid. The police insignia on the medal bar is mounted to a steel plate and attached by two prongs. The crossed swords and police eagle devices on the ribbon bar are all brass with a gold finish. Notice how the reddish-orange of the Olympic Medal and the green of the Bulgarian Medal have faded on the ribbon bar. This is an indication that the ribbon bar was worn more often, and exposed to more sunlight than the medal bar.

The reverse of the medal bar is backed with black wool. The pin and catch are made of flat metal stock. All metal hardware on this bar is magnetic. Although they look like brass, the pin, catch, and mounting plates are all made of steel with a bronzed finish.

*Opposite: Four-place German Police medal bar and matching ribbon bar. The medals on this bar are from (L-R): 1914-1918 Cross of Honor with Swords, 1936 Olympic Games Commemorative Medal, 25-Year Police Long Service Cross, and the Bulgarian World War I Commemorative Medal. Medal bar: $350-375. Ribbon bar: $40-50.*

1914
1918

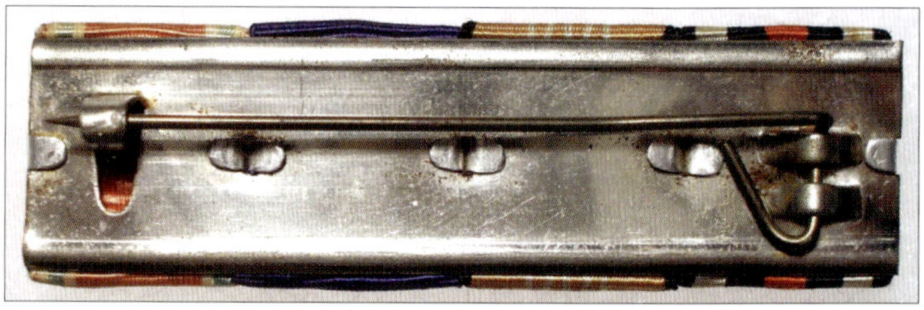

*Police ribbon bar. (Obverse and Reverse)*

Ribbon bars are almost as complicated in their construction as medal bars. Each of these four, narrow ribbon widths were wrapped around an individual front plate and stitched down. Each front plate has two locking tabs which are bent over, locking it to the back plate. The metal devices were attached to the ribbons by two metal prongs. The ribbon bar has a steel pin and nickel-plated steel mounting plates. The catch and hinge are an integral part of the rear mounting plate. Notice the eight, bent over metal tabs that locked the front plates and ribbons into the mounting. All four ribbons were clipped into the bar individually.

This three-place medal bar (**below**) also has the matching ribbon bar. Both items are in excellent condition, showing only the slightest amount of aging. In fact, other than the darkening of the silver frames on the Iron Cross, the bars look as if new. As mentioned previously though, it is not unusual to find original medal bars in this kind of condition. Ribbon bars usually show more age and wear because they were worn on a daily basis, in lieu of the actual medals. But this particular ribbon bar looks to be in mint condition. Chances are that the owner had more than one ribbon bar so that he would not have to transfer it from one tunic to the other. Or this one may have been a spare, which was kept in a drawer and never actually worn. On the medal bar, notice that the ribbon for the Cross of Honor has a salmon-colored central stripe rather than red. It is not due to fading on this example, but is attributable to the ribbon manufacturer. With original ribbons, shades of color can very to some degree, especially with the reds. All of the medals on this bar are constructed from the standard materials and have the typical finishes. The Cross of Honor has the same maker marking as the cross in the previous example, "N. & H." for Noelle &

*Three-place German Police medal bar with matching ribbon bar. The medals are from (L-R): 1914 Iron Cross Second Class, 1914-1918 Cross of Honor with Swords, and the Police 25-Year Long Service Cross. Medal bar: $250-275. Ribbon bar: $30-35.*

Reverse of medal and ribbon bars.

Police ribbon bar. (Obverse)

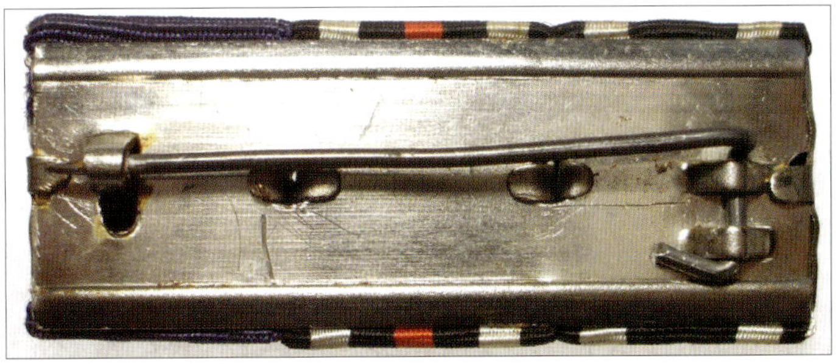

Police ribbon bar (Reverse)

Hueck. The police insignia on the medal bar is a separate piece of ribbon, doubled over and sewn in place. The medal bar has a brass pin and catch. There is no part of the mounting plate visible on this bar, but they are definitely non-magnetic and most likely made of zinc. The backing cloth is black, ribbed cotton twill. It is completely sewn down on all sides so nothing underneath can be seen. This is a real quality assembly. Notice how the large size and nice gathering of the ribbon rosettes enhances the overall appearance.

On the ribbon bar, both the crossed swords and police emblem are iron with a gold finish. The ribbon bar for a non-combatant Cross of Honor would have no swords device on it. The ribbon bar for an 18-Year Police Long Service Cross would have a metal police device, finished in silver. The 8-Year Police ribbon bar would be a plain blue ribbon, without a police emblem. All of the mounting and attachment hardware on the ribbon bar is nickel-plated steel.

This police medal bar (**top page 76**) is made up of three common medals, but the grouping as a whole is rare because the 8-Year Police Long Service Medal is hard to find on a medal bar. Because it is a rare combination of awards, the value of the medal bar should exceed the value of the individual medals. All three medals are non-magnetic. The 8-Year Police Medal is tombak with a frosted silver finish. The Medal for the Annexation of Austria is bronze with a silver finish, and the Medal for the Annexation of Czechoslovakia is unfinished bronze. The medals are all correctly mounted, according to the regulations for wear. This bar is a real gem!

*A scarce example of a German Police medal bar. Medals are from (L-R): 8-Year Police Long Service Medal, Medal for the Annexation of Austria, and the Medal for the Annexation of Czechoslovakia. The 8-Year Medal is seldom seen on a medal bar. Right: Medal bar reverse. Courtesy of and photo by Jody Beltram. $225-250.*

On the reverse, the medal bar mounting plate is backed with gray colored wool felt. The backing cloth has a pinking shear cut along the bottom edge. The mounting plates are zinc, and both the pin and catch are brass. There are no magnetic parts on this bar.

I recently found this two-place police medal bar (**below**) at a local gun show. I bought it because the price was reasonable, and for that I was willing to overlook the fact that the bar as a whole is somewhat questionable. In the first place, I can say with certainty that the medals, ribbons, and all the other assembly components are genuine to the Third Reich Period. I am also convinced that this bar was assembled during the period. However, I believe that this bar was originally mounted with an Armed Forces 4-Year Long Service Medal, or possibly an 18 or 25-Year Police Long Service Cross rather than the 8-Year Police Medal. If you look at the long service ribbon, you can see that there are two holes in it. The holes are most likely from where an armed forces eagle device or an 18/25-year police insignia device was once attached. There is also some evidence of the ribbon having been disturbed at the area where the medal is suspended. Remember that these items we collect have been around for many decades. Unless you are getting the items from the actual veteran that owned them, most of these artifacts have changed hands numerous times. The more an item exchanges hands, the greater the chance that something will get messed with. This kind of thing does happen, and

*Two-place German Police medal bar. Medals are from (L-R): 1914-1918 Cross of Honor with Swords, and the 8-Year Police Long Service Medal. This bar was most likely changed around post-war. Notice the two holes in the long service ribbon. Right: Medal bar reverse. $125.*

*Four-place German Police medal bar. Medals are from (L-R): 1914 Iron Cross Second Class, 1914-1918 Cross of Honor with Swords, 18-Year Police Long Service Cross, and the Luftschutz Honor Award Second Class. Below: Medal bar reverse. Courtesy of and photo by Jody Beltram. $300-325.*

Five-place German Police medal bar. Medals are from (L-R): 1914 Iron Cross Second Class, 1914-1918 Cross of Honor with Swords, 18-Year Police Long Service Cross, 1936 Olympic Games Commemorative Medal, and the World War I Commemorative Medal for Hungary. Below: Medal bar reverse. $350-375.

for any number of reasons: A dealer removes a medal or other part from a medal bar to sell it individually. A collector buys a medal bar that is missing a medal and attaches a replacement to make it complete again. Curiosity causes a person to take things apart. Careless handling causes something to break. Children latch onto the item and use it for a toy. (I was guilty of this last example as I always played with my dad's war souvenirs when I was growing up.) Yes, there is always the slim possibility that this medal bar was converted during the Third Reich Period, but it is more likely a bar that was messed with and changed post-war. Examine and scrutinize every purchase beforehand. Understand exactly what you are buying so that you will not be disappointed later.

The 1914-1918 Cross of Honor is bronzed iron. On the reverse it is maker marked with "L. NBG." This marking was used by the firm L. Ch. Lauer of Nürnberg. The 8-Year Police Long Service Medal is tombak with a frosted silver finish. The mounting plate is covered with dark gray wool felt. The mounting plates are zinc, and the pin and catch are brass. This bar has steel hooks on the front for attaching the medals.

This is a fine example of a German Police medal bar in mint condition (**page 77**). The 1914 Iron Cross has a magnetic core and nickel-silver frames. The Cross of Honor is bronzed steel. It was made by a firm of the Pforzheim conglomerate. The 18-Year Police Long Service Cross is tombak with a finish of matt silver and burnished highlights. The Luftschutz Medal is the early, aluminum type. The reverse of the bar is backed with dark blue wool. The mounting plates are made of steel and have a bright nickel finish. The pin and catch are also made of steel. A bar such as this would have belonged to a municipal policeman that was involved in the protection of the local population during air raids. The man was probably in his forties or fifties during the Second World War.

Here is one last example of a German Police Medal bar (**opposite**). The medals are nicely mounted, and their arrangement is according to regulations. The Iron Cross is a standard three-part example. The Cross of Honor is bronzed iron. On the reverse of the upper cross arm it has the stamped marking, "JK" within a triangle. The Police Long Service Cross is made of tombak and finished in matt silver. The highlights of the cross have a polished effect. The Olympic Games Commemorative Medal is iron with a silver finish. In the photos you will notice several rust spots on both the obverse and reverse. The World War I Commemorative Medal for Hungary is a non-magnetic base metal, finished in darkened silver. All of the mounting and attachment hardware is made of steel. The back plate has an integral hinge/catch setup. The steel pin shows traces of a brass or bronze colored finish. Green wool was used for the backing material.

## CHAPTER FOUR

# MEDAL BARS OF THE GERMAN ARMED FORCES

This chapter will cover medal bars that were worn by members of the German Armed Forces during the Third Reich Period. It includes those of the German Army, Navy, and the Air Force. Some of the medal bars shown in this chapter belonged to those that served in the military during both world wars. They are usually the larger bars that have a more interesting display of medals. Other medal bars shown (usually the smaller ones) were to younger members of the military that served exclusively during World War II. This chapter will also show a few examples of award documents pertaining to long service in the military. At places within the chapter, some period photographs will show medal bars being worn by members of the armed forces.

Here is a four-place medal bar (**opposite**) that belonged to either a member of the German Kriegsmarine (Navy) or the Heer (Army). It is impossible to know for sure because both the Kriegsmarine and Heer used the same type of national eagle device attached to the ribbon of their Long Service Medals. It is also impossible to tell whether the recipient of these awards was an enlisted man, non-commissioned officer, or a commissioned officer. In World War II, Germany did not award different types of medals to officers and enlisted men, and the individual's rank did not determine the class of medal awarded. All ranks of the military were eligible to receive these medals based on heroism, merit, time in service, and participation. Those were the deciding factors, not the status of the individual.

From looking at this bar, we can tell that the recipient was decorated for bravery in combat, by virtue of the Iron Cross. He also had at least four, but less than twelve years of service in the military, and he served in either the Navy or Army. The last two medals show that he took part in the occupation of Czechoslovakia in October 1938, and also the occupation of the Memel District of East Prussia in March of 1939. This medal bar combination is scarce because of the last medal on the bar. There were just over 31,000 Memel Medals awarded, and most of the awards were to naval personnel. The Iron Cross is a three-part construction type, having the center core sandwiched between the obverse and reverse frames. The core on this particular Iron Cross is unusual as it is non-magnetic. Most Iron Crosses have cores made of iron, and they will attract a magnet. The Long Service Medal is made of iron with a matt silver finish. The medal is magnetic, which is typical for the majority of these. Czech Occupation Medals were normally struck from a bronze alloy. This example, however, is very unusual as it is die-stuck iron and magnetic. The Memel Medal is made of bronze and is non-ferrous. This is typical for most, if not all Memel Medals.

The steel mounting plate for this medal bar is covered with very dark, almost black-looking, navy blue wool. The color of this cloth backing could be an indication that this bar belonged to a member of the Navy rather than the Army. The color would certainly be a better match to a naval uniform. Some collectors believe that medal bars were backed in dark blue for Navy, blue-gray for Air Force, and field-gray for Army. This may have been true in some cases, but it certainly was not true in all cases. Many other colors and types of backing were also used. I think that in most cases, it just depended on who did the work, and what they had available at the time. The backing cloth was just there to protect the tunic when the medal bar was worn. The long pin on this bar is made of round, brass stock and the catch is steel. The ribbons are nicely furled and form rosettes at the bottom.

This medal bar (**page 82**) is the same style as the previous example, and it shows the same combination of awards. This bar has the more standard type of 1939 Iron Cross, having a magnetic core. The Long Service Medal is magnetic, while the eagle device, attached to the ribbon, is not. This medal bar also has a Czech Medal that is magnetic and made of die-struck iron. Again, a magnetic Czech Annexation Medal is seldom encountered. The Memel Medal is bronze. On the reverse, this bar has a steel pin and catch. The backing cloth is dark blue wool.

*A four-place German medal bar. (Most likely to a naval enlisted man or officer.) Medals are from (L-R): 1939 Iron Cross Second Class, Armed Forces 4-Year Long Service Medal, Medal for the Annexation of Czechoslovakia, and the Medal for the Return of the Memel District. Below: Medal bar reverse. $325-375.*

*This four-place medal bar has the same combination of awards as the previous example. Below: Medal bar reverse. $325-375.*

**Are there two different patterns of Memel Medals?**

Because of the relatively small number of Memel Medals awarded, these medals have always been the subject of much debate. Although only about 31,000 were awarded, a considerably greater number were produced.[1] It is not reasonable to think that only one manufacturer produced these medals using a single die. There are scarcer awards, such as the Knight's Cross and German Cross, which clearly involved several different manufacturers using their own sets of tooling. It would have been the same for the Memel Medal. Small details will differ from one manufacturer's piece to another. Look at the reverse of the Memel Medal in (Example A). This type has been pictured in reference books as far back as I can recall. However, many collectors believe that this type is not original by virtue of the shape of the letter "G" in the word "ERINNERUNG" and the shape of the letter "M" in "MEMELLANDES" and "MÄRZ." In my opinion, this is an acceptable type, attributable to a different manufacturer using their tooling. Yes, there are good quality copies of the Memel Medal in circulation that resemble this pattern. However, given the fact that this particular example is mounted and sewn into a medal bar that is unquestionably an original wartime assembly, I can only conclude that this Memel Medal is genuine.

The Memel Medal shown in (Example B) is the type that most collectors will agree is original. If you look at the letter "G" in this example, you will see that the leg of the "G" is angled inward, whereas on (Example A) it is vertical. In addition, the legs of the letters "M" have less inward curve than on (Example A). Again, a different manufacturer used different tooling. **The same type of medal produced by different manufacturers will look similar, but they will not always be identical in each and every detail**. One thing I have learned in this hobby is never to believe absolute statements such as, "All Memel Medals must have an angled G to be real." or "All Iron Crosses must be magnetic." These absolutes are never true.

This four-place medal bar (**page 84**) belonged to a veteran of the First World War who had quite a number of years of service in the

*This German Navy Petty Officer wears his medals on his wedding day. The medals are the 1939 Iron Cross, Armed Forces 4-Year Long Service Medal, Medal for the Annexation of Czechoslovakia, and the Medal for the Return of the Memel District. Below the medals he wears the Minesweeper Badge. Notice that only the 4-Year Medal is mounted in parade form. The other medals have the ribbons simply folded over and pinned to the uniform. No doubt the Iron Cross, Czech and Memel Medals were recently awarded, and the man had yet to find time to have a new medal bar made.*

*Reverse of Memel Medal. 32.20mm in diameter. (Example A)*

*Reverse of Memel Medal. 32.25mm in diameter. (Example B)*

*A four-place medal bar consisting of (L-R): 1914 Iron Cross Second Class on combatant ribbon, 1914-1918 Cross of Honor without Swords, Wehrmacht 12-Year long Service Medal, and the Wehrmacht 4-Year Long Service Medal. Below: Medal bar reverse. $200-225.*

German Armed Forces. After serving in the First World War, he probably returned to military duty in the late 1930s, and continued to serve during the Second World War. From looking at the bar, we can tell that the recipient was decorated for bravery in World War I. In the mid 1930s he was awarded the Honor Cross without Swords, meaning that he had been a non-combatant in World War I. This is quite unusual because even though a non-combatant during the First World War, he was decorated for bravery and permitted to wear his Iron Cross on a combatant ribbon. (The non-combatant ribbon would have the colors reversed.) He may have been a doctor or medic, performing a difficult task in even more difficult surroundings. The Iron Cross is the typical three-part construction, with a magnetic iron core. The other medals on this bar are magnetic as well, including the eagle devices attached to the ribbons of the Long Service Medals. The Cross of Honor is bronzed iron. The 12-Year medal is matt gold-finished iron and the 4-Year Medal is matt silver-finished iron. The owner of this bar had at least 12, but less than 18 years of service in the military at the time that this bar was assembled. It was probably made in the late 1930s, just prior to World War II. Regulations allowed members of the Armed Forces to wear two long service medals on their medal bar if so qualified.

The reverse of this medal bar is covered with black or navy blue wool. It is neatly stitched in place with cotton thread. Here again, the color of the wool backing may indicate that the bar belonged to a member of the Navy, but we cannot be certain of this. The metal mounting plate on this bar is made of zinc and is non-magnetic. Both the pin and catch on this example are made of brass. The pin is round wire stock, and the catch was stamped out of brass sheeting. If you look at the right edge of this bar, you can see that a small part of the zinc mounting plate is visible. Along the left edge of the bar, you will notice some white, fibrous material. This is cotton batting, which was used to puff up the ribbons. It gives the medal bar a nice, padded look from the front. The ribbons have an overlapping wrap on the front, and at the bottom they are gathered into semi-circular rosettes. Notice that on this mounting, the medals hang down partly below the ribbon rosettes. On the two medal bars shown previously, the medals completely nest within the rosettes. The Cross of Honor (also known as the Hindenburg Cross) is maker marked on the reverse, lower cross arm. The marking reads, "R.V. 67. PFORZHEIM." Most Hindenburg Crosses were maker marked, and it is quite unusual to find one without a marking. Because so many of these crosses were awarded, there were more manufacturers involved in the production of Hindenburg Crosses than of any other award produced during the Third Reich Period. About 6.2 million were awarded to combatants, about 1.1 million to non-combatants, and about 700,000 to either the widow or parents of the fallen.[2]

The 1914-1918 Cross of Honor is by far the most common award to be found on a medal bar of the Third Reich Period. Although it looks like a World War I award, it is actually a commemorative medal that was instituted during the Third Reich. Even if all the other awards on a medal bar are from the Imperial Period, the presence of a 1914-1918 Cross of Honor makes it a Third Reich Period medal bar.

The Cross of Honor is an ideal medal for beginning collectors. Because of the large number of crosses awarded, they are inexpensive and easy to find. Since they are so common and inexpensive, there has been no serious attempt at reproducing them. Beginners can still buy these with the assurance that they are getting an original medal. One thing I would suggest, though, is to check the medal with a magnet to insure it is made of iron. Another thing to be aware of is that the cross for widows/parents is the least common and therefore it usually costs more. Since the widow/parent cross is identical to the non-combatant cross, except for the finish, it is easy for someone to take a non-combatant cross, paint it black, and then pass it off as a widow/parent cross.

*There were three versions of the 1914-1918 Cross of Honor (Hindenburg Cross). Shown from (L-R): for combatants, for non-combatants, and for the widow or parents of the fallen. The combatant cross features crossed swords and a wreath of laurel leaves. The non-combatant cross is without swords and has a wreath of oak leaves. The cross for widows/parents is identical to the non-combatant cross, except that it is finished in black lacquer. Most of these crosses were struck from iron so they should be magnetic. Notice that both the combatant and non-combatant crosses have the same ribbon while the widow/parent cross has the colors reversed. Combatant: $5-10. Non-combatant: $10-15. Widow/parent: $25-30.*

Another nice thing about the Cross of Honor, is the wide range of maker markings that can be found on them. Some collectors enjoy finding all the different makers of a medal. It would take much time and effort to acquire all the different makers of the Cross of Honor. The pictures will show just a small sampling of some of the markings that can be found. Maker markings can be *relief, stamped, or incuse-relief*. Relief means that the marking is raised from the surface of the medal. A stamped marking means that the design is impressed into the surface of the medal. Incuse-relief means that the design has an impressed area, and within that area there are raised markings. (The pictures show examples of each type of mark.)

*Marking used by Wilhelm Deumer of Lüdenscheid. The marking is in relief.*

*An unknown marking in relief. The letter "O" probably stands for Ordenshersteller (medal manufacturer).*

*Another unknown marking, also in relief. The letter "G" probably stands for Gesellschaft (company).*

*Marking used by Ochs & Bonn of Hanau a.Main. The marking is stamped.*

*Marking used by L. Chr. Lauer of Nürnberg. The marking is in relief.*

*A stamped marking used by Wagner & Sohn of Berlin.*

*An unknown marking in relief.*

*Another unknown maker mark, also in relief.*

*A marking to an unknown company of the Pforzheim manufacturing conglomerate. The letters "R.V." stand for Reichs Verband (empire association).*

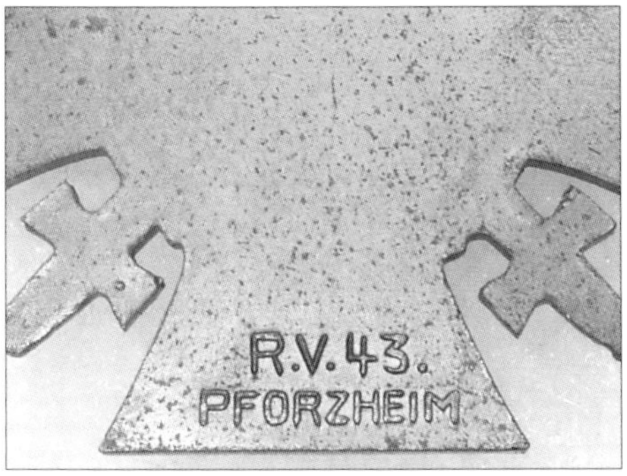


*Another unknown company of the Pforzheim conglomerate. The marking is in relief.*

*A relief marking used by Gebrüder Wegerhoff of Lüdenscheid.*

*Another Pforzheim conglomerate marking.*

*Marking used by C. Th. Dicke of Lüdenscheid. The marking is in relief.*

*Relief marking used by Werner Redo of Saarlautern.*

*This marking was possibly used by Berg & Nolte of Lüdenscheid. The marking is in relief.*

*Another relief marking of a manufacturer based in Pforzheim.*

*I have been unable to determine the manufacturer that used this logo. Several possibilities exist. The marking is in relief.*

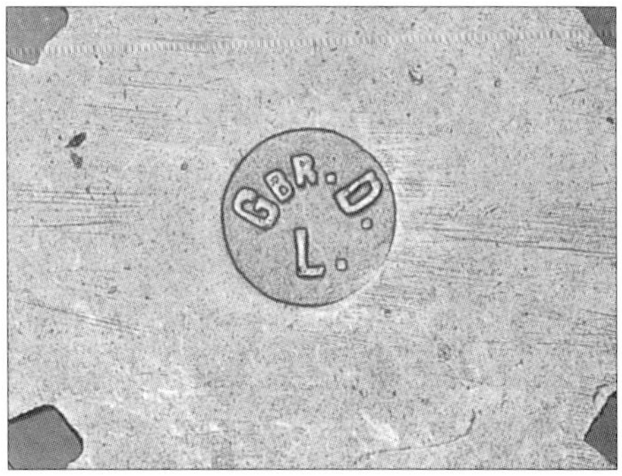


*This marking was used by Gebrüder Dornbach of Lüdenscheid. The marking is incuse-relief.*

*A marking used by Noelle & Hueck, located in Lüdenscheid. This marking is in relief.*

*A stamped logo used by an unconfirmed manufacturer. It could be that of Kerbach & Israel of Dresden. (The German letter "I" was formed like the letter "J" much of the time.)*

*This logo was used by Paul Schulze & Co. of Lübeck. The marking is in relief.*

This stamped marking was used by Kallenbach, Meyer, and Franke of Luckenwalde.

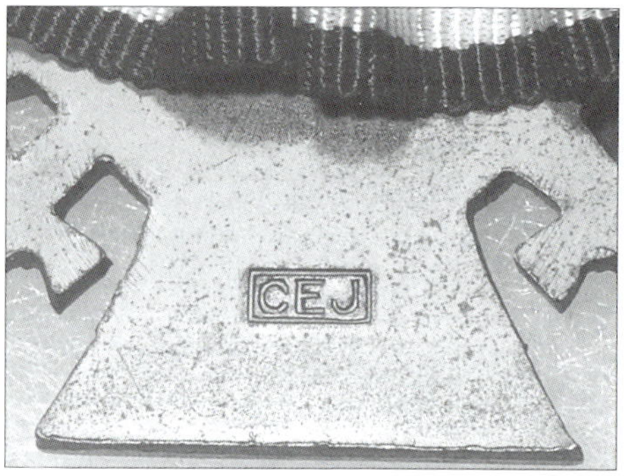


This stamped marking was used by C. E. Juncker of Berlin.

This marking was possibly used by Richard Sieper & Söhne of Lüdenscheid. The marking is in relief.

This beautifully made, six-place medal bar (**below**) belonged to a German Officer from Saxony. He was a veteran of World War I, and was inactive from military service for a number of years. At some point, he returned to active duty for service in World War II. Obviously, the owner of this bar was very brave. In World War I, three German States decorated him for bravery: Prussia, the Kingdom of Saxony, and the Grand Duchy of Mecklenburg-Schwerin. Then in World War II, he was decorated for bravery with the 1939 War Merit Cross with Swords. This bar was surely worn with much pride. Over the years, it was also well cared for. Despite the age of this bar, you can see that it is still in excellent condition. This is not uncommon for medal bars. Many original bars can be found in this condition because they were not worn on a daily basis. On the service uniform, only a ribbon bar was worn. The medal bar would only be worn on the dress uniform for special occasions. Most medal bars were worn only a few times.

The Iron Cross on this bar has silver frames and a magnetic, iron core. The 1939 War Merit Cross is an early-war example, die-struck from bronze. The Albert Order was struck from silver and the swords are gold-plated. It features opaque enamel work of white and royal blue. The maker marking "G" is stamped into the edge of the lower cross arm. This is the marking of Glaser & Sohn. Glaser manufactured Albert Orders between 1911 and 1918.[3] This Order was only awarded to officers. The Mecklenburg-Schwerin War Merit Cross is bronze with a gilded finish. The Cross of Honor is bronzed iron and the Long Service Medal is iron with a matt silver finish. The eagle attached to the ribbon is magnetic. On the reverse of the medal bar, dark forest green wool covers the zinc mounting plate. The long pin and catch are steel. The maker markings are visible on the reverse of the Cross of Honor: "R.V. 38 PFORZHEIM."

Six-place medal bar to a Saxon Officer. The medals are from (L-R): 1914 Iron Cross Second Class, 1939 War Merit Cross Second Class with Swords, Saxon Order of Albert- Knight's Cross Second Class, Mecklenburg-Schwerin War Merit Cross Second Class on combatant ribbon, 1914-1918 Cross of Honor with Swords, and the Armed Forces 4-Year Long Service Medal. $600-650.

*Above: Medal bar reverse. Right: This photo shows a nice, custom touch to a well made medal bar. The eagle device, attached to the ribbon of the Long Service Medal, has been vaulted so that it makes a neater fit to the ribbon. It is therefore less likely to snag onto something. It is the small details like this that really add character to a medal bar. The eagle devices can be either magnetic or non-magnetic. They were die-struck from iron, brass, or tombak. They were usually attached to the ribbon by two metal prongs.*

Both of these three-place medal bars (**page 90**) show the same combination of awards. This combination is common, and the awards are typical for a junior officer, non-commissioned officer, or enlisted man that fought against the Soviets on the Eastern Front. On (Example A), the War Merit Cross is the later type, made of die-struck zinc with a bronze color wash. The War Merit Cross on (Example B) is the early type, made of solid bronze. On both bars, the Russian Front Medals are fine zinc, with darkened centers, and silver-washed helmets and medal rims. Both of the Czech Medals are bronze. On medal bar (A), the suspension rings of the medals are sewn down to the mounting, underneath the ribbons. The medals cannot be removed unless the stitching is cut apart. On (B), the medals are attached by metal clips, below the ribbons. With some effort, the medals could be removed.

The reverse of these two medal bars show some similarities as well as differences. Both of these bars have brass wire attachment pins and stamped-out brass catches. The mounting plates on both bars are bare zinc. On (Example A), a small portion of the mounting plate is visible on the right. Both bars have wool backings, neatly hand-stitched in place. The cotton thread matches the colors of the wool backings. Medal bar (A) is backed with reed green wool, while (B) has a backing of courser grade, charcoal gray wool. In looking at the rosettes, we see that (A) uses a simplified gathering of the ribbon, which gives them an angular, sided appearance. Medal bar (B) has a traditional gathering of the ribbon, giving the rosettes a nice, semi-circular and rippled appearance. Bar (A) has the medals neatly aligned along the bottom plane, while (B) has the medals in staggered fashion. Although these two bars essentially look the same, the details of construction and workmanship make each one unique. I still do not know which one I like better. These medal bars belonged to soldiers of the German Army, who fought in the East. Many such soldiers never got the chance to wear their medals, or even have them mounted.

*Three-place medal bar. (Example A) Medals are from (L-R): 1939 War Merit Cross Second Class with Swords, Medal for the 1941/42 Winter Battle in the East, and the Medal for the Annexation of Czechoslovakia. $125-150.*

*Three-place medal bar with same combination of awards. (Example B) $125-150.*

*Reverse of medal bar. (Example A)*

*Reverse of medal bar. (Example B)*

1914
1918

While not an uncommon grouping of awards, this medal bar (**opposite**) shows something truly remarkable. The man was just an ordinary soldier, but he did his duty over the course of two world wars. Certainly not the medal bar of a man who made a lifetime career out of the military, but one of a man who could be counted on to serve when needed. He was obviously a front-line fighter in World War I. After surviving the trenches of the First World War, he returned to a civilian life and occupation. Then in the Second World War, he once again became a soldier, now twenty-plus years and one war older. The second time around had to be even more difficult than the first, given his age and the fact that he had seen the horrors of war once before. In World War II, he probably had some support-related assignment as opposed to front-line combat. Still, whatever role he had, it brought him close enough to danger that he was awarded the 1939 War Merit Cross with Swords. The placement of the medals on the bar is exactly per regulations, with the two valor/merit decorations worn before the 1914-1918 Cross of Honor. The ribbons on this bar have some rust staining near the top: probably because the bar got wet at some point, and the moisture caused the steel mounting hardware underneath to rust.

Shown above the medal bar is the matching *Bandspange* or (ribbon bar). This is what was worn on the service and combat uniforms in lieu of the actual medals. This ribbon bar features a single width of ribbon, with the colors of all three awards printed together. This was sometimes done for common award combinations, and it would surely simplify the assembly of the ribbon bar. For the most part though, ribbon bars were assembled using separate, narrow widths of ribbon for each award on the bar. The two crossed sword devices on the bar are iron. Close examination shows that both were struck from the same die.

Both the ribbon bar and medal bar are backed with field gray wool. The backing cloth on the medal bar has a zigzag cut across the bottom, from large size pinking shears. Both have steel mounting plates. The pin and catch are steel on the ribbon bar, and they are brass on the medal bar. In looking at this picture, you can see that almost as much work went into the making of the small ribbon bar as the full-size medal bar. It definitely took some skill and effort to assemble these bars. The work was seldom sloppy, as most workers seemed to take pride in the job they did. The only time a bar might show sub-par workmanship is if it was a homemade job, done by the recipient himself or a family member. Medal and uniform shops did quality work.

This medal bar (**below**) may have belonged to a member of the German Armed Forces in World War II, or a civilian that was working in the service of the armed forces. Regardless, the man was a veteran of World War I and won the Iron Cross for bravery. In World War II, he may have been a member of the German Red Cross or other social welfare organization. Whatever job he held, his work brought him close enough to the front that he was recognized for bravery with the War Merit Cross. All the medals and ribbons on this bar are in excellent condition. The Iron Cross is three-part construction with a magnetic core. The frames of this Iron Cross have not darkened much over the years, so they are probably made of nickel-silver rather than genuine silver. The War Merit Cross is an early-war example of solid bronze. The Cross of Honor is magnetic, having a bronze finish over iron. It is maker marked on the reverse with a "G.3" in relief. The Tyrolean Commemorative Medal is bronze gilt. This medal was awarded by Austria, to Tyroleans who served in World War I. It was also awarded to Germans who helped defend the Tyrol Province during

*Opposite: A three-place medal bar with matching ribbon bar. Medals are from (L-R): 1914 Iron Cross Second Class on combatant ribbon, 1939 War Merit Cross Second Class with Swords, and the 1914-1918 Cross of Honor with Swords. Bottom: Reverse of medal bar and matching ribbon bar. Medal bar: $100. Ribbon bar: $15-20.*

*Above: A five-place medal bar consisting of from (L-R): 1914 Iron Cross Second Class, 1939 War Merit Cross Second Class with Swords, 1914-1918 Cross of Honor with Swords, the Tyrolean Commemorative Medal, and the Social Welfare Medal. $175-225.*

*Reverse of five-place medal bar.*

the war. The medal was instituted in February of 1928. About 120,000 were awarded between 1928 and 1940.[4] The Social Welfare Medal is an early-quality example, made from tombak and having an antiqued-silver finish. Later versions of the award were struck from zinc and finished with a silver wash. The zinc examples tend to lose their finish over the years. They usually appear dull and dark gray in color. When given to members of the armed forces, the rank of the recipient determined the class of the Social Welfare Decoration that was awarded. There was a first class decoration for Generals, a second class decoration for Colonels and Lieutenant Colonels, a third class for Majors and Captains, and the medal (as seen on this bar) which was awarded to Lieutenants and below. This system was the exception rather than the standard for the issuance of awards during the Third Reich Period. Almost all other medals awarded by Germany during World War II had no such stipulation of rank. The Social Welfare Decorations were instituted in May of 1939.[5] They were intended to replace the previously instituted decorations of the German Red Cross.

The reverse of the medal bar is covered with red wool felt. The mounting plate is steel, with a nickel-plated finish. The attachment pin is brass, and the pin catch is steel.

This beautiful, five-place medal bar (**opposite bottom**) belonged to a German Officer from the Kingdom of Saxony. He was a veteran of the First World War. He was in-active in the period between the wars, but was recalled to active duty in World War II. The Iron Cross is the usual three-part construction and the core is magnetic. The Merit Order is quite rare, and was only awarded to officers. The Order was instituted by King Friedrich August of Saxony in 1815. Originally, the Order was without swords, but swords were authorized in 1866. After that, it could be awarded either with or without swords. The Merit Order seen on this medal bar is the type that was manufactured between 1911 and 1918. There were only about 1,800 of these awarded during that period.[6] The Merit Order is made of silver and the swords are silver-gilt. The enamel is white and should be opaque. The center medallion on the front shows the Crest of Saxony, surrounded by, "Friedrich August King of Saxony," as well as the original date of institution. The center medallion on the reverse has the inscription, "for merit and loyalty." On this example, the edge of the lower cross arm is stamped with the letter, "R." This maker marking was used by the Dresden firm of Alfred Rösner. The Albert Order is also struck in silver and has gold-plated swords. It has white and blue enamel, which is opaque. The front, center medallion shows the profile of Albert the Stout-Hearted. The center medallion on the reverse shows the Crest of Saxony and the year of institution: 1850. This example is marked on the edge of the lower cross arm with the letter, "G." This marking was used by Glaser & Sohn of Dresden. Notice that the Merit Order has the reversed ribbon colors of the Albert Order. Both of these Saxon Orders were awarded exclusively to officers. The Friedrich August Cross was awarded by the Grand Duchy of Oldenburg. It was a bravery decoration and was Oldenburg's equivalent to the Iron Cross of Prussia. It is estimated that at least 60,000 of these were awarded during World War I.[7] The Friedrich August Cross could be awarded to both officers and enlisted men. This example is made of die-struck iron and has a black-painted finish. The 1914-1918 Cross of Honor is made of iron and has the usual bronze finish. On the reverse, the cross is marked, "GHO." This marking was used by the Dresden firm, G.H. Osang.

The reverse of the medal bar is backed with dark green wool. The mounting plates are made of zinc and the pin and catch are brass. Large ribbon rosettes are formed at the bottom and the medals hang only slightly below.

The protective box for the medal bar is a hard to come by item. This box was supplied by the shop that assembled the bar. It is made of cardboard and covered with a textured paper of bluish-gray. The interior is lined with burgundy flocking. The name and address of the shop is embossed on the lid in gold.

*Social Welfare Medal (Obverse). These medals were die-struck from either tombak or zinc. Example shown here is an early-quality type, made of tombak. 38.22mm in diameter. $55.*

*Social Welfare Medal (Reverse). The inscription on the reverse reads, "Medal for German Social Welfare." The medal could be awarded to members of the armed forces, as well as to civilians.*

*A five-place medal bar with storage box, to an army officer from Saxony. The medals are from (L-R): 1914 Iron Cross Second Class on combatant ribbon, Saxon Merit Order- Knight's Cross Second Class with Swords, Saxon Order of Albert- Knight's Cross Second Class with Swords, Oldenburg Friedrich August Cross Second Class on combatant ribbon, and the 1914-1918 Cross of Honor with Swords. Courtesy of Edward Maroli. $1200-1400.*

*Medal bar reverse. Courtesy of Edward Maroli.*

*Obverse of the Saxon Merit Order- Knight's Cross Second Class (left) and the Saxon Albert Order- Knight's Cross Second Class (right). These enameled orders were awarded only to commissioned officers. The orders were stuck from genuine silver, and finished in gold-plate. The enamel work on both orders is opaque. Courtesy of Edward Maroli.*

*Reverse of the Albert Order (left) and Merit Order (right). Courtesy of Edward Maroli.*

*Opposite: The medal bar is shown with its protective storage box from the shop that mounted the medals. The shop is that of Oskar Rössler, located in Leipzig. A storage box such as this is a very scarce item to find in today's collector market. In the portrait photo, the original owner of the medal bar is seen beside his son. The officer wears the matching ribbon bar to this medal bar, with the addition of the ribbon to the 1939 War Merit Cross Second Class with Swords. Below the ribbon bar, he wears the 1914 Iron Cross First Class. He also wears the ribbon to the 1914 Iron Cross Second Class diagonally, through the second buttonhole of the tunic. Courtesy of Edward Maroli.*

### Armed Forces Long Service Awards

The German Armed Forces awarded medals for four, twelve, eighteen, twenty-five, and forty years of service. All of the awards were suspended from a cornflower blue ribbon. Attached to the ribbon of each medal was a national emblem (eagle). The medals were identical for all three branches of the military. For awards to the Army and Navy, a straight-winged eagle insignia was attached to the ribbon. The Air Force used their characteristic flying eagle insignia on the ribbon.

The 4-Year Medal was round and finished in matt silver. The 12-Year Medal was also round, but finished in matt gold. The 18-Year Medal was in cross form and finished in silver. The 25-Year Medal was also in cross form, but finished in gold. The 40-Year Award was nothing more than the 25-Year Cross but with the addition of a gold-finished oak leaves device, attached to the ribbon. The color of the national eagle device on the ribbon matched the color of the medal/cross. The 4 and 18-Year Awards had a silver eagle device, while the 12, 25, and 40-Year Awards had a gold eagle device.

Regulations allowed for members of the armed forces to wear two long service awards on their medal bar if so qualified. The 12-Year Medal could be worn with the 4-Year Medal. Once the 18-Year Cross was awarded, regulations specified that it be worn with the 4-Year Medal. When the 25-Year Cross was awarded, it was to be worn with the 12-Year Medal. Likewise, the 40-Year Cross was to be worn with the 12-Year Medal.

The majority of Armed Forces Long Service Awards were die-struck from iron, so most will be magnetic. However, non-magnetic originals also exist and they were made from tombak. The eagle devices that were attached to the ribbons can be either magnetic or non-magnetic.

*This type of eagle insignia was used by both the German Army and the Navy.*

*The flying eagle insignia was used by the German Air Force.*

*Obverse of the Armed Forces 4-Year Long Service Medal. This example is die-struck iron with a matt silver finish. The inscription reads, "Faithful service in the Armed Forces." 30.02mm in diameter.*

*Reverse of the Armed Forces 4-Year Long Service Medal. The reverse shows the numeral "4" within a wreath of oak leaves.*

*Obverse of the Armed Forces 12-Year Long Service Medal. Other than the color of finish, it is identical to the obverse of the 4-Year Medal. 30.27mm in diameter.*

*Reverse of the 12-Year Medal. The reverse has the numeral "12" encircled by oak leaves. This example is also die-struck iron.*

*Obverse of the Armed Forces 18-Year Long Service Cross. This example is the less encountered version, die-stuck from tombak. The cross arms should be smooth and the center stippled. 36.32mm square.*

*Reverse of the 18-Year Cross. The reverse has the numeral "18" in the center.*

*Obverse of the Armed Forces 25-Year Long Service Cross. The 25-Year Cross is larger, and both the center area and the cross arms are stippled. This example is also made of tombak. 39.95mm square.*

*Reverse of the 25-Year Cross. The reverse has the numeral "25" in the center. The central field and the cross arms are stippled as they are on the obverse.*

This medal bar (**below**) shows the wearing of the 12 and 4-Year Long Service Medals according to regulations. Both of these medals, and the eagle devices on the ribbons, are magnetic and made of iron. The highest long service award always took precedence on the medal bar and it was worn to the viewer's left. Notice that the 12-Year Medal has a gold eagle on the ribbon and the 4-Year Medal has a silver one. This style of eagle device tells us that the bar belonged to either a member of the German Army or Navy. The bar features a simple ribbon wrap without rosettes. The medals were clipped onto hooks on the front mounting plate. The only stitching done on this type of mount was a few passes of heavy thread across the ribbon ends. The medal bar has no cloth covering on the reverse. The attachment pin is brass. All other mounting hardware is made of steel. The back plate has a gray finish to it. The finish may just be paint, but it looks more like an anodized-type finish. The hinge and the catch are integral parts of the back plate. The catch shape was cut into the plate and simply bent outward. The four tabs that locked the medals into the bar are bent over on the reverse.

*A two-place medal bar consisting of the Armed Forces 12-Year Long Service Medal and the Armed Forces 4-Year Long Service Medal. $125-150.*

This five-place medal bar (**below**) belonged to a World War I veteran and member of the German Luftwaffe (Air Force). He was either a non-commissioned officer or an officer, but it is impossible to tell for sure from the medals on the bar. The Iron Cross is three-part construction and has an iron core. The frames of this Iron Cross are unusual in that they are made of silver-finished brass, instead of the usual silver or nickel-silver. The Hessen Honor Medal is made of solid .800 silver. This medal was awarded by the Grand Duchy of Hessen as a general honor decoration for bravery. It was the Hessen equivalent to the Prussian Iron Cross Second Class. The medal was awarded without regard to rank, so officers and enlisted men were eligible to receive it. About 150,000 of these medals were awarded during World War I.[8] The 1914-1918 Cross of Honor is iron with a bronze finish. It is maker marked on the reverse, "G18." The 12-Year Long Service Medal is iron with a matt gold finish. The ribbon eagle is brass and has a gold finish. The 4-Year Medal is iron with a matt silver finish. The ribbon eagle is silver-finished brass. Both eagle devices are the Luftwaffe type, but each one has slightly different details.

On the reverse of the medal bar, the mounting plate is covered with black wool, hand-stitched into place. The pin, catch, and mounting plates are all made of steel. There are also steel hooks on the front for hanging the medals from the bar. The hook is visible on the Cross of Honor and partially visible on the Iron Cross. The other hooks are hidden, underneath the ribbons.

*Five-place Luftwaffe medal bar. The medals are (L-R): 1914 Iron Cross Second Class, Hessen Honor Medal, 1914-1918 Cross of Honor with Swords, Luftwaffe 12-Year Long Service Medal, and the Luftwaffe 4-Year Long Service Medal. $250-275.*

*Right: Notice that each of these long service eagles is slightly different from the other. Just as it was with medals, many different manufacturers made small insignia, so there are bound to be differences in the small details. Both of these devices are non-magnetic and appear to be brass or tombak. The eagle at the left still retains its gold finish. The eagle on the right has lost most of its silver finish.*

*Below: Obverse of the Hessen Honor Medal. The medal is made of solid silver. The obverse shows a profile of Ernst Ludwig and reads, "Ernst Ludwig Grand Duke of Hessen."*

*Reverse of the Hessen Honor Medal. The reverse has the inscription, "for bravery." The inscription is surrounded by a wreath of laurel and oak leaves.*

This three-place bar (**page 104**) is in excellent condition. Both of the Long Service Medals are magnetic and made of iron. The eagle devices on the ribbons are tombak and non-magnetic. These eagle devices are unusual because they do not have the typical two prongs on the reverse. Instead, they have an eyelet soldered to the center reverse. This allowed the eagle devices to be sewn in place instead of having to push prongs through the ribbon. The Defense Wall Honor Award (also known as the West Wall Medal) is die-struck bronze. The West Wall Medal was awarded to members of the Armed Forces and to civilians who were involved in the planning, construction, and defense of the German fortifications in the west. Early issues of this award were solid bronze and later issues were made of zinc. The reverse of the medal bar is backed with red wool felt. The mounting plates are zinc, and the attachment pin and catch are brass. The ribbons have nicely gathered rosettes at the bottom. This would be considered a traditional style German mount.

*Opposite: This Luftwaffe Oberst (Air Force Colonel) wears a six-place medal bar consisting of the 1914 Iron Cross Second Class, Hohenzollern House Order, 1914-1918 Cross of Honor with Swords, Luftwaffe 12-Year Long Service Medal, Luftwaffe 4-Year Long Service Medal, and an unconfirmed award (possibly the Austrian Military Merit Cross). Below the medal bar he wears the 1914 Iron Cross First Class, a cut-out type World War I Wound Badge, and two other badges. On the lower part of his right breast pocket, he wears the Austro-Hungarian Field Pilot's Badge of the 1913-1916 type. Courtesy of George Robinson.*

*A three-place German Army medal bar. The medals are from (L-R): Wehrmacht 12-Year Long Service Medal, Wehrmacht 4-Year Long Service Medal, and the Defense Wall Honor Award. $150-175.*

*Medal bar reverse.*

This five-place medal bar (**opposite**) belonged to either an officer or non-commissioned officer with at least eighteen, but less than twenty-five years of service in the military. He could have been a member of the Army or the Navy. The medals are nicely mounted and placed exactly according to the regulations. (Notice that the 18-Year Cross is worn with the 4-Year Medal, and that the 18-Year Cross is placed before the 4-Year Medal.) The Iron Cross has a magnetic core and the silver frames are heavily tarnished. The War Merit Cross is a later-war piece, struck from zinc. There is wear to the bronze color wash, revealing the gray-colored base metal underneath. The Cross of Honor is iron and finished in bronze. It is maker marked on the reverse with the logo, "PSL" within a circle. The marking is in relief. This logo was used by the manufacturer, Paul Schulze & Company, located in Lübeck. The 18-Year Cross is the less encountered, non-magnetic version. It is made of tombak and finished in silver. The 4-Year Medal is magnetic and made of iron. Both eagle devices are magnetic. They are silver-finished iron.

On the reverse of the medal bar, the zinc mounting plate is covered with black wool. The wool is neatly stitched in place with black thread. Both the pin and catch are made of brass. The ribbons are gathered into large rosettes at the bottom, but the medals hang down partially below them. I refer to this style of mount as the "modified traditional" pattern.

A five-place medal bar. The medals are from (L-R): 1914 Iron Cross Second Class on combatant ribbon, 1939 War Merit Cross Second Class with Swords, 1914-1918 Cross of Honor with Swords, Wehrmacht 18-Year Long Service Cross, and the Wehrmacht 4-Year Long Service Medal. $325-350.

Im Namen
des Führers und Reichskanzlers
verleihe ich

dem Uffz. Albrecht Georg
(Dienstgrad, Vor- und Zuname)

Kavallerieschützenregiment 10
(Truppenteil)

für 4 jährige treue Dienste in der Wehrmacht

die Dienstauszeichnung
IV. Klasse

Wien, den 1. Mai 1939

Generalmajor
u. Kommandeur 4. leichte Division

(Dienststempel)

*This is an example of an award document for the Wehrmacht 4-Year Long Service Medal, awarded to an Army NCO in Cavalry Protection Regiment 10. The document is signed by Generalmajor Alfred Ritter von Hubicki, as Commander of the 4th. Light Division.[9] There was a multitude of variations for Wehrmacht Long Service documents. This award was given in Vienna, Austria on May 1, 1939. The document refers to the 4-Year Medal as the Fourth Class. $35-40.*

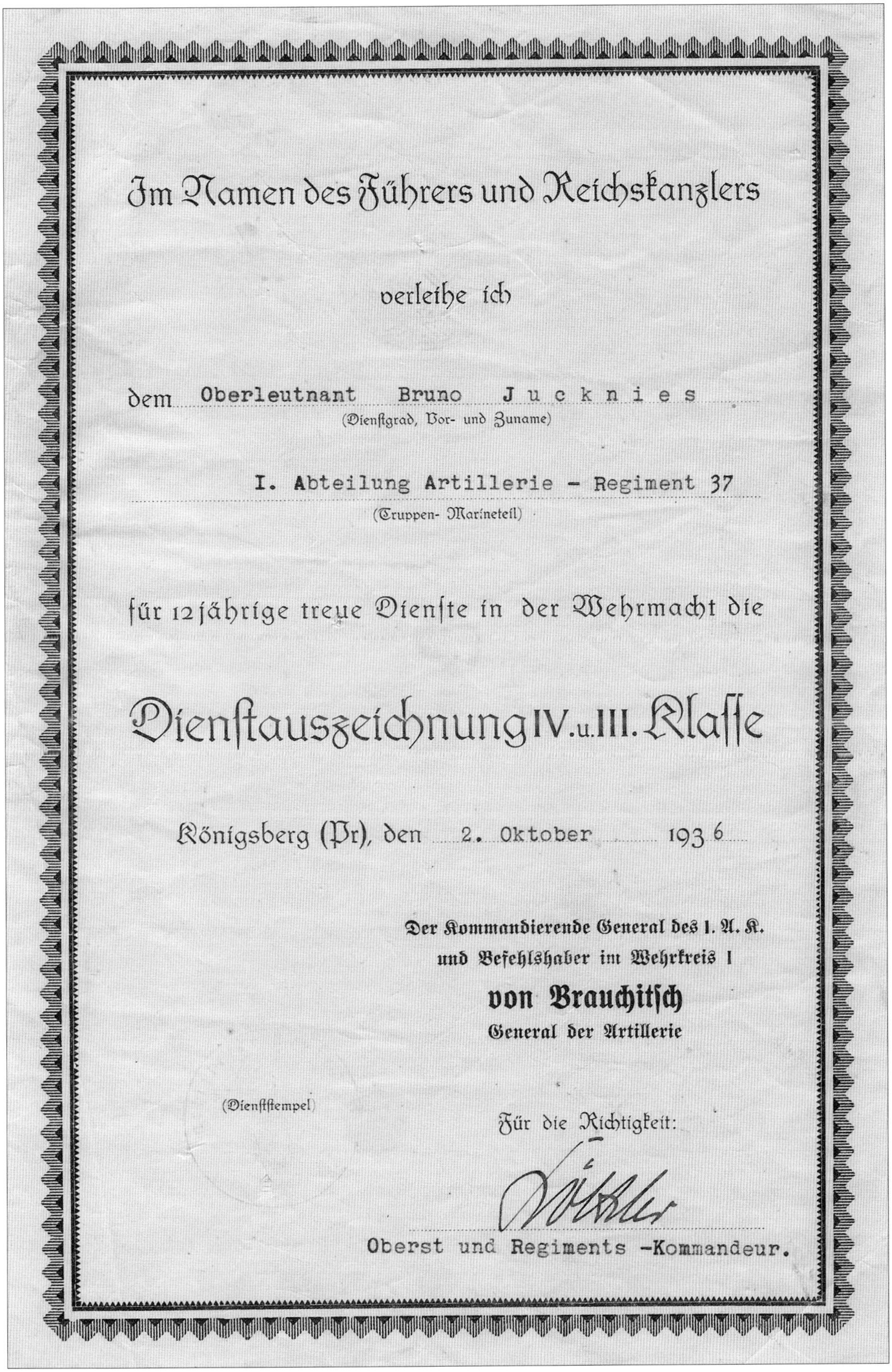

Im Namen des Führers und Reichskanzlers

verleihe ich

dem Oberleutnant Bruno J u c k n i e s

(Dienstgrad, Vor- und Zuname)

I. Abteilung Artillerie – Regiment 37

(Truppen- Marineteil)

für 12jährige treue Dienste in der Wehrmacht die

Dienstauszeichnung IV. u. III. Klasse

Königsberg (Pr), den 2. Oktober 1936

Der Kommandierende General des I. A. K.
und Befehlshaber im Wehrkreis I
von Brauchitsch
General der Artillerie

(Dienststempel)

Für die Richtigkeit:

Oberst und Regiments -Kommandeur.

*This document is to an Oberleutnant (First Lieutenant) in Artillery Regiment 37. The document is for the simultaneous awarding of both the 4-Year (Fourth Class) and the 12-Year (Third Class) Medals. The award was made in Königsberg on October 2, 1936. The document is signed by the Oberst (Colonel) and Regimental Commander. As a further note: The 18-Year Long Service Cross was referred to as the Second Class and the 25-Year Cross as the First Class. The 40-Year Long Service Cross was referred to as the First Class with oak leaves. $65-75.*

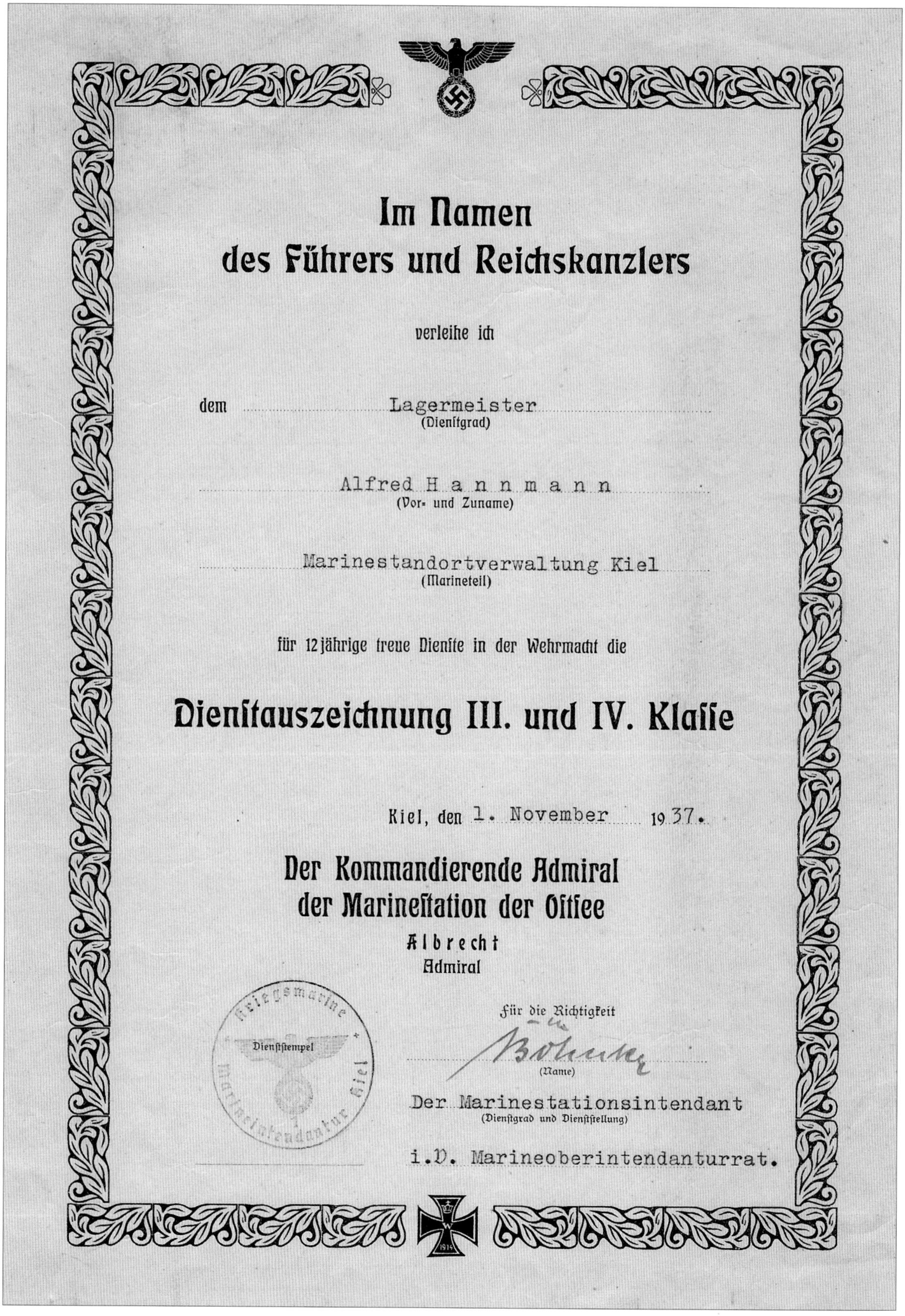

Im Namen
des Führers und Reichskanzlers

verleihe ich

dem Lagermeister
(Dienſtgrad)

Alfred H a n n m a n n
(Vor- und Zuname)

Marinestandortverwaltung Kiel
(Marineteil)

für 12 jährige treue Dienſte in der Wehrmacht die

Dienſtauszeichnung III. und IV. Klaſſe

Kiel, den 1. November 1937.

Der Kommandierende Admiral
der Marineſtation der Oſtſee
Albrecht
Admiral



Für die Richtigkeit
(Name)
Der Marinestationsintendant
(Dienſtgrad und Dienſtſtellung)
i.V. Marineoberintendanturrat.

*This document is also for the simultaneous awarding of both the 4 and 12-Year Long Service Medals, but in this case it is to a Naval Official. The awards were given in Kiel on November 1, 1937. Documents also exist where three, and even all four classes were awarded simultaneously. The Wehrmacht Long Service Awards were instituted in March of 1936 and awards were retroactive for prior service time. By the end of 1940, awarding of the Armed Forces Long Service Medals had apparently ceased. I have never seen one dated after December of 1940. $70-80.*

This six-place bar (**below**) belonged to either an officer or non-commissioned officer in the German Luftwaffe (Air Force). He was a World War I veteran and career military man with at least eighteen years of service at the time this medal bar was assembled. The medals are beautifully mounted. This is an interesting medal bar, not only because of the two Finnish medals worn to the right, but also because it shows the long service awards mounted contrary to the regulations. The placement of the medals is correct, except for the two long service awards, which should actually be switched around in order. The 18-Year Cross should be worn before the 4-Year Medal, not after it. Whether this was a simple mistake, a misinterpretation of the regulations, or intentionally done to give the bar a more balanced look is purely a matter of speculation. The Iron Cross is a standard three-part example with a magnetic core. The Cross of Honor is bronze-finished iron and is maker marked, "KM&F." This marking was used by Kallenbach, Meyer & Franke of Luckenwalde. The 4-Year Medal is iron with a matt silver finish and the 18-Year Cross is silver-finished tombak. Both of the eagles on the ribbons are non-magnetic. The Finnish Medal of Liberty is made of bronze. On the front it has the inscription, "for gallantry" in both Finnish and Swedish. The reverse has the inscription, "from the people of Finland 1918." This medal was awarded to NCOs and other ranks for bravery in the field.[10] The Liberation War Medal is magnetic and made of blackened iron. This medal was awarded simply for participation in the War for the Liberation of Finland.[11] The owner of this medal bar was almost certainly a member of the German Baltic Division, which assisted Finland in securing their independence in 1918.

The reverse of the medal bar shows the same quality of assembly that is present on the front. The ribbons are formed into nicely-gathered rosettes at the bottom. The mounting plates are non-magnetic and made of zinc.

*A very interesting six-place Luftwaffe medal bar showing long service awards worn contrary to regulations. The medals are from (L-R): 1914 Iron Cross Second Class on combatant ribbon, 1914-1918 Cross of Honor with Swords, Luftwaffe 4-Year Long Service Medal, Luftwaffe 18-Year Long Service Cross, the Finnish 1918 Medal of Liberty Second Class, and the Finnish Liberation War Medal of 1918. Below: Medal bar reverse. Courtesy of George Robinson. $425-475.*

*A close up, obverse view of the 1918 Finnish Medal of Liberty and the Finnish Liberation War Medal of 1918. These two medals are not often seen on a German medal bar. Courtesy of George Robinson.*

The back plate is visible below the bottom edge of the cloth backing. Both the pin and catch are made of brass. The backing cloth is green wool and it has a zigzag cut to both the top and bottom edges. Attached to the cloth backing is a maker label, which is actually a metal button that is riveted to the cloth. The button is silver with lettering in black. The lettering reads, "WOLFG.ROB.SCHWARZ-DIREKT AM WEDDINGPLATZ." In my opinion, this is one of the more frequently encountered labels. Over the years, I have noticed quite a few medal bars with the assembler label/button of Wolfgang Robert Schwarz. Every example that I have seen has been well made. Schwarz usually provided a protective storage box with the medal bars they assembled. The box was plain cardboard with a pull off lid. The Schwarz logo, company name, and address were printed on the lid in black.

This beautiful medal bar (**below**) belonged to either a Luftwaffe officer or a non-commissioned officer, and certainly to one who made a career out of the military. Although at first glance it looks like a six-place medal bar, this one is actually considered a seven-place bar because of the 1939 Iron Cross Clasp, which is attached to the ribbon of the 1914 Iron Cross. The medal bar is nicely mounted and is in excellent condition considering its age. The Iron Cross is magnetic. It has an iron core and silver frames. The 1939 Clasp, attached to the ribbon of the 1914 Iron Cross, looks to be made of nickel-silver. It is attached to the ribbon by two metal prongs. The clasp signifies that the owner of this bar was decorated with the Iron Cross Second Class in both World War I and World War II. The Cross of Honor is made of iron and finished in bronze. It is maker marked on the reverse, "G&S." This marking was used by Glaser & Sohn

*A German Luftwaffe medal bar consisting of from (L-R): 1914 Iron Cross Second Class on combatant ribbon and to which is attached the 1939 Clasp to the Iron Cross Second Class, 1914-1918 Cross of Honor with Swords, Luftwaffe 25-Year Long Service Cross, Luftwaffe 12-Year Long Service Medal, the World War I Commemorative Medal for Austria, and the World War I Hungarian Commemorative Medal. $500-525.*

*Medal bar reverse.*

*The 1939 Clasp to the 1914 Iron Cross Second Class signifies that the wearer was awarded the Iron Cross Second Class in World War I and again in World War II. This clasp is not often seen on a medal bar. This example is a half-size version. It measures 15mm x 15mm. The full-size clasp was about 30mm x 30mm. There was also a "Prinzen" version of the clasp that was about 25mm x 25mm.*

*The quality of this 25-Year Long Service Cross is quite remarkable. From looking at this photo, it is hard to believe that this cross is made of iron and can have such a beautiful finish. Try taking a magnet to some of your medals. Some that you would never think were made of iron are just that. You may really be surprised.*

of Dresden. The 25-Year Long Service Cross is magnetic and made of iron. This example is the nicest one I have ever seen. It has a flawless gold finish and burnished highlights. The 12-Year Long Service Medal is also made of iron. It is finished in matt gold. Both of the ribbon eagles are non-magnetic and attached by two prongs. The Austrian Commemorative Medal is bronze. The crossed swords device on the ribbon looks to be brass with a gold finish. The Hungarian Medal is a non-magnetic base metal with an antiqued silver finish. Notice how the reds in the ribbons of the Austrian and Hungarian Medals have faded. This medal bar is mounted per regulations with no error in the placement of any of the awards. On the reverse, the medal bar is backed with dark green wool. The pin and the catch are both made of brass. The mounting plates are sheet steel, but they have a brass or gold-colored finish to them.

This six-place medal bar (**below**) belonged to another career military man serving in either the Army or Navy. He was either an officer or non-commissioned officer. We cannot know for sure because there are no decorations on this bar that were exclusive to officers. The bar is nicely mounted and all of the medals are aligned at the bottom. This is an interesting medal bar because it shows two long service crosses being worn contrary to the regulations. According to the regulations, the 25-Year Long Service Cross was to be worn with the 12-Year Medal. Therefore, in a perfect world, we should never see the 25-Year Cross being worn with the 18-Year Cross. But did it ever happen? Yes, of course it did, and this bar is a good example of how the regulations were not always followed to the letter by everyone. This could have been nothing more than a simple mistake, due to ignorance or misinterpretation of the regulations. On the other hand, the owner of this bar may have been a stubborn individual who wanted to wear his two long service crosses together, and nothing, or no one was going to tell him otherwise. After all, the crosses are more impressive looking than a round medal aren't they? Even in a rigid military society, where everything is structured and individualism obscured, the character of the individual will still reveal itself from time to time.

The Iron Cross has an iron core and silver frames. The lower arm of the cross is secured with heavy thread. The War Merit Cross is an early-issue, made of bronze. The Cross of Honor is iron with a bronze finish. It is maker marked, "G&S" on the reverse of the lower arm. Both of the long service crosses are magnetic and made of iron. The 25-Year Cross is finished in gold and the 18-Year Cross is finished in silver. Both of the ribbon eagles are non-magnetic and finished to match the crosses that they are paired with. The Hungarian Commemorative Medal is a non-magnetic base metal and has a darkened-silver finish. The medal bar reverse is

*A Six-place medal bar showing two long service crosses worn contrary to regulations. The medals are from (L-R): 1914 Iron Cross Second Class, 1939 War Merit Cross Second Class with Swords, 1914-1918 Cross of Honor with Swords, Armed Forces 25-Year Long Service Cross, Armed Forces 18-Year Long Service Cross, and the World War I Hungarian Commemorative Medal. Below: Medal bar reverse. $400-425.*

*Both the 25-Year and 18-Year Crosses shown here are magnetic and made of iron. Iron was used in the making of many more medals than collectors realize. The fact that they are iron does not mean that they are late-war quality either. The majority, if not all, of the Armed Forces Long Service Awards were produced in the years from 1936 until 1939, so regardless of the base metal, they must all be considered early-quality. By the end of 1940, these awards were no longer being given out.*

backed in black wool. The bottom edge of the backing has a zigzag cut to it. The mounting plates are zinc and non-magnetic. The pin and catch are made of brass.

This seven-place medal bar (**below**) shows a terrific combination of awards to a long-time, career military man. While it does show the proper display of the two long service awards, the bar is not entirely within regulations because of the incorrect placement of the 1939 War Merit Cross. This is also an interesting medal bar because it has a non-combatant 1914 Iron Cross. A non-combatant Iron Cross is seldom seen on a medal bar. This medal bar may have belonged to a combat medic in World War I, who remained in the military between the wars and then continued to serve as a medic in World War II. The Iron Cross is a standard three-part construction with a magnetic core. There is no difference between a combatant and a non-combatant Iron Cross. The only thing which distinguishes one from the other is the ribbon from which the cross is suspended. Notice that the ribbon on this Iron Cross has the colors reversed: The combatant ribbon is predominately black with two white stripes while the non-combatant ribbon is predominately white with two black stripes. The Merit Cross for War Aid is die-struck zinc. This award was instituted in December of 1916.[12] It could be awarded to men and women, regardless of their status, for meritorious assistance in the war effort. The Cross of Honor is iron with a bronze finish. It is maker marked, "G&S" for Glaser and Sohn of Dresden. The 1939 War Merit Cross is an early-issue type, made of solid bronze. The War Merit Cross should actually be placed second on this bar, immediately after the Iron Cross and before the War Aid and Honor Crosses. Again, this may have been just a mistake, but it could also be that the owner of this bar felt his contributions in World War I were far more significant than anything he did in World War II. He therefore valued all of his World War I decorations more than the 1939 War Merit Cross. The Silesian Eagle Second Class is die-stuck iron with a painted finish of black

*A seven-place medal bar. The medals are from (L-R): 1914 Iron Cross Second Class worn on a non-combatant ribbon, Prussian Merit Cross for War Aid, 1914-1918 Cross of Honor without Swords, 1939 War Merit Cross Second Class with Swords, the Silesian Eagle Second Class, the Armed Forces 25-Year Long Service Cross, and the Armed Forces 12-Year Long Service Medal. $525-550.*

*Above: Medal bar reverse.*

*The Silesian Eagle Second Class is made of iron and is magnetic. It is a single-piece construction and considered the standard issue type. There are also non-magnetic and enameled versions of this award, which are considered to be private-purchase types. The inscription on the banner, held in the eagle's talons reads, "For Silesia." The reverse of the medal is plain. The medal was suspended from a yellow ribbon having a white central stripe.*

and silver. This award was instituted in June of 1919.[13] Between 1919 and 1921, there were several uprisings by Polish Nationals against the Germans in Silesia. The award was given to those that defended Silesia and served in the area for three months. It is considered a non-official award because it recognized *Freikorps* (free corps) paramilitary units that were not part of the regular army. The Silesian Eagle was one of only two *Freikorps* awards that were permitted to be worn during the Third Reich Period. (The other was the Baltic Cross.) Both of the Long Service Awards, and the attached eagle devices, are iron with a gold finish. The reverse of the medal bar has a backing of red wool. The wool has a zigzag cut along the bottom edge. The pin is brass, but the catch is zinc. All of the mounting plates are zinc and non-magnetic.

This large, eight-place medal bar (**opposite**) is another fine example showing the service and accomplishments of a career military man. This medal bar shows the correct placement of all awards, exactly per regulations. All of the medals but one are made of the standard materials and have the typical finishes. Both of the long service awards and the ribbon eagles are magnetic. The only non-standard item on this bar is the Silesian Eagle, which is a non-magnetic example and thought to be a private purchase type. Rather than being finished in black, the eagle has a gold-toned finish. The reverse of the medal bar is backed with red wool. The pin and catch are made of brass. The mounting plates are non-magnetic and made of zinc. The reverse of the 1914-1918 Cross of Honor is marked, "R.V. PFORZHEIM 29."

*An eight-place medal bar. The medals are from (L-R): 1914 Iron Cross Second Class on combatant ribbon, Hamburg Hanseatic Cross, 1914-1918 Cross of Honor with Swords, Silesian Eagle Second Class, Armed Forces 25-Year Long Service Cross, Armed Forces 12-Year Long Service Medal, the World War I Commemorative Medal for Hungary, and the World War I Commemorative Medal for Bulgaria. Courtesy of George Robinson. $525-550.*

*Right: This Silesian Eagle Second Class is thought to be a deluxe quality, private-purchase type. It is of multi-part construction. The crescent and Silesia banner are separate attachments, riveted in place. This example is non-magnetic. Courtesy of George Robinson.*

*Medal bar consisting of from (L-R): 1914 Iron Cross Second Class, 1914-1918 Cross of Honor with Swords, Armed Forces 4-Year Long Service Medal, and the Medal for the Annexation of Czechoslovakia. Below: Medal bar reverse. $150-175.*

This four-place medal bar (**opposite**) is nicely mounted in the modified traditional style. The Iron Cross has a magnetic center core and the frames are silver. The upper arm of the cross was once secured with heavy thread, but it has since broken away. There are four holes present in the ribbon of the Iron Cross. At one time this medal bar must have had a 1939 Iron Cross Clasp attached to the ribbon. It is a pity that the clasp is no longer present. What happened to it is anybody's guess. It is highly unlikely that it fell off, so it must have been intentionally removed by someone. This kind of thing happened frequently in past years. People would remove items from medal bars, and even completely dismantle them, so that they could sell off the items individually. Selling the items separately would usually yield more money so people didn't think twice about taking bars apart. This is sad but true. It still happens today, but to a much lesser degree. Collectors and even most dealers realize now that an intact medal bar is more valuable than a pile of parts. The Cross of Honor is iron with a bronze finish. The cross is secured with heavy thread at the sword ends, just above the laurel wreath. The reverse is marked with the letters "CEJ" within a rectangle. This marking was used by C. E. Juncker of Berlin. The 4-Year Long Service Medal is iron with a matt silver finish. The ribbon eagle is tombak with a silver finish. The Czech Annexation Medal is bronze and non-magnetic. The medal bar reverse is backed with dark gray wool. The attachment pin is heavy gauge brass and the catch is brass sheet. The mounting plates are non-magnetic and made of zinc.

The medal bar shown at the top of page 119 displays a nice combination of awards. I find it very appealing because of the predominate reds in all of the ribbons. This is considered a seven-place medal bar because of the Prague Castle Bar, attached to the ribbon of the Czech Annexation Medal. It is an interesting and desirable medal bar because all of the awards are of the Third Reich Period. An all-Third Reich medal bar of this size is seldom seen. Most of the larger medal bars were to those that served in both World

*If you look at this picture closely, you will see four holes in the ribbon of the 1914 Iron Cross. These holes mark the spot where the prongs of the 1939 Iron Cross Clasp were once attached to the ribbon. Why the clasp was removed, one can only guess. Removing an item from the medal bar will substantially reduce the overall value. From the spacing of the four holes, it is obvious that this bar once had the full-size Iron Cross Clasp attached. These were typically about 30mm wide x 30mm high.*

*A 1939 Clasp to the 1914 Iron Cross Second Class, similar to the one shown here, was once attached to the medal bar. This example measures 30.58mm wide x 30.86mm high. The weight of this clasp is 8.7 grams, including the ribbon to which it is attached. $175-200.*

*Four, flat metal prongs were soldered to the reverse of the clasp. The prongs were pushed through the ribbon and then bent over to secure the clasp.*

*This 1939 Clasp is an example of the later-war type. It is made of die-struck zinc, rather than the tombak or nickel-silver of the earlier types. The finish on these was little more than a silver color wash and it typically fades away over time, leaving an unattractive, dark gray appearance. This clasp also has four metal prongs soldered on the reverse. The reverse is marked, "L/11." This marking was the commercial production code used by the manufacturer: Wilhelm Deumer of Lüdenscheid. The clasp shown here is attached to a sales sample board, which was used by the Deumer firm for promoting their wares.*

*The Medal for the Crusade against Communism was awarded by Romania to a large number of Germans that fought on the Russian Front. Since it is a foreign award, it should always be placed last on the medal bar. The medal was struck in bronze. The front of the medal features a fist, clutching an upraised sword, superimposed over a Balkan cross. Around the outer portion of the medal is the inscription, "Crusade against Communism." Although instituted in 1942, the medal bears the date 1941, which signifies the year in which the invasion of the Soviet Union began.*

War I and World War II, and thus display a combination of Imperial and Third Reich Period awards. The medals are nicely mounted and correctly placed per regulations. Notice that the Iron Cross is worn first (to viewer's left) on the bar because it is a combat valor decoration. The Russian Front Medal was given a high order of precedence on the medal bar, so it was worn immediately after any valor decorations. The two annexation medals are placed next, and the Austrian Annexation is worn before the Czech Annexation Medal. This is because Austria was annexed in March of 1938 and Czechoslovakia was annexed in October of 1938. Annexation medals were worn on the medal bar by date of occurrence. The commemorative medal is placed after the annexation medals and the foreign award is placed last on the bar. Notice that there is no Armed Forces Long Service Award on this bar. The owner of this medal bar was probably working in a civilian capacity at the time of the 1936 Olympic Games. By the time of the annexation of Austria and Czechoslovakia, he may have been in the military, but he could have also earned those awards as a civilian. Even if he had entered the military in 1937, by the time he would have been eligible to receive the 4-Year Long Service Medal, the Armed Forces had discontinued awarding them.

The Iron Cross has a magnetic core made of iron and the frames are nickel-silver. The Russian Front Medal is made of zinc. The silver wash on the rim and helmet of the medal have faded and only traces remain. The Austrian Annexation Medal is bronze with a silver finish. The Czech Annexation Medal and the Prague Castle Bar are bronze. The Olympic Games Commemorative Medal on this medal bar is uncommon. Whereas most were struck from iron and silvered, this example is non-magnetic. It is made of tombak and finished in silver. The Romanian Medal for the Crusade against Communism is solid bronze. This medal was instituted in April of 1942 and awarded through 1944.[14] After that, Romania came under Soviet control and therefore the medal ceased to exist. It could be awarded to all ranks and was given for distinguished service on the Eastern Front. Romania awarded these to a large number of Germans fighting in the east. The inscription on the front of the medal reads, "Crusade against communism." The reverse inscription reads, "Romania is grateful."[15] All of the mounting and attachment hardware is made of steel. The medal bar is backed with dark green wool.

*A medal bar consisting of all-Third Reich Period awards. Medals are from (L-R): 1939 Iron Cross Second Class, Medal for the 1941/42 Winter Battle in the East, Medal for the Annexation of Austria, Medal for the Annexation of Czechoslovakia with the Prague Castle Bar attached, the 1936 Olympic Games Commemorative Medal, and the Romanian Medal for the Crusade Against Communism. $365-380.*

*Below: Medal bar reverse. Right: The Prague Castle Bar signified that the recipient was involved in the occupation of the Sudetenland as well as Bohemia and Moravia. The bar is die-struck bronze with a matt gold finish. It was attached to the ribbon by two metal prongs that were soldered to the reverse. This example measures 31.09mm x 11.05mm.*

This is another medal bar (**below**) consisting of awards that are all from the Third Reich Period. It is considered a five-place medal bar because of the bar attached to the Czech Annexation Medal. The Iron Cross is a typical example with a magnetic core and nickel-silver frames. There is no maker marking on the suspension ring. The War Merit Cross is an early issue type, made of solid bronze. Likewise, there is no marking on the suspension ring. The 4-Year Long Service Medal is iron and the attached eagle device is silver-finished tombak. Both the Czech Annexation Medal and the attached Prague Castle Bar are made of bronze. This example of the Prague Castle Bar measures 30.81mm long x 10.77mm high. The medal bar has nickel-plated, steel clips on the front for attaching the medals. On the reverse, the bar has a backing of red wool felt. The cloth backing has a pinking shear cut along the lower edge. The mounting plates are zinc with an integral catch and hinge. The attachment pin is brass.

*Another example of a medal bar with all awards of the Third Reich Period. Medals are from (L-R): 1939 Iron Cross Second Class, 1939 War Merit Cross Second Class with Swords, Armed Forces 4-Year Long Service Medal, and the Medal for the Annexation of Czechoslovakia with the Prague Castle Bar. $250-275.*

A four-place medal such as this (**below**) may have belonged to a young officer or non-commissioned officer. The bar was probably assembled in 1940 or 1941. All of the medals are from the Third Reich Period. The Iron Cross has an iron core and the frames are nickel-silver. The War Merit Cross is the early-quality type, made of bronze. The 4-Year Medal is iron with a silver finish. Unfortunately, the eagle device is missing from the ribbon. The two holes from the prongs of the eagle device are visible. The Defense Wall Honor Award is also an early-quality example, made of solid bronze. The medal bar is backed with gray-green wool. The mounting plates are zinc and the catch is an integral part of the back plate. The attachment pin is made of brass.

*Four-place medal bar consisting of the 1939 Iron Cross Second Class, 1939 War Merit Cross Second Class with Swords, Armed Forces 4-Year Long Service Medal, and the Defense Wall Honor Award. $200-225.*

*Three-place medal bar. Medals are from (L-R): 1939 Iron Cross Second Class, Armed Forces 4-Year Long Service Medal, and the Medal for the Annexation of Czechoslovakia. $160-175.*

This three-place medal bar (**opposite**) is a common grouping of awards. This medal bar would have belonged to either a member of the Army or Navy, and most likely an NCO or young officer. The 1939 Iron Cross has a magnetic core. The frames of this cross are either silver-plated or genuine silver. While many 1914 Iron Crosses had frames of genuine silver, the frames of most 1939 Iron Crosses were only silver-plated or nickel-silver. The Armed Forces 4-Year Long Service Medal is die-struck iron and magnetic. The eagle device on the ribbon is non-magnetic. The Czech Annexation Medal is die-struck bronze. On the reverse, the medal bar is backed with dark blue wool. The mounting plates are zinc, while the attachment pin and catch are made of brass. Black colored cotton fiber was used to pad the ribbons. In the accompanying wartime wedding photo, a German Army NCO is seen wearing a medal bar with the same combination of awards.

This Luftwaffe medal bar and matching ribbon bar (**below**) are in excellent condition. Because of the presence of the 4-Year Long Service Medal, I would suspect that the owner entered the military no later than 1936, and that he was either an NCO or junior officer. The Iron Cross is the typical three-part construction. The core is magnetic and the frames are nickel-silver. The 4-Year Medal and the eagle device are non-magnetic. The Czech Annexation Medal and the attached Prague Castle Bar are tombak bronze with a gold finish. The ribbon bar has non-magnetic eagle and Prague Castle devices. Both the medal bar and ribbon bar have sheet steel mounting plates, with integral hinge/catch setups. The attachment pins are also steel. All metal hardware has a nickel-plated finish.

This three-place bar (**page 124**) features an iron 4-Year Long Service Medal. The eagle device is missing from the ribbon, but from the impression that remains, you can tell that it was a Luftwaffe type eagle. The Czech Annexation Medal is tombak with a golden bronze finish, and the Defense Wall Honor Award is the early, solid bronze type. The front of the bar has steel clips for attaching the medals. The reverse of the medal bar is backed with blue-gray wool felt. The mounting plates are zinc. The pin, hinge, and catch are all made of brass.

*This army non-commissioned officer wears a three-place medal bar on his parade dress uniform. Medals are from (L-R): 1939 Iron Cross Second Class, Armed Forces 4-Year Long Service Medal, and the Medal for the Annexation of Czechoslovakia.*

*Luftwaffe medal bar and matching ribbon bar. Medals are from (L-R): 1939 Iron Cross Second Class, Luftwaffe 4-Year Long Service Medal, and the Medal for the Annexation of Czechoslovakia with the Prague Castle Bar. Medal bar: $225-250. Ribbon bar: $25-30.*

*A three-place medal bar consisting of the Luftwaffe 4-Year Long Service Medal, Medal for the Annexation of Czechoslovakia, and the Defense Wall Honor Award. Note the missing eagle device from the long service ribbon. From the impression that is left in the ribbon, you can clearly see that it was a Luftwaffe style eagle. $125.*

This five-place, all-Third Reich medal bar (**opposite**) has a three-piece Iron Cross with a magnetic core and nickel-silver frames. The Medal for the Winter Battle in the East is zinc. The silver color wash to the medal rim and helmet has faded. Both the 4-Year Long Service Medal and the eagle device are non-magnetic. The Defense Wall Honor Award and the Czech Annexation Medal are bronze. The reverse of the medal bar is backed with brown wool. The mounting plates are zinc, with an integral hinge/catch setup. The attachment pin is steel. The medal bar is a bit contrary to regulations because the Czech Annexation Medal should be placed before the Defense Wall Award, not after it. I have read in a couple of references that members of the armed forces were not eligible for the Defense Wall Honor Award if they had already received the Czech Annexation or Memel Medals. If this is true, then this medal bar and the three-place bar shown previously are contradictions to the regulation. The presence of the 4-Year Long Service Medal would eliminate the possibility that one or both of the medals were awarded while in civilian service. I'm not sure what to make of this regulation. I do know that the Chief of the SS and German Police, Heinrich Himmler, had the Austrian Annexation, Czech Annexation with Prague Bar, Memel, and Defense Wall Medals on his medal bar.[16] Of course, the same rules probably did not apply to somebody like Himmler. I also recall seeing original ribbon bars that had both the Czech Annexation and Defense Wall ribbons. There is also photographic evidence that seems to contradict this regulation.[17]

Here is an interesting six-place medal bar (**page 126**) displaying all awards of the Third Reich Period. The medals, ribbons, and other assembly components are all original to the period, but in my opinion the medal bar was assembled post-World War II. The 1939 Iron Cross has a magnetic core and nickel-silver frames. The 1939 War Merit Cross is zinc with a bronze color wash. Both the Medal for the Winter Battle in the East and the Campaign Medal for the Spanish Volunteers in Russia are made of die-forged zinc. The Austrian Annexation Medal is tombak with a silver finish and the Czech Annexation Medal is tombak with a gold finish. The medal bar has steel mounting plates and a steel catch. The pin is made of brass. On the reverse, the bar is backed with black wool. The reason I believe this bar was assembled post-World War II is because of the presence of the Campaign Medal for the Spanish Volunteers in Russia. As far as I know, this medal was only awarded to Spanish volunteers that fought for Germany. I think it highly unlikely that a Spanish volunteer would have been awarded the Austrian and Czech Annexation Medals. The Medal for the Spanish Volunteers in Russia was instituted in January of 1944.[18] Originals (at least those made in Germany during World War II) should be in zinc only. The central stripe on the ribbon should actually be yellow, but the color has faded away and now appears white. On the reverse, the yellow color is still present. Apparently it was more protected from the bleaching effect of exposure to light.

*A five-place medal bar. Medals are from (L-R): 1939 Iron Cross Second Class, Medal for the 1941/42 Winter Battle in the East, Armed Forces 4-Year Long Service Medal, Defense Wall Honor Award, and the Medal for the Annexation of Czechoslovakia. Courtesy of Edward Maroli. $250-275.*

*A six-place medal bar consisting of all-Third Reich Period awards. Medals are from (L-R): 1939 Iron Cross Second Class, 1939 War Merit Cross Second Class with Swords, Medal for the 1941/42 Winter Battle in the East, Campaign Medal for the Spanish Volunteers in Russia, Medal for the Annexation of Austria, and the Medal for the Annexation of Czechoslovakia. This bar has all original medals, ribbons, and other assembly components, but in my opinion it was assembled in the post-war period. $300-325.*

The preceding three medal bars show a 1939 Iron Cross Second Class paired with another medal. These are all considered common groupings, and typical for younger members of the armed forces. Most would have been awarded only two or three ribboned medals during World War II. The larger medal bars were usually to those that had a long career in the military and served in both world wars. The first bar shows a 1939 Iron Cross in combination with a Czech Annexation Medal. The medals are of the usual construction and base materials. The front has steel attachment clips for the medals. The bar has a zinc mounting plate with applied brass hinge and catch. The pin is also made of brass. The backing material is gray-green wool. The second, two-place medal bar and matching ribbon bar, has a 1939 Iron Cross paired with a 1939 War Merit Cross. The Iron Cross is typical for the period and the War Merit Cross is the early-war, solid bronze type. This bar also has steel clips for attaching the medals. The reverse is backed with gray wool. The mounting plate is zinc, with an integral catch and brass pin. The ribbon bar has steel plates with an integral hinge/catch setup. The steel plates have a gold-colored finish. The pin is also steel. The ribbon bar is backed with light gray felt. The crossed swords device is made of iron. The third bar shows a 1939 Iron Cross in combination with an Armed Forces 4-Year Long Service Medal. The Iron Cross is magnetic as is the 4-Year Medal. The eagle device for the 4-Year Medal is non-magnetic. Again, there are steel clips on the front for medal attachment. The reverse is backed with black wool, having a zigzag cut to all four edges. The mounting plate is zinc with applied, brass attachment components. The following three wartime photographs show two-place medal bars featuring the 1939 Iron Cross.

*A two-place medal bar consisting of the 1939 Iron Cross Second Class and the Medal for the Annexation of Czechoslovakia. $125-150.*

*Two-place medal bar with matching ribbon bar. Medals are from (L-R): 1939 Iron Cross Second Class and the 1939 War Merit Cross Second Class with Swords. Medal bar: $125-150. Ribbon bar: $10-15.*

*Two-place medal bar consisting of the 1939 Iron Cross Second Class and the Armed Forces 4-Year Long Service Medal. $135-155.*

Both of these two-place bars (**below, next page**) feature the Armed Forces 4-Year Long Service Medal in combination with the Defense Wall Honor Award. The first bar is a trapezoid clasp. The 4-Year Medal is magnetic and the Luftwaffe eagle device is non-magnetic. The Defense Wall medal is the early type, made of bronze. The mounting plates, pin, and catch are nickel-plated steel. The back plate has an integral hinge and catch mounts. On the second example, the medals are mounted in modified traditional style. The 4-Year Medal and the eagle device are magnetic. The Defense Wall Medal is the later type, made of zinc. The medal bar is backed with dark green wool felt. Both the mounting plate and pin are made of steel. The plate has an integral catch and hinge.

*Opposite*
*Bottom left: This German Navy Petty Officer wears a two-place medal bar consisting of the 1939 Iron Cross Second Class and the Armed Forces 4-Year Long Service Medal. He also wears a marksmanship lanyard on his right side.*

*Bottom right: This German Army Oberleutnant (First Lieutenant) wears a two-place medal bar consisting of the 1939 Iron Cross Second Class and the Medal for the 1941/42 Winter Battle in the East. He also wears officer's aiguillettes, officer's brocade belt, and sword.*

*Right: This German Army NCO wears a two-place medal bar consisting of the 1939 Iron Cross Second Class and the Defense Wall Honor Award. The medal bar is a Bavarian style clasp that has removable medals. Below his medal bar, the NCO wears a 1937 type National Sport Badge, a 1939 Wound Badge in Black, and the SA Sport Badge.*

*Below: A two-place Luftwaffe medal bar of the trapezoid clasp type. Medals are from (L-R): Luftwaffe 4-Year Long Service Medal and the Defense Wall Honor Award. $90-100.*

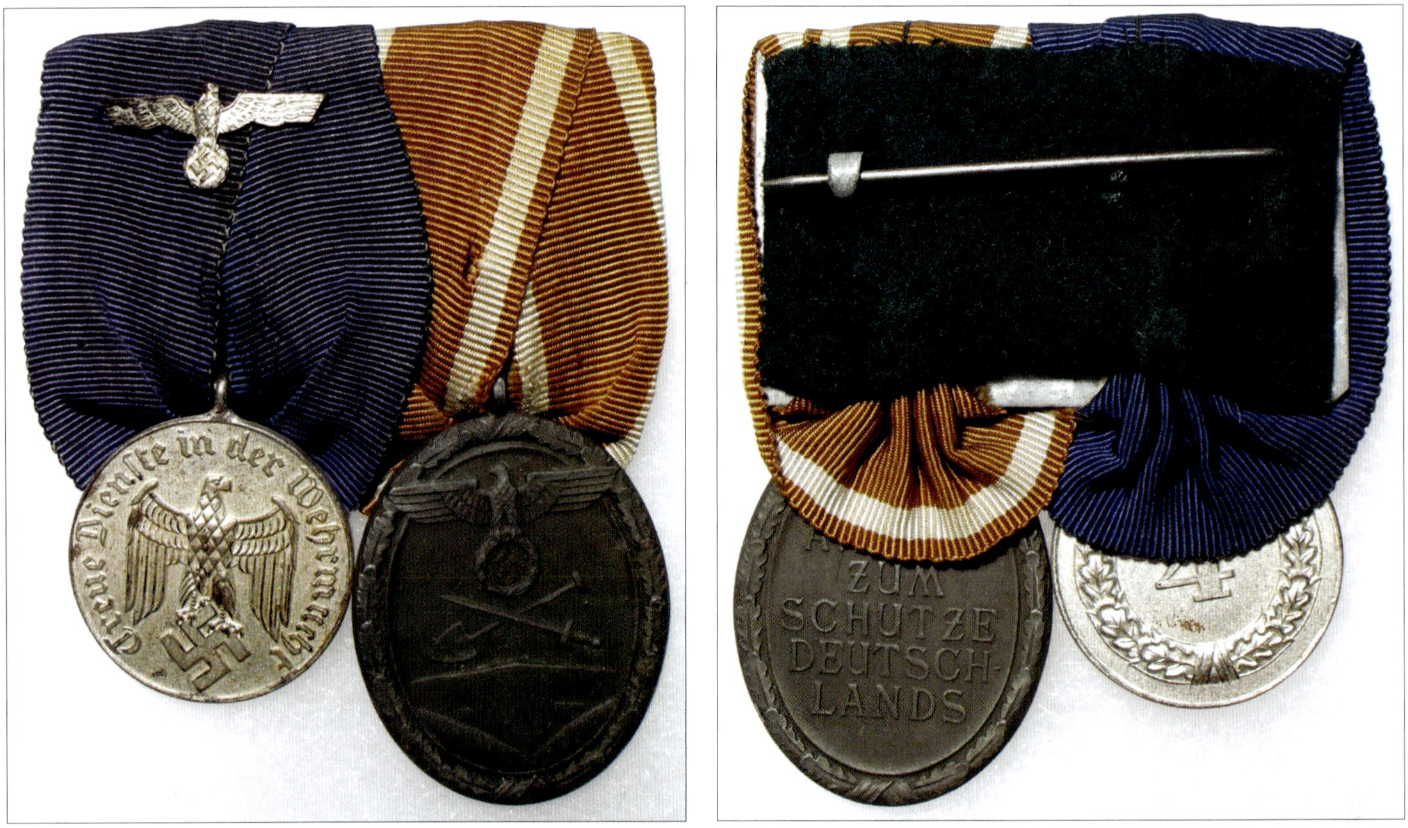


*Two-place medal bar in modified traditional style. Medals are from (L-R): Armed Forces 4-Year Long Service Medal and the Defense Wall Honor Award. $85-100.*

*A two-place bar consisting of (L-R): Armed Forces 4-Year Long Service Medal and the Medal for the Annexation of Czechoslovakia. $85-100.*

This two-place medal bar (**opposite bottom**) has a 4-Year Long Service Medal paired with a Medal for the Annexation of Czechoslovakia. The 4-Year medal is magnetic but the eagle device on the ribbon is non-magnetic. The Czech Annexation Medal is die-struck bronze. On the reverse, brown wool felt covers the steel mounting plate. The integral catch is missing, but the brass attachment pin still remains. In the accompanying photograph, a Luftwaffe NCO is seen wearing a two-place medal bar with the same awards, but incorrectly placed. The Long Service Medal should always be placed before an Annexation Medal. The regulations were quite clear on this particular point, yet the mistake was still made. If a mistake like this was made on a simple two-place bar, just imagine the potential for errors on the larger medal bars. This is period photographic evidence that mistakes did occur. So to emphasize a point made previously: A medal bar should never be called a reproduction solely on the basis that a medal is placed incorrectly with regard to the order of precedence. Always remember to evaluate every part of the bar and make a determination based on the "big picture."

This medal bar/clasp (**below**) has removable medals. The Medal for the 1941/42 Winter Battle in the East is zinc, with a darkened finish to the center and silver-finished medal rim and helmet. Notice the bubbled finish, which is typical of plated, zinc pieces. This medal is maker marked "25" on the suspension ring. This code number was assigned to the manufacturer: Abeitsgemeinschaft der Graveur-Gold und Silber-schmiede-Innungen, located in Hanau on the Main. (Work union of the gold and silver engravers and smiths guilds.) The medal measures 36.11mm in diameter and weighs 18 grams. The Medal for the Return of the Memel District is solid bronze.

*In this photo, a Luftwaffe NCO is seen wearing a two-place medal bar consisting of the Medal for the Annexation of Czechoslovakia and the Luftwaffe 4-Year Long Service Medal. This is an interesting photo because it shows an error in the placement of the medals. The Long Service Medal should be placed first on this bar. Even with a simple two-place bar like this, mistakes were made.*

*Below: A medal bar/ribbon bar combination clasp consisting of the Medal for the 1941/42 Winter Battle in the East and the Medal for the Return of the Memel District. $200.*

It measures 32.21mm in diameter and weighs 13.9 grams. The medal bar is backed with pink colored wool. The mounting plate is zinc. The hinge, catch, pin, and medal suspension hooks are all made of brass.

Each of these two-place medal bars and matching ribbon bars (**below and opposite**) feature a 1939 War Merit Cross in combination with another medal. The first bar has an early example of the War Merit Cross, made of solid bronze. It is paired with a Czech Annexation Medal that is made of tombak. On the reverse, dark green wool felt covers the steel mounting plates. The back plate has an integral hinge/catch setup, and the pin is steel. The ribbon bar has an iron, crossed swords device on the front. On the reverse, the bar is backed with gray wool felt. The back plate is zinc with an integral catch and a steel attachment pin. The second medal bar has a 1939 War Merit Cross in combination with a Defense Wall Honor Award. Both medals are early-quality and made of bronze. The medal bar has steel clips on the front for attaching the medals. On the reverse, the bar is backed with cream-colored wool felt. Notice the assembler label and the way the ribbon was given a simplified fold, rather than the semi-circular rosette form. The mounting plate is steel with a gold-colored finish. The pin and catch are made of brass. The matching ribbon bar has a non-magnetic crossed swords device on the front. It has zinc mounting plates with an integral hinge and catch. The pin is made of steel. On the back plate, there is a stamped maker marking, "TZ" within a circle. As far as I know, the manufacturer is still unknown.

*Right: This Luftwaffe non-commissioned officer wears a three-place medal bar. The medals are the 1939 War Merit Cross Second Class with Swords, Luftwaffe 4-Year Long Service Medal, and the Czech Annexation Medal with the Prague Castle Bar. (Technically, it is considered a four-place medal bar.)*

*Two-place medal bar with matching ribbon bar. Medals are from (L-R): 1939 War Merit Cross Second Class with Swords and the Medal for the Annexation of Czechoslovakia. Medal bar: $80-90. Ribbon bar: $10-15.*

*Above: Two-place medal bar and ribbon bar. Medals are from (L-R): 1939 War Merit Cross Second Class with Swords and the Defense Wall Honor Award. Medal bar: $80-90. Ribbon bar: $10-15.*

*Right: The 1939 War Merit Cross and the Defense Wall Honor Award as issued. Once awarded, it was up to the recipient to have the medals mounted for wear. In many cases, the paper issue packets were simply thrown away. Surviving issue packets are sometimes found with the name of the original recipient penciled in.*

This is a real attractive looking medal bar (**below**) in that all of the awards are in cross form. The medal bar was to a World War I combatant that was inactive between the wars, but then recalled for duty in World War II. The 1914 Iron Cross has a magnetic center core and frames of genuine silver. The 1939 War Merit Cross with Swords is an early-issue, made of bronze. The Mecklenburg-Schwerin War Merit Cross is bronze with a gilded finish. It is mounted on a combatant ribbon. The 1914-1918 Cross of Honor is iron with a bronze finish. The cross is marked, "39 R.V. Pforzheim" on the lower reverse. The medal bar has a zinc mounting plate with applied hinge and catch, made of brass. The attachment pin is also brass. The mounting plate is covered with dark blue wool.

*A four-place medal bar. Medals are from (L-R): 1914 Iron Cross Second Class on combatant ribbon, 1939 War Merit Cross Second Class with Swords, Mecklenburg-Schwerin War Merit Cross Second Class on combatant ribbon, and the 1914-1918 Cross of Honor with Swords. Courtesy of Edward Maroli. $225-250.*

This impressive, six-place medal bar (**below**) belonged to a Bavarian non-commissioned officer. He obviously had a long and distinguished military career. The Iron Cross is magnetic and the frames are silver. The Bavarian Military Merit Cross First Class with Swords is gold-plated bronze. The central disc on the front is a separate attachment. The black and white enamel is opaque. The Military Merit Cross First Class is a very rare decoration. Only about 700 of these were awarded.[19] The 1914-1918 Cross of Honor is bronzed iron. This one has the manufacturer's logo of Wilhelm Deumer on the reverse. The 1905 Prince Regent Luitpold Military Jubilee Medal is made of bronze. This medal was awarded by the Crown Prince of Bavaria to all commissioned officers in the Bavarian military. It was also awarded to career-oriented enlisted personnel. Since the owner of this medal bar was an enlisted man (NCO in this particular case) he must have been in the military for several years prior to 1905, or he would not have received this medal. Both of the long service awards and the eagle devices are die-struck iron with gold finishes. The medal bar has steel mounting plates with a nickel-plated finish. Both the pin and catch are brass. The bar is backed with white, silk-like material. In all likelihood, a senior NCO with this much time in service would have been bumped up to commissioned officer rank. He probably held the rank of *Leutnant ausser Dienst* at the time he was recalled for duty in World War II. I would guess that he was about 55 to 60 years old during the war.

*A rare, six-place medal bar to a Bavarian non-commissioned officer. Medals are from (L-R): 1914 Iron Cross Second Class, Bavarian Military Merit Cross First Class with Swords, 1914-1918 Cross of Honor with Swords, Prince Regent Luitpold Military Jubilee Medal (1905 type), Armed Forces 25-Year Long Service Cross, and the Armed Forces 12-Year Long Service Medal. Courtesy of Edward Maroli. $650-700.*

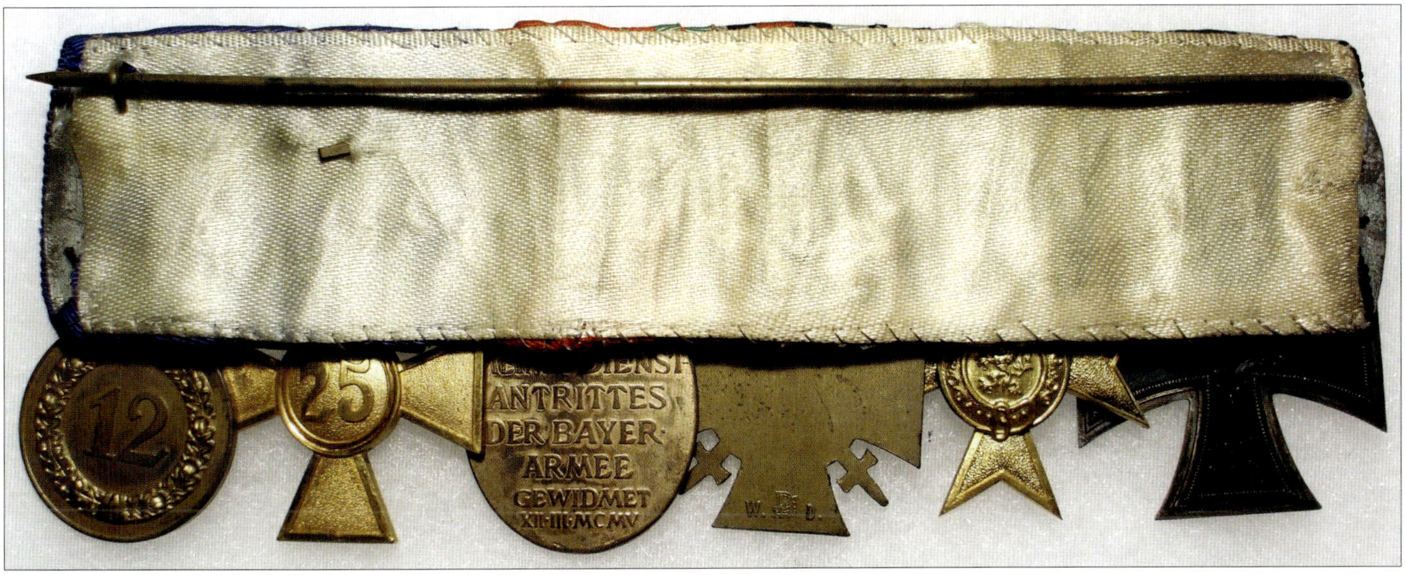

*Close up of the Bavarian Military Merit Cross First Class with Swords. The cross is gold-plated and the enameled central disc is a separate attachment. Courtesy of Edward Maroli.*

*Both long service awards and the eagle devices are iron. Courtesy of Edward Maroli.*

Here is another six-place Bavarian medal bar (**below**). This one is a commissioned officer's bar and it reportedly belonged to a Bavarian *Oberst* (Colonel). The Iron Cross has the usual magnetic core and silver frames. The Bavarian Military Merit Order Fourth Class with Swords is a beautiful looking piece. These were only awarded to commissioned officers. The Order was struck from silver and it features royal blue, black, and white enamel work. The white and black enamel is opaque, but the blue enamel should be translucent. You should be able to see the striations in the cross arms through the blue enamel. The King Ludwig cipher on the front and the rampant lion on the reverse are either gold or gold-plated. The crossed swords are a separate piece, riveted in place. Usually a maker marking will be found on the reverse of the swords. This

*Another six-place Bavarian medal bar. This one reportedly belonged to an Oberst (Colonel). Medals are from (L-R): 1914 Iron Cross Second Class, Bavarian Military Merit Order Fourth Class with Swords, 1914-1918 Cross of Honor with Swords, Prince Regent Luitpold Military Jubilee Medal (1905 type), Armed Forces 18-Year Long Service Cross, and the Armed Forces 4-Year Long Service Medal. $700-750.*

particular example is maker marked, "GH 900." This marking was used by Gebrüder Hemmerle of Munich. The "900" is the silver content number. The 1914-1918 Cross of Honor is iron with a bronze finish. The reverse is marked, "G3." The presence of the 1905 Prince Regent Luitpold Medal on this bar indicates that this man was a commissioned officer by 1905. The 18-Year Long Service Cross and the 4-Year Medal are both iron with a silver finish. The ribbon eagles are also made of iron. On the reverse, the bar is backed with dark green wool. The mounting plates are zinc and the pin and catch are steel.

From what I was told, this medal bar belonged to a known recipient. The person that sold me this bar said that the owner was an *Oberst*, and that he had the name written down somewhere at home. Unfortunately this information has not materialized and it may now be lost forever. From the medals on this bar, there is no doubt that the original owner was an officer of considerable rank. If you own any items that are to a known recipient, it is important to keep that information intact. Having a name associated to a piece of militaria not only enhances the historical significance of the item, but it can also increase its value.

*Medal bar reverse.*

*The Bavarian Military Merit Order Fourth Class is made of .900 silver. This order was awarded exclusively to commissioned officers. The royal blue enamel should be translucent. Notice that the v-shaped striations of the cross arms are visible through the enamel.*

*Both the 18-Year Cross and 4-Year Medal are iron. The eagle devices are also made of iron.*

Here is an eight-place medal bar (**below**) to a known recipient. After a bit of research by a person whom I consider to be the most knowledgeable and helpful on the subject, this medal bar was identified as having belonged to *Generaloberst* Otto Deßloch of the German Luftwaffe.[20] Otto Deßloch's military career began in 1911. He was an officer candidate and then platoon leader in the 5th. Bavarian Mounted-Rifles Regiment.[21] When World War I began, he held the rank of *Leutnant*. He was wounded in 1914 and spent two months in the hospital recovering. Shortly after his release from the hospital, Deßloch received training as an aerial observer. For most of 1915, he served as an aerial observer with Field-Flying Battalion 8b.[22] Deßloch then received pilot training. He returned to Field-Flying Battalion 8b and served as a pilot, flying two-seat observation aircraft. After a few months of flying observation aircraft, he was trained on single-seat fighter aircraft. For the remainder of World War I, Deßloch had several assignments as a fighter pilot, fighter squadron leader, and flying school leader. He reportedly scored one confirmed aerial victory during the war, for which he was awarded the Honor Goblet for the Victor in Air Combat. Deßloch remained in the military after World War I. He had assignments as a signals officer, staff officer, and special advisor. He was promoted to *Hauptmann* in 1921, *Major* in 1932, *Oberstleutnant* in 1934, and *Oberst* in 1936.[23] By January of 1939, Deßloch had attained the rank of *Generalmajor*. At the beginning of World War II he was commanding the 6th. Flying Division. His other wartime assignments included Commanding General of the Second Flak Corps, Commanding General of the First Flak Corps, Commander in Chief of Air Fleet 4, Commander in Chief of Air Fleet 3, and Commander in Chief of Air Fleet 6. During World War II, he was promoted to *Generalleutnant* in 1940, to *General der Flakartillerie* in 1942, and to *Generaloberst* in 1944.[24] He survived the war, surrendering in May of 1945. After being held for several years, Deßloch was released from captivity in 1948.

This medal bar was probably assembled in 1939, at which time Deßloch held the rank of *Generalmajor*. The 1914 Iron Cross has an iron core and nickel-silver frames. The Bavarian Military Merit Order Fourth Class with Crown and Swords is a very scarce order. The large crown above the swords signifies the second awarding of the Bavarian Military Merit Order. (Deßloch was awarded the Merit Order with Swords on April

*A Bavarian, Luftwaffe General's medal bar. Medals are from (L-R): 1914 Iron Cross Second Class, Bavarian Military Merit Order Fourth Class with Crown and Swords, 1914-1918 Cross of Honor with Swords, Luftwaffe 25-Year Long Service Cross, Luftwaffe 12-Year Long Service Medal, Medal for the Annexation of Austria, Prince Regent Luitpold Military Jubilee Medal (1911 type), and the Golden Anniversary Medal of the Royal Wedding. This medal bar belonged to Generaloberst Otto Deßloch. $3000-3500.*

19, 1915 and the Merit Order with Crown and Swords on November 9, 1917.)[25] Deßloch's Military Merit Order is maker marked on the reverse of the swords, "W.Co. 900.' This marking was used by Weiss & Company of Munich. Weiss manufactured Bavarian Orders from the 1880s until 1918.[26] The "900" is the silver content number. The 1914-1918 Cross of Honor is bronzed iron. It is maker marked "G&S" on the reverse, for the Dresden firm of Glaser & Sohn. The 25-Year Long Service Cross is tombak, with a fire gilded finish. The 12-Year Long Service Medal is iron with a matt gold finish. Both Luftwaffe eagle devices are tombak and have a gold finish. The Medal for the Annexation of Austria is tombak with a matt silver finish. The presence of the Austrian Annexation Medal is a clear indication that this medal bar was not assembled prior to 1938. I'm not sure when Deßloch was awarded his Austrian Annexation Medal, but most of these were awarded in late 1938 or early 1939. The Prince Regent Luitpold Medal is made of bronze. It is the type that was awarded in 1911, even though the reverse bears the 1905 date. The last medal on the bar is the Golden Anniversary Medal of the Royal Wedding. This medal is die-struck iron with a black lacquer finish. It was awarded in 1921 by the Royal Family as a special token to those in attendance at the funeral of King Ludwig III. The medal bar has a brass mounting plate, brass hinge, and brass catch. The attachment pin is steel. The medal bar is backed in Luftwaffe blue-gray wool.

It is not known for sure if Deßloch had another medal bar made during World War II, but in my opinion it is highly unlikely. He would have only had a single Bavarian Military Merit Order with Crown and Swords, so making a new medal bar would require the partial dismantling of his old medal bar. Bavarian Orders were not produced after 1918, and commercial replacements for this Order were neither available nor authorized. Two subsequent awards that could have been on his medal bar are the 1939 Clasp to the 1914 Iron Cross Second Class and the Medal for the 1941/42 Winter Battle in the East. We can be sure that this medal bar was made prior to May 5, 1940, as this is when Deßloch was awarded the 1939 Clasp to the 1914 Iron Cross Second Class. The medal bar would surely have had the 1939 Clasp attached if assembled after that date. There is a wartime color photograph which exists, showing Deßloch wearing his decorations.[27] The photograph was taken sometime between March and May of 1944, based on the fact that he is wearing the rank insignia of *Generaloberst* (promoted to that rank on March 1, 1944) but does not yet have the Oakleaves (awarded on May 10, 1944) attached to his Knight's Cross. In the photograph, he is wearing the ribbon bar which is an exact match to his medal bar. He did not add the ribbon of the East Medal to his ribbon bar but instead wears it diagonally, through the second button hole of his tunic. In addition to all of the ribboned awards worn on the medal bar, Deßloch was awarded with the following neck decorations and breast badges: 1939 Knight's Cross to the Iron Cross with Oakleaves, Commander's Grade of the Romanian Aeronautical Virtue Order with War Decoration and Swords, 1914 Iron Cross First Class, 1939 Clasp to the 1914 Iron Cross First Class, Bavarian Observer's Badge, Bavarian Pilot's Badge, Wound Badge in Black (1918 type), Combined Pilot/Observer's Badge with Diamonds, and the Kuban Campaign Shield.[28] On page 77 of his book, *The Luftwaffe*, Bender shows an excellent photograph of Deßloch wearing his Knight's Cross with Oakleaves, as well as the Romanian Aeronautical Virtue Order.

*Close up of the Bavarian Merit Order Fourth Class with Crown and Swords. Note again that the v-shaped striations of the cross arms are visible through the royal blue enamel.*

*On Deßloch's medal bar, the 25-Year Cross is tombak (non-magnetic) and the 12-Year Medal is iron (magnetic). Both Luftwaffe eagle devices are non-magnetic.*

*Notice that the Prince Regent Luitpold Military Jubilee Medal and the Golden Anniversary Medal of the Royal Wedding are worn on the same kind of ribbon.*

*Top right: Reverse view of Deßloch's medal bar showing the 1914 Iron Cross, Military Merit Order, and the 1914-1918 Cross of Honor.*

*Right: Reverse view of Deßloch's medal bar showing the two long service awards.*

*Reverse view of Deßloch's medal bar showing the Austrian Annexation Medal, Luitpold Medal, and the Golden Anniversary Medal of the Royal Wedding. Even though the Luitpold Medal has the "1905" date on the reverse, it is the type that was issued in 1911.*

Although nowhere near as impressive as a medal bar belonging to a Luftwaffe *Generaloberst*, this is another fine example of medals to a member of the Luftwaffe (**below**). I would suspect that this medal bar was assembled in the late 1930s, shortly before World War II. Given the fact that he was a World War I veteran and also had at least four years service in the military, he must have been a non-commissioned officer at the very least.

The 1914 Iron Cross Second Class is non-magnetic and a single-piece striking. It is made of nickel-silver with a black-finished center. Finding a single-piece Iron Cross on a medal bar is always a welcome sight for me. They are scarce in relation to the standard three-part crosses and just as nicely made. The 1914-1918 Cross of Honor is iron with a bronze finish. Unlike most, it has no maker marking on the reverse. The Luftwaffe 4-Year Long Service Medal is silver-finished iron, while the eagle device is silvered tombak. Both of the World War I commemorative medals are non-magnetic. The Austrian Medal is bronze with a gilt finish. The crossed swords are also non-magnetic. They are either brass or tombak with a gilt finish. The Hungarian Medal is finished in darkened silver. On the reverse, blue-gray wool was used for the backing material. The mounting plate is nickel-plated steel with an integral hinge. The catch is also made of steel. Brass wire was used for the attachment pin. Notice that instead of having circular rosettes, this medal bar has square folds to the lower portions of the ribbons. The uniform age and fading present on this medal bar are good indicators of its authenticity. The natural, unaltered look should be immediately apparent to the trained eye.

*A five-place Luftwaffe medal bar. Medals are from (L-R): 1914 Iron Cross Second Class, 1914-1918 Cross of Honor with Swords, Luftwaffe 4-Year Long Service Medal, World War I Commemorative Medal for Austria with Swords, and the World War I Commemorative Medal for Hungary. $200-225.*

The last medal bar in this chapter is a very recent acquisition and one of my new favorites (**below**). It is actually a small grouping of items that belonged to *Hauptmann* Gotthold Oehlschlägel of the German Luftwaffe. The grouping consists of his medal bar, ribbon bar, and his document for promotion to *Hauptmann*. Other than these three artifacts, I could not find any information on Oehlschlägel. What happened to him in World War II is unknown. But from looking at his medal bar, several inferences can be made about his military career. During World War I, he was decorated for bravery on several occasions. He was awarded valor decorations from both the Kingdom of Prussia and the Kingdom of Saxony. The Silver Medal of the Military Order of St. Heinrich and the Order of Albert make for an interesting combination on this medal bar. The Medal of the Order of St. Heinrich was a bravery decoration that was only awarded to enlisted personnel. The Order of Albert, on the other hand, was only awarded to commissioned officers. This leads me to believe that Oehlschlägel was an enlisted man who became an officer later in the war. He must have been commissioned prior to the end of World War I otherwise it would have not been possible for him to be awarded the Order of Albert. After World War I, he retained his commission as a reserve officer, but was probably on inactive status until the late 1930s. The Long Service Medal confirms that he had at least four, but less than twelve years of military service at the time the medal bar was assembled. This medal also confirms that he was on active duty, in the Luftwaffe. The Czech Annexation Medal shows that he was either involved in the occupation of the Sudetenland or Bohemia/Moravia. In my opinion, this medal bar was assembled in 1939, shortly after Oehlschlägel received his promotion to Hauptmann.

The Iron Cross is a standard example, made in three parts. The center core is iron and the frames are silver. The Medal of the Military Order of St. Heinrich is made of genuine silver. This medal is very scarce as there were only about 9,500 awarded between 1840 and 1918.[29] The Order of Albert- Knight's Cross Second Class is also made of genuine silver, and the swords are gold-plated. The white and blue enamel is opaque. This particular example was made by Alfred Rösner of Dresden. The rim of the lower cross arm has the stamped marking, "R." Only about 11,000 of these were awarded.[30] The 1914-1918 Cross of Honor is bronzed iron. On the reverse, lower cross arm is the stamped marking "ERK" within a cartouche. The 4-Year Long Service Medal is iron with a silver finish. The Luftwaffe eagle device is also made of iron. The Czech Annexation Medal is tombak with a golden bronze finish. The medal bar has steel mounting plates and a steel catch. The attachment pin is non-magnetic and appears to be stainless steel. Dark blue wool covers the back plate.

The matching ribbon bar has non-magnetic devices. The crossed swords are either brass or tombak with a gilt finish. The Luftwaffe eagle is silvered tombak. On the reverse, gray-green wool covers the back plate. The mounting plate is zinc, with an integral hinge and catch. The attachment pin is brass-plated steel.

*A six-place, Saxon officer's medal bar and matching ribbon bar. Medals are from (L-R): 1914 Iron Cross Second Class, Silver Medal of the Military Order of St. Heinrich, Saxon Order of Albert- Knight's Cross Second Class with Swords, 1914-1918 Cross of Honor with Swords, Luftwaffe 4-Year Long Service Medal, and the Medal for the Annexation of Czechoslovakia. This medal bar belonged to Hauptmann Gotthold Oehlschlägel. Medal bar: $650-700. Ribbon bar: $55-65*

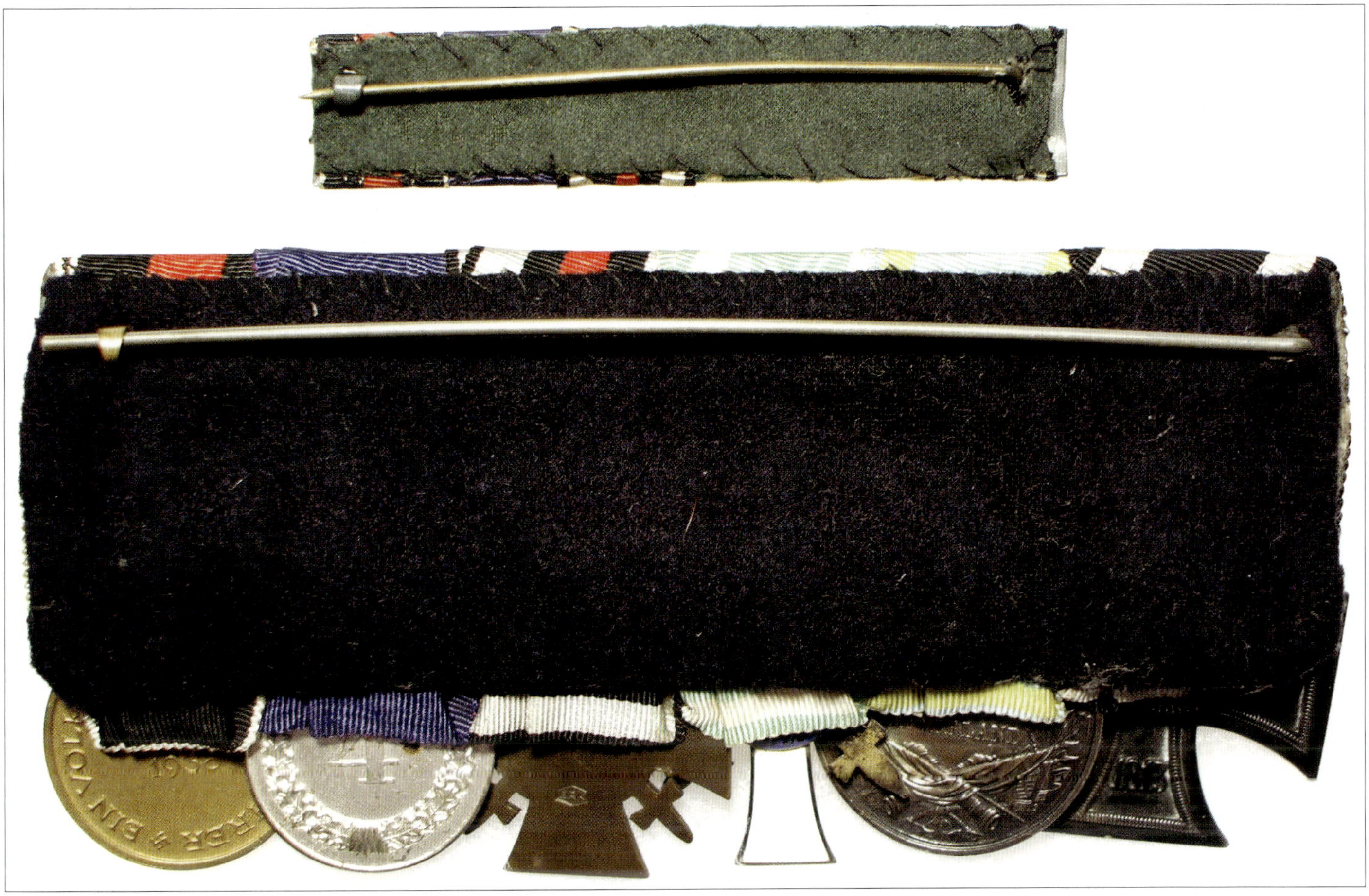

Reverse of Hauptmann Oehlschlägel's medal and ribbon bar.

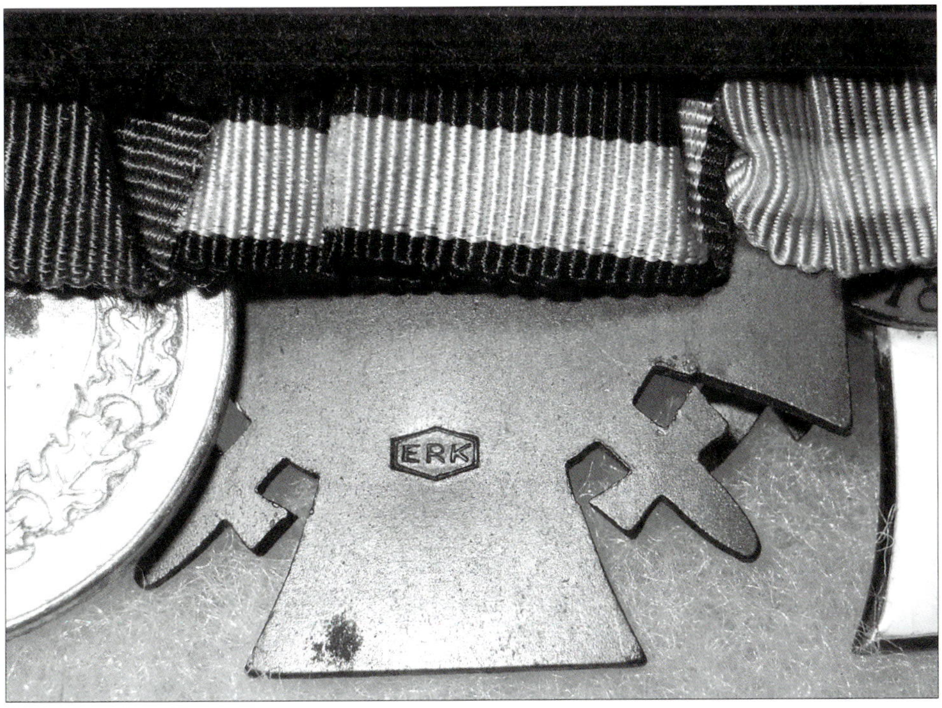


The reverse of the Cross of Honor has the stamped marking "ERK" within a cartouche. The manufacturer is unknown.

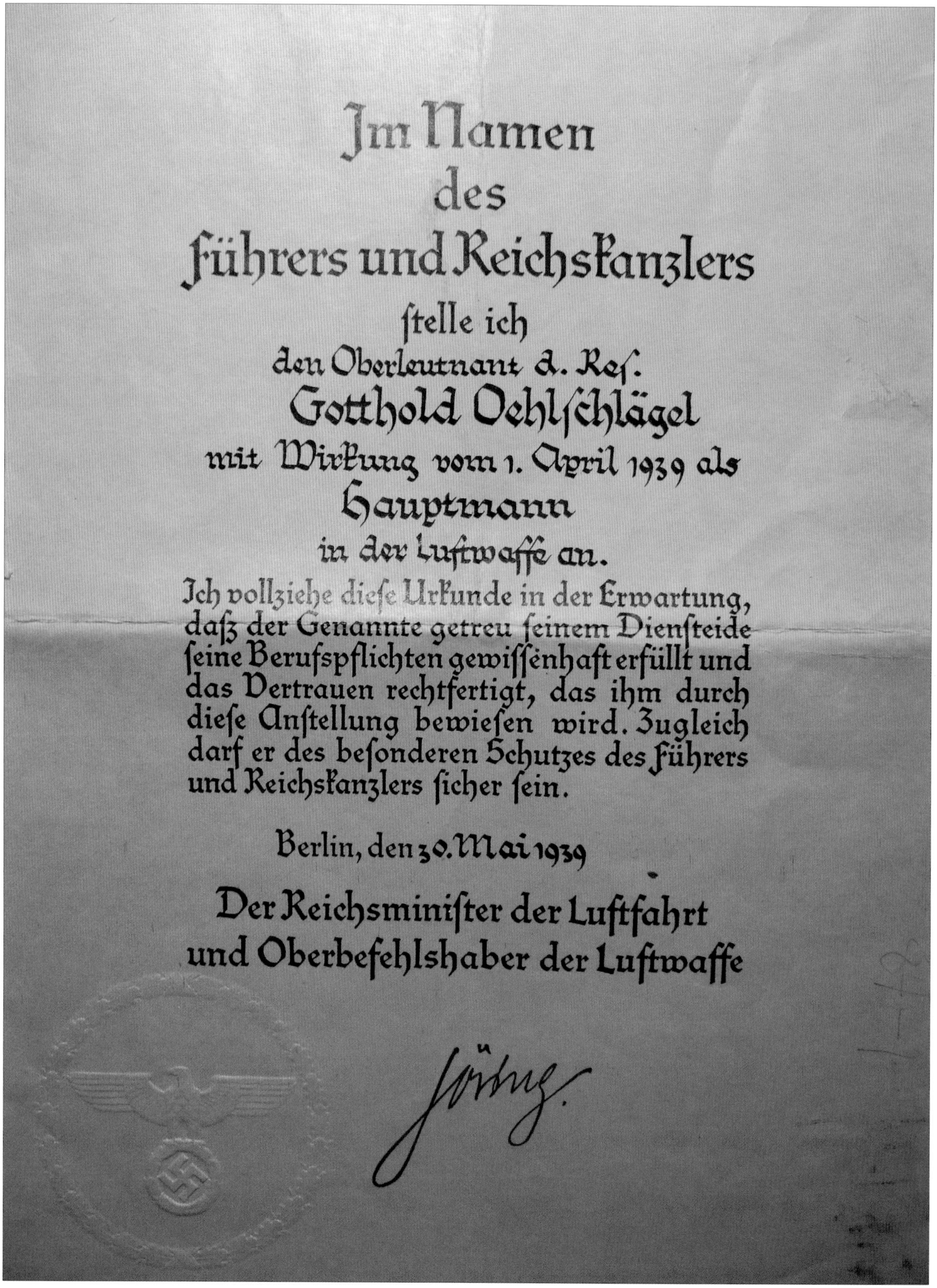

Im Namen des Führers und Reichskanzlers stelle ich den Oberleutnant d. Res. Gotthold Oehlschlägel mit Wirkung vom 1. April 1939 als Hauptmann in der Luftwaffe an.

Ich vollziehe diese Urkunde in der Erwartung, daß der Genannte getreu seinem Diensteide seine Berufspflichten gewissenhaft erfüllt und das Vertrauen rechtfertigt, das ihm durch diese Anstellung bewiesen wird. Zugleich darf er des besonderen Schutzes des Führers und Reichskanzlers sicher sein.

Berlin, den 30. Mai 1939

Der Reichsminister der Luftfahrt und Oberbefehlshaber der Luftwaffe

Göring.

*Gotthold Oehlschlägel was promoted from Oberleutnant der Reserve to the rank of Hauptmann, effective as of April 1, 1939. This promotion document was presented to him in Berlin, on May 30, 1939. The document has the facsimile signature of Hermann Göring, as Minister of Aviation and Supreme Commander of the Luftwaffe. It also displays a large, embossed eagle and wreath at the lower left corner. 254mm x 355mm. $35-40.*

# POLITICAL AND CIVIL MEDAL BARS

This chapter will cover political and civil medal bars. Many of the bars in this chapter will show prior military service in World War I. The main objective though, is to show medal bars that belonged to persons who held civilian jobs or governmental/political positions during the Third Reich Period. Medals were by no means limited to members of the military. Medals were awarded to persons of all occupations as a way of promoting national pride, hard work, and sacrifice. During the Third Reich Period, almost everyone had some type of uniform, and where there were uniforms there were medals.

This two-place medal bar (**below**) belonged to a World War I veteran and NSDAP (National Socialist German Workers Party) member. Although a combatant in World War I, he did not receive any valor decorations during his time in service. This is not unusual, as many soldiers never received recognition for risking life and limb in combat. Eventually, the man joined the Nazi Party. At the time that this medal bar was assembled, he had at least ten, but less than fifteen years of active membership in the party. NSDAP Long Service Crosses were awarded for 10, 15, and 25 years of membership. These awards were instituted in April of 1939, but the first awards were not given until January of 1940.[1] Service time was retroactive to February of 1925. In addition, any membership time between February of 1925 and February of 1933 counted double.[2] This was done to recognize those that were party members in the early days, when the party was struggling to gain power in Germany. The Cross of Honor is the usual bronzed iron. It is maker marked "G.3" on the reverse. The NSDAP Long Service Cross is die-struck zinc, with a bronze color wash that has all but faded away. The loss of finish is very common on these pieces, as zinc has a poor ability to hold a finish. The medal is a two-part construction. The center medallion (eagle and wreath) is a separate attachment that was soldered into place. These medals can also be found in single and three-part constructions. NSDAP 10-Year Crosses were manufactured from either zinc or aluminum. The zinc crosses are thick and heavy, while the aluminum ones are thin and lightweight.

*A two-place medal bar to a NSDAP (Nazi Party) member. Medals are from (L-R): 1914-1918 Cross of Honor with Swords and the 10-Year NSDAP Long Service Cross. $150-175.*

*Another two-place medal bar to a NSDAP member. Medals are from (L-R): 10-Year NSDAP Long Service Cross and the Medal for the Annexation of Austria. Courtesy of George Robinson. $175-200.*

On the reverse of the medal bar, "political brown" wool was used to cover the mounting plate. This was the color used for many of the political uniforms. All the attachment and mounting hardware is magnetic. The pin is steel wire, and the mounting plate and catch is thin sheet steel. The catch on this example is actually an integral part of the mounting plate. The catch was cut from the mounting plate and simply bent outwards. Cost-cutting and timesaving steps such as this became more of a necessity as the war raged on. This is obviously a wartime assembly. Since no NSDAP Long Service Crosses were awarded before 1940, it could not have been assembled before that year. From the sub-par quality of this bar, I would say it was made even later in the war.

This two-place medal bar (**above**) belonged to a member of the Nazi Party that apparently had no military service in World War I. He was an active party member for at least ten, but less than fifteen years when this bar was assembled. He was also involved in the annexation of Austria in some civilian capacity. The 10-Year NSDAP Long Service Cross is a two-piece, die-forged example made of zinc. The finish on the cross has held up fairly well, except on the separately applied eagle/wreath, which has faded to gray. The Austrian Annexation Medal is tombak with a matt silver finish. The medals are mounted in Bavarian style, characterized by furled ribbons and the absence of ribbon rosettes. The medal bar has zinc mounting plates and a brass pin and catch. On the reverse, the mounting plate is backed with purplish-gray ribbon of mercerized cotton. The reverse of the Austrian Annexation Medal has the inscription, "one people, one empire, one leader." In the center is the date when Austria became part of the German Empire.

This three-place medal bar (**opposite**) belonged to a World War I veteran and long-time Nazi Party Member. This bar could not have been assembled anytime before January 30, 1940, as this is when the first NSDAP Long Service Awards were given. Any original medal bar sporting one or more of these awards is therefore a wartime assembly and definitely not pre-World War II. The owner of this bar was probably an active party member at least as far back as 1929. If this was the case, he would have had double credit for service between 1929 and 1933 (eight years credit) and the additional seven years from 1933 to 1940, making him eligible for the 15-Year NSDAP Cross in 1940.

The Cross of Honor is iron with a bronze finish. The reverse has a stamped maker mark, showing a letter "G" within a larger letter "G." This logo may have been used by Gebrüder Godet & Company of Berlin, or possibly by Gebrüder Gengenbach & Company of Pforzheim. The 15-Year NSDAP Cross is a *schwere Ausführung* (heavyweight version) made of die-struck tombak. It has a silver-plated finish and translucent, deep blue enamel work. The eagle/wreath on the front is a separate attachment, as is the wreath on the center reverse. The 10-Year NSDAP Cross is a *leichte Ausführung* (lightweight version). It is made of die-struck aluminum with a bronze finish. The aluminum version was a single-piece construction. The bronze finish on these aluminum crosses holds up well when compared to the zinc ones, which typically have a faded finish.

This three-place political medal bar is backed with dark blue wool felt. All of the attachment and mounting hardware is magnetic. The pin, catch, and mounting plate are steel and have a bright, nickel-plated finish. The nickel finish on these parts is very durable. In many cases, the finish will look almost like new. The lower portions of the ribbons are gathered into large rosettes, and the medals rest completely on top of the rosettes. This is considered a traditional German style medal bar.

Regulations allowed for more than one NSDAP Long Service Cross to be worn. In fact, the recipient could wear all three crosses together if he rated them. The 10-Year NSDAP Cross is somewhat common. The 15-Year Cross is scarce, and the 25-Year Cross is very scarce. The 25-Year NSDAP Cross is identical in design to the 15-Year Cross, except that it is

*Three-place medal bar to World War I veteran and NSDAP member. Medals are from (L-R): 1914-1918 Cross of Honor with Swords, 15-Year NSDAP Long Service Cross, and the 10-Year NSDAP Long Service Cross. $525-550.*

finished in gold and has white enamel. The ribbon is predominately red, with white and gold edge stripes. NSDAP Long Service Awards were very well made, especially the 15 and 25-Year Crosses. There are fairly good quality fakes of these medals, so be sure to examine them carefully. The fakes fall short in overall appearance and quality. It is near impossible to find a medal bar with the 25-Year Cross on it. The Nazi Party did not even exist for 25 years. However, since double credit was given for membership between the years 1925 and 1933, it could be earned by those who were members back in 1925 or 1926. Those that joined the party after 1926 would never have been eligible to receive the 25-Year Cross. With the end of the war in 1945, the Nazi Party was abolished so the required amount of service time could not have been achieved.

*NSDAP long service ribbon bar. (Obverse) Awards represented are from (L-R): 1914 Iron Cross Second Class, 1914-1918 Cross of Honor with Swords, 25-Year NSDAP Long Service Cross, 15-Year NSDAP Long Service Cross, 10-Year NSDAP Long Service Cross, Medal for the Annexation of Austria, and the Medal for the Annexation of Czechoslovakia. The quality of workmanship and the amount of detail is superb. Notice that the ribbons are furled. This would be considered a "Bavarian style" ribbon bar. $325-375.*

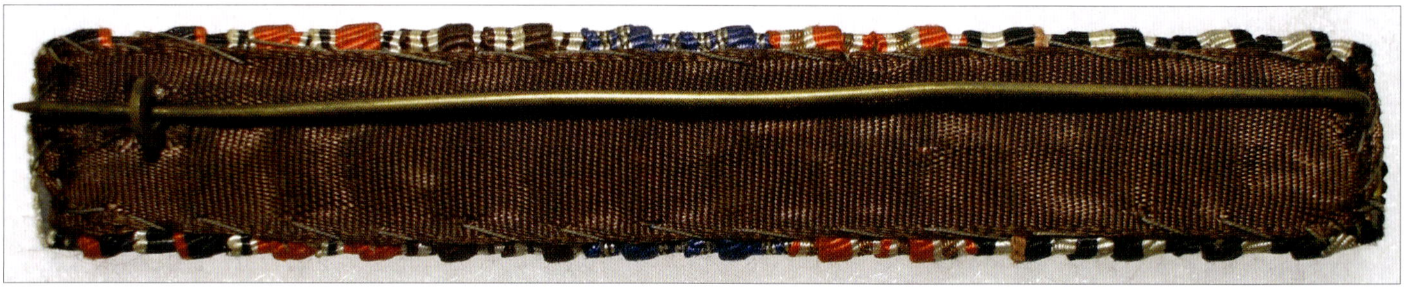

This ribbon bar (**above**) is an original and very rare example showing the wear of all three NSDAP Long Service Crosses simultaneously. The owner of this bar was an active member of the party from the earliest days of its existence. The ribbon bar must have been assembled sometime between 1942 and 1945. All of the metal devices are non-magnetic, and plated with their respective finishes: gold for the 25-Year, silver for the 15-Year, and bronze for the 10-Year. On the reverse, the bar is backed with a dark brown grosgrain, silk-like ribbon. The pin and catch are brass and the mounting plate is zinc. A ribbon bar such as this is worth several hundred dollars. A medal bar with this combination of awards would be worth about $3300. Remember that a combination like this is very rare so careful examination is required.

## NSDAP Long Service Crosses

A five-place medal bar such as this (**page 153**) would have belonged to a First World War veteran and party member having ten, but less than fifteen years of active membership. Again, we know that this medal bar was assembled sometime after January of 1940. This medal bar is made nicer by the fact that it is still paired with its matching ribbon bar. A set like this should remain together and not be sold individually. The 1914 Iron Cross has a magnetic core and silver frames. The 1914-1918 Cross of Honor is iron with a bronze finish. The reverse is marked, "O8." The 10-Year NSDAP Long Service Cross is a heavyweight, three-piece version, made of zinc. The center medallions on the front and reverse are separate pieces, soldered in place. The Hungarian Commemorative Medal for World War I is a non-magnetic base metal with an antiqued silver finish. The Bulgarian Commemorative Medal for World War I is also a non-magnetic base metal, but finished in bright gilt. The medal bar has zinc mounting plates. The pin and catch are made of brass. The reverse of the medal bar is backed with black wool.

*Opposite*

*Top left: 10-Year NSDAP Long Service Cross. (Obverse) This is a singe-piece, lightweight version made of die-struck aluminum. It weighs 14.4 grams and measures 42.92mm square. $150.*

*Top right: 10-Year NSDAP Long Service Cross. (Reverse) The crosses struck in aluminum retain their finish quite well. The inscription reads, "Faithful for leader and people."*

*Bottom left: 10-Year NSDAP Long Service Cross. (Obverse) This is a two-part, heavyweight construction made of die-struck zinc. The central eagle/wreath is separately attached. This example weighs 35.7 grams and measures 42.85mm square. $125-150.*

*Bottom right: 10-Year NSDAP Long Service Cross. (Reverse) This one has retained its finish better than most zinc examples. Notice that there are some areas where the finish has bubbled. This is often seen on zinc pieces that have been plated.*

Treue
für Führer
und
Volk

Treue
für Führer
und
Volk

*This 10-Year NSDAP Long Service Cross sits inside an original box of issue. The box is cardboard, covered with dark brown, textured paper. The interior has a golden colored flocking. On the box lid, an eagle is embossed in gold.*

*Below: The bottom of the box is stamped with the "RZM" logo, and the manufacturer's code of "M1/143." This code number was for the manufacturing firm of Gebrüder Jäger, located in Gablonz a.d.Neisse.[3] The "RZM," or Reichszeugmeisterei, was the national procurement office, responsible for selecting suppliers and sellers of all party-related uniforms, equipment, and accessories.[4]*

*The 15-Year NSDAP Long Service Cross. (Obverse) These were die-struck in tombak and finished in silver. The royal blue enamel should be translucent. You see be able to see the stippling of the cross arms though the enamel. This example is a three-piece, heavyweight construction. The weight is 39.0 grams and it measures 42.47mm square. $325-350.*

*Right: 15-Year NSDAP Long Service Cross. (Reverse) Although nowhere near as rare as the 25-Year Cross, I think the 15-Year Cross is by far, the nicest looking.*

*Left: 25-Year NSDAP Long Service Cross. (Obverse) These were die-struck in tombak and fire-gilded. The white enamel should be opaque. This example is a three-piece, lightweight version produced by E. Ferd Wiedmann of Frankfurt a.Main. The suspension ring is marked "19." This example weighs 23.6 grams and it measures 42.26mm square. Courtesy of George Robinson. $2500.*

*Above: The case interior was compartmented for the cross and the ribbon. The narrow width of ribbon seen in this picture was used for the miniature version of the cross, and for making ribbon bars. Below: The case for the 25-Year Cross showing the gold eagle embossed on the lid. Courtesy of George Robinson. Case only: $500.*

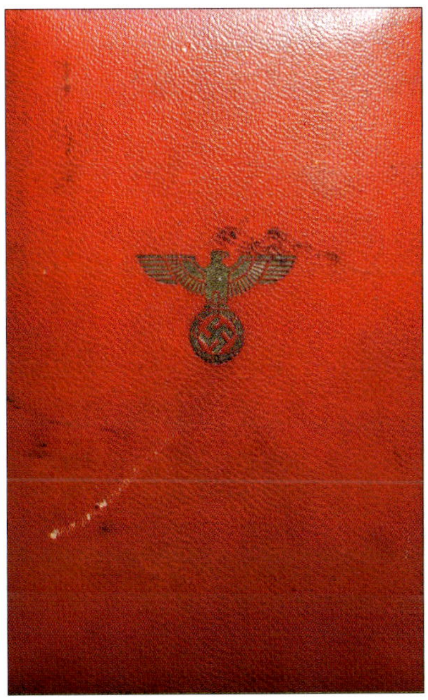

Besitzurkunde

Dem Parteigenossen

Georg Schlapp

verleihe ich hiermit

die Dienstauszeichnung

der NSDAP in Bronze

für 10 jährige aktive

Dienstzeit in der NSDAP

München, den 20.4.1940

NATIONALSOZIALISTISCHE DEUTSCHE ARBEITERPARTEI

*Award documents for the NSDAP Long Service Crosses are not often seen in the collector market. The 25-Year document is practically unobtainable, but even the 10 and 15-Year documents are rare. The example shown above is an original document for the 10-Year Long Service Cross. It is a large document, printed in black and reddish-brown ink on heavy parchment. The document features a large, embossed eagle at the top and an embossed seal of "der Führer" at the bottom. The recipient's name and the date of award is hand-done calligraphy. At the lower right is the facsimile signature of Adolf Hitler. $200.*

The ribbon bar shows the same combination of awards. The ribbons for the 1914-1918 Cross of Honor, Hungarian Commemorative Medal and Bulgarian Commemorative Medal all have crossed swords devices. The ribbon for the 10-Year NSDAP Cross does not have a wreath and eagle device on it. From looking more closely, there is no evidence of it ever having one either. The ribbon bar mounting plates are steel, and the back plate has an integral catch and hinge. The pin is also steel. There is quite a bit of rust on the ribbon bar, so it was obviously exposed to the weather.

*A five-place political medal bar with the matching ribbon bar. Medals are from (L-R): 1914 Iron Cross Second Class, 1914-1918 Cross of Honor with Swords, 10-Year NSDAP Long Service Cross, Hungarian Commemorative Medal for World War I, and the Bulgarian Commemorative Medal for World War I. Medal bar: $250-275. Ribbon bar: $30-40.*

The medal bar/ribbon bar combination clasp was designed with hooks on the back plate so that the medals could be easily removed. For special occasions, the medals would be worn on the bar. At all other times, the bar would be worn without the medals as an oversize ribbon bar. With this type of medal bar, be extra careful when examining the medals. The ease at which the medals can be removed makes it an ideal bar for someone to remove genuine pieces and replace them with fakes. This clasp (**right**) would have belonged to a party member that was also a member of the German Red Cross, or possibly another social welfare organization engaged in visiting the sick or wounded. The Medal for German Social Welfare is the early type, made of tombak and finished in darkened silver. The medal measures 38.02mm in diameter and it weighs 22.3 grams. The 10-Year NSDAP Long Service Cross is a heavyweight, two-piece version made of zinc. This example is 42.52mm square and it weighs 31.9 grams. The mounting plates are nickel-plated steel and the back plate has an integral catch and hinge. The pin is also steel. The back plate is stamped "DRGM" at the lower center. This is the abbreviation for Deutsches Reich Gebrauchsmuster (German Empire registered design).

On this two-place clasp (**opposite top**), the 1939 War Merit Cross is made of solid bronze. The suspension ring of the medal is marked, "60." This code number was assigned to the manufacturer, Katz & Deyhle of Pforzheim. The cross measures 48.89mm square and it weighs 18.2 grams. The 10-Year NSDAP Long Service Cross is a one-piece version, made of aluminum. This cross measures 43.07mm square and weighs 14.1 grams. The mounting plate and medal suspension hooks are made of steel with a nickel-plated finish. The catch and pin is actually a single-piece, safety pin type setup. The pin is made of brass. This type of pin was used primarily on German tinnies and day badges, but was also used occasionally on single-place or small, multi-place medal bars. The clasp is backed with orange colored wool. The ribbons are furled in the Bavarian style.

A medal bar such as this (**opposite bottom**) would have belonged to a veteran of World War I that had at least 25 years of loyal service in a civilian occupation. The 1914 Iron Cross is a three-part example. The core is iron and the frames are silver. The 1914-1918 Cross of Honor is bronzed iron. On the reverse, the lower cross arm is marked, "1 R.V. Pforzheim." The 25-Year Faithful Service Decoration is made of tombak bronze. It has a matt silver finish with polished highlights. The swastika at the center is black enamel. This award was instituted in January of 1938, and given in recognition of loyal civilian service.[5] Credit for civilian service time was retroactive, and started from the age of 18. Any breaks in civilian service due to military duty counted towards the total number of years.[6] Therefore, the owner of this medal bar had to be at least 43 years old. The medal bar has steel mounting plates with an integral hinge and catch. The attachment pin is also steel. On the reverse, gray-green wool covers the back plate. The matching ribbon bar has non-magnetic devices made of tombak. The silver finish is worn on the 25-Year device. The ribbon bar mounting plates are steel, with an integral hinge/catch setup. The pin is also steel.

*Two-place medal bar/ribbon bar combination clasp consisting of the Medal for German Social Welfare and the 10-Year NSDAP Long Service Cross. $200.*

*Another example of a medal bar/ribbon bar combination clasp. Medals are from (L-R): 1939 War Merit Cross Second Class without Swords and the 10-Year NSDAP Long Service Cross. $175-200.*

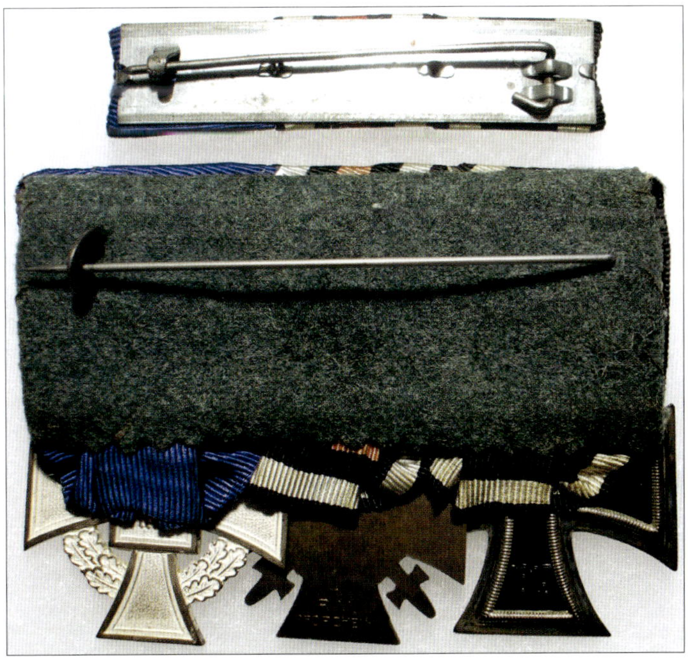

*Three-place medal bar and matching ribbon bar. Medals are from (L-R): 1914 Iron Cross Second Class, 1914-1918 Cross of Honor with Swords, and the 25-Year Faithful Service Decoration. Medal bar: $95-110. Ribbon bar: $15.*

*Three place medal bar consisting of the 1914 Iron Cross, 1914-1918 Cross of Honor with Swords, and the 40-Year Faithful Service Decoration. $110-130.*

While similar to the medal bar previously shown, this bar (**above**) has the 40-Year Faithful Service Decoration. The recipient of this award had to be at least 58 years old at the time the medal bar was assembled. (Receiving this award at 58 would mean that his service began at the age of 18, and that he had no break in service time other than his military duty in World War I.) The 1914 Iron Cross on this medal bar is rather interesting. It is non-magnetic and made in one piece, rather than the usual three. **Remember that there are original Iron Crosses that are non-magnetic, and there are also original one-piece Iron Crosses.** The 1914-1918 Cross of Honor is the usual bronzed iron. This example is marked on the reverse, "R.S.L." This marking was most likely used by the manufacturer, Richard Sieper of Lüdenscheid. The 40-Year Faithful Service Decoration is made of tombak bronze, with a fire-gilded finish. Other than the color of the finish, the 40-Year Decoration is identical to the 25-Year Decoration. It would be unusual to see a medal bar with more than one Faithful Service Decoration on it. However, I do recall seeing a couple of examples that had both the 40-Year and 25-Year Decorations and they appeared to be period assemblies. I'm not sure what the regulations were on this matter, but I think in most cases only one was worn. All of the mounting and attachment hardware on the medal bar is made of steel with a nickel-plated finish.

Faithful Service Decorations (**below**) are well made and impressive looking. They all seem to have been made from tombak and should therefore be non-magnetic. I have never encountered any originals made from iron or zinc. The 25-Year Decoration has a silver finish while the 40-Year is finished in gold. There is also a 50-Year Decoration which has

*Obverse of the 40-Year (left) and 25-Year (right) Faithful Service Decorations. The 40-Year is 41.35mm square. $50-55. The 25-Year is 40.97mm square. $30-35.*

*Reverse of the 40-Year and 25-Year Faithful Service Decorations. The majority of these awards were issued with brooch pin mounted ribbons as shown.*

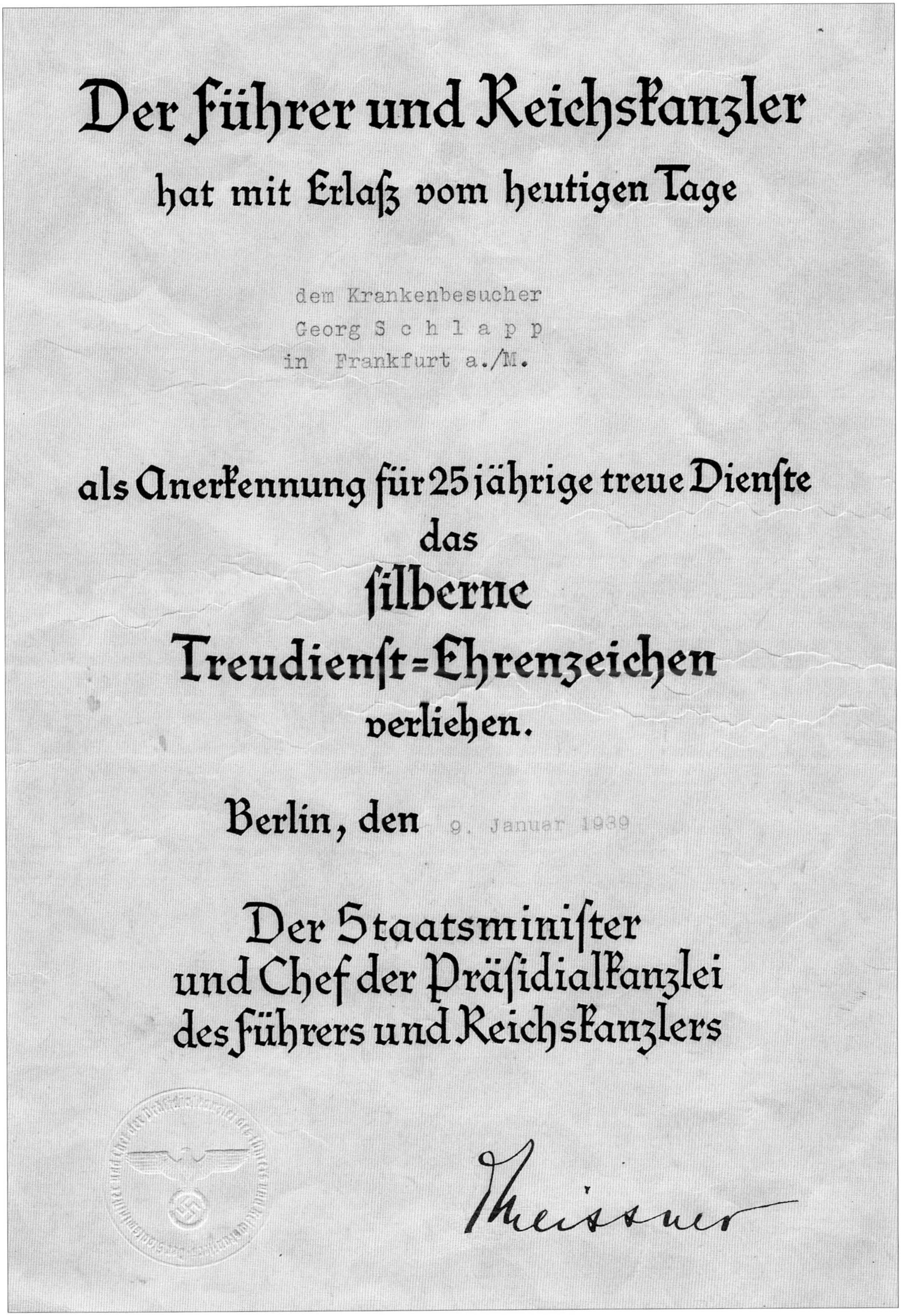

Der Führer und Reichskanzler

hat mit Erlaß vom heutigen Tage

dem Krankenbesucher
Georg S c h l a p p
in Frankfurt a./M.

als Anerkennung für 25jährige treue Dienste

das

silberne

Treudienst=Ehrenzeichen

verliehen.

Berlin, den 9. Januar 1939

Der Staatsminister
und Chef der Präsidialkanzlei
des Führers und Reichskanzlers

Meissner

*Example of an award document for the 25-Year Faithful Service Decoration. This document was awarded on January 9, 1939 to a visitor of the sick, residing in Frankfurt on the Main. The document has the embossed seal of the State Minister at the lower left and the facsimile signature of Otto Meissner. 209mm x 296mm. $25-30.*

a silver cross, gold wreath, and a gold numeral "50" added to the upper cross arm. The 25-Year Decoration was referred to as the second class, the 40-Year was the first class, and the 50-Year was called the special class. All three classes have a large, black enameled swastika on the front. The 25 and 40-Year Decorations are common, but the 50-Year is very scarce. I have never seen a 50-Year Faithful Service Decoration on a medal bar. The reverse of the 25 and 40-Year Decorations bear the inscription, "for faithful service." The 50-Year has the inscription, "for faithful work."

Some references indicate that these awards measure 42mm square. However, according to one author, originals can measure anywhere between 40.5 and 42mm.[7] This would be more accurate as many different manufacturers produced these awards so the dimensions would no doubt vary. I measured six original specimens and recorded their measurements. From smallest to largest they measure: 40.89mm, 40.97mm, 41.27mm, 41.30mm, 41.35mm, and 41.55mm.

This well made, two-place medal bar (**below**) is mounted in the traditional style. The recipient was a veteran of the First World War but he did not receive any valor or merit decorations. The 1914-1918 Cross of Honor is iron with a bronze finish. On the reverse of the lower cross arm is the manufacturer logo of Wilhelm Deumer of Lüdenscheid. The 25-Year Faithful Service Decoration is tombak with a frosted silver finish and burnished highlights. On the reverse, the medal bar is backed with crimson colored wool. The wool has a deep, pinking shear cut along the bottom edge. The mounting plate, catch, and hinge are steel. The pin is unusual as it appears to be made of stainless steel. The ribbon rosettes are nicely formed and the medals rest completely upon them.

This four-place, Bavarian style medal bar (**opposite**) belonged to a man that had served in World War I, then had a civilian occupation in the years between the wars. He was obviously from Bavaria. In World War I, he was an enlisted man below the rank of NCO. The Iron Cross is the typical three-piece construction. The core is made of iron and the frames are silver. The Bavarian Military Merit Cross Third Class with Swords is bronze with a copper finish. This was Bavaria's valor and merit decoration for enlisted personnel below the rank of Sergeant. A Sergeant was normally awarded this same award, but with the addition of a large crown above the swords. An enlisted man of lesser rank had to earn the Military Merit Cross on two separate occasions in order to receive the crown. The 1914-1918 Cross of Honor is bronzed iron. The reverse, lower cross arm is marked, "O.2." The 25-Year Faithful Service Decoration is the usual base metal and finish. On the reverse, the medal bar has a zinc mounting plate with an applied hinge and catch, made of brass. The attachment pin is also made of brass. Red wool felt was used as the backing material.

*Two-place medal bar consisting of the 1914-1918 Cross of Honor with Swords and the 25-Year Faithful Service Decoration. $45-50.*

*Opposite: Four-place, Bavarian style medal bar. Medals are from (L-R): 1914 Iron Cross Second Class, Bavarian Military Merit Cross Third Class with Swords, 1914-1918 Cross of Honor with Swords, and the 25-Year Faithful Service Decoration. $125-140.*

1914
1918

Für treue Dienste
1866

W
1914
1914
1918

OKTOBER
1938
R.V. 24
PFORZHEIM

The World War I veteran that owned this medal bar (**opposite**) had many years of service in a civilian occupation. His civilian service may have continued through World War II, although it is possible that he was recalled to military duty. Since the 25-Year Faithful Service Decoration could be awarded for just about any kind of civilian job, it is impossible to know for sure what occupation he had. If he was awarded the Czech Annexation Medal as a civilian, I would think that he was some sort of civil servant or government official.

The 1914 Iron Cross on this medal bar is a scarce example of a one-piece cross, struck from a non-magnetic alloy. The center is finished in black lacquer and the edges appear to be silver-plated. The Cross of Honor is die-struck iron with a bronze finish. On the reverse it is maker marked in relief, "24 R.V. Pforzheim." The 25-Year Faithful Service Decoration is tombak with a matt silver finish that has darkened in places. The Czech Annexation Medal is also made of tombak but finished in a golden bronze. On the reverse, the medal bar has a backing of beige wool felt. The mounting plates, catch, and hinge are all made of steel and have a nickel-plated finish. Underneath, the ribbons are padded with white cotton fibers. When looking at this medal bar, you will notice little clues that attest to its age. There are a few spots that show chemical reactions and abrasive effects between medals. There is a dark spot on the flag of the Czech Annexation Medal that was caused by continual contact with the right cross arm of the Faithful Service Decoration. There is also some brown discoloration to the center of the Faithful Service Decoration, probably caused by a metal reaction between tombak and iron. In addition, the right arm of the Cross of Honor has caused surface abrasion to the enameled swastika on the Faithful Service Decoration. And lastly, the upper point on the right arm of the Iron Cross has worn away some of the bronze finish on the Cross of Honor's left sword tip. These subtle clues can be very helpful when evaluating a medal bar. Of course, they cannot offer absolute proof that a medal bar was assembled during the Third Reich, but they certainly attest to the fact that the medals have been mounted together for a long period of time.

This is a very interesting medal bar (**page 162**). It is composed of four, common medals, but the combination of awards is scarce because of the 1939 War Merit Medal. The medal bar is also unusual because the 1914 Iron Cross is worn on a combatant ribbon, contradictory to the 1914-1918 Cross of Honor without Swords, which was for non-combatants. The 1914 Iron Cross is iron with silver frames. The 1939 War Merit Medal is die-struck, solid bronze. This medal was instituted in August of 1940 and almost 5 million were awarded during World War II.[8] Despite the huge number of awards, the War Merit Medal is seldom seen on a medal bar. The 1914-1918 Cross of Honor without Swords is iron with a bronze finish. The reverse is marked with the letters, "A S" and a sword logo. The manufacturer that used this logo has not been determined. The 25-Year Faithful Service Decoration is tombak with a matt silver finish and burnished highlights. The reverse of the medal bar is backed with red wool. The mounting plates and catch are steel. The attachment pin is brass. The bar has an assembler label from H. Acker of Stuttgart. The matching ribbon bar has zinc mounting plates. Both the pin and catch are made of brass. The ribbon bar is backed with dark green silk-like ribbon.

*Opposite: A four-place, modified traditional style medal bar. Medals are from (L-R): 1914 Iron Cross Second Class, 1914-1918 Cross of Honor with Swords, 25-Year Faithful Service Decoration, and the Medal for the Annexation of Czechoslovakia. $140-150.*

*Above: This medal bar features a single-piece 1914 Iron Cross Second Class. The cross is non-magnetic. The quality is every bit as good if not better than most multi-part Iron Crosses. Notice that the blackened area of the cross is stippled; a feature common to most one-piece Iron Crosses.*

The 25-year device is tombak with a silver finish. This medal bar and ribbon bar would have belonged to a veteran of the First World War who served in some non-combatant capacity, yet was decorated for bravery and permitted to wear his Iron Cross on a combatant ribbon. The Faithful Service Decoration indicates that he was a civilian between the wars and probably into the Second World War as well. The presence of the 1939 War Merit Medal confirms that he remained in a civilian capacity during World War II as this medal was only awarded to civilians. This medal bar could not have been assembled prior to late 1940. More likely, it was assembled in 1942 or later because the War Merit Medal is placed before the Cross of Honor. Prior to 1942, the regulations specified that the War Merit Medal was worn after the Cross of Honor.

This three-place medal bar (**page 163**) probably belonged to some sort of civil service official. It is a well constructed medal bar and I would suspect that it was assembled in 1940 or 1941. The 1939 War Merit Cross without Swords is an early issue type, made of bronze. The 25-Year Faithful Service Decoration is tombak, with a matt silver finish and polished highlights. Both the Czech Annexation Medal and the Prague Castle Bar are non-magnetic, die-struck solid bronze. The reverse of the medal bar is backed with red wool felt. There is a zigzag cut to the bottom edge of the backing material. The mounting plate is made of zinc, with an applied catch and hinge made of brass. The attachment pin is brass wire. It is unusual to see a medal bar having the 25-Year Faithful Service Decoration, but showing no service in World War I.

*Four-place medal bar with matching ribbon bar. Medals are from (L-R): 1914 Iron Cross Second Class on combatant ribbon, 1939 War Merit Medal, 1914-1918 Cross of Honor without Swords, and the 25-Year Faithful Service Decoration. Medal bar: $140-160. Ribbon bar: $25-30.*

*Medal bar consisting of from (L-R): 1939 War Merit Cross Second Class without Swords, 25-Year Faithful Service Decoration, and the Medal for the Annexation of Czechoslovakia with the Prague Castle Bar. Courtesy of George Robinson. $150-175.*

The owner of this medal bar (**below**) was from Saxony and was a commissioned officer in the First World War. He had a civilian occupation after World War I, but was almost certainly recalled for military duty in the Second World War. This medal bar was definitely assembled during World War II, probably in 1940 or later. We can be certain of this because the medal bar displays the 1939 War Merit Cross, which was not instituted until late 1939. Since the War Merit Cross has the swords, it is a good indication that the man was back in the military during World War II. Civilians would have normally received the War Merit Cross without Swords. The medal bar has a 1914 Iron Cross with a magnetic core and nickel-silver frames. The 1939 War Merit Cross is an early-issue example in solid bronze. The Saxon Order of Albert is genuine silver with gold-plated swords. The blue and white enamel is opaque. This example has the maker mark, "G" on the bottom edge of the lower cross arm. This marking was used by Glaser and Sohn of Dresden. Glaser must have been a prolific manufacturer of this Order. The majority of Albert Orders pictured in this book were made by Glaser. Albert Orders were also produced during World War I by Gustav Scharffenberg, Alfred Rösner, Christian Rothe, and Godet of Berlin.[9] The 1914-1918 Cross of Honor is bronzed iron. This example was made by the same company that produced the Albert Order on this medal bar: Glaser and Sohn. On the reverse of the lower cross arm is the incuse marking, "G&S." It seems that Glaser also produced the Cross of Honor in large quantities, as quite a few of the examples shown in this book display the G&S logo. The World War I Commemorative Medal for Austria is non-magnetic and has a matt gold finish. The crossed swords device on the ribbon is also non-magnetic. The 25-Year Faithful Service Decoration is the typical base metal and finish. Brown silk-like grosgrain ribbon was used as the backing material. The mounting plate is zinc with

*A six-place Saxon officer's medal bar. Medals are from (L-R): 1914 Iron Cross Second Class, 1939 War Merit Cross Second Class with Swords, Saxon Order of Albert- Knight's Cross Second Class, 1914-1918 Cross of Honor with Swords, World War I Commemorative Medal for Austria with Swords, and the 25-Year Faithful Service Decoration. $550-600.*

an integral hinge/catch setup. The pin is brass wire. On this medal bar, the placement of the medals is exactly according to the regulations. One would think that the Commemorative Medal for Austria should be placed last on the bar. However, the wartime regulations listed its precedence after the Cross of Honor and before long service awards.[10] The World War I Commemorative Medal for Austria was even rated higher than the extremely rare Lifesaving Medal. It doesn't seem to make much sense to me, but it is true.

This beautiful, five-place medal bar (**below**) belonged to a commissioned officer from Baden, who served in World War I. After the war, he apparently left the military and worked in some civilian occupation. I would think that this medal bar was assembled early in 1939, prior to the start of the Second World War. At this particular time he may have still been a civilian, but in all likelihood he would have been recalled to active duty in World War II. The medal bar is shown in this chapter because of the 25-Year Faithful Service Decoration, which was

*Five-place Baden officer's medal bar. Medals are from (L-R): 1914 Iron Cross Second Class, Baden Order of the Zähringen Lion-Knight's Cross Second Class, 1914-1918 Cross of Honor with Swords, 25-Year Faithful Service Decoration, and the Medal for the Annexation of Austria. $750-800.*

*Obverse of the Baden Order of the Zähringen Lion- Knight's Cross Second Class. The order is made from genuine silver and has translucent green cut glass in the arms of the cross.*

*Reverse of the Baden Order of the Zähringen Lion. Note that the swords are attached by rivets. The swords are gold-plated silver.*

awarded for civilian service. In addition, there is no Third Reich valor or merit decoration on the bar to confirm military service in World War II. The 1914 Iron Cross has a magnetic center and silver frames. The Order of the Zähringen Lion is made of genuine silver and the swords are gold-plated silver. Inserted into each arm of the cross, is a piece of emerald green cut glass. The center medallion on the obverse shows the Zähringen Castle on a white enameled field. This artwork on the obverse is actually hand-painted. The medallion on the reverse has a gold rampant lion on a field of translucent red enamel. The Zähringen Lion was the primary Order awarded by the Grand Duchy of Baden for bravery and military merit. The Order was only awarded to commissioned officers. According to records, about 6,300 of these were awarded during World War I.[11] The 1914-1918 Cross of Honor is magnetic. It is maker marked in relief on the reverse, "G19." The 25-Year Faithful Service Decoration is tombak with

*Two-place medal bar consisting of the 1939 War Merit Cross Second Class with Swords and the 4-Year Long Service Award of the National Labor Service. $110-140.*

a frosted silver finish, polished highlights, and enameled swastika. The Medal for the Annexation of Austria is tombak with a matt silver finish. On the medal bar reverse, black wool covers the back plate. The plates are steel, with an integral hinge and catch. The attachment pin is made of brass. The medals are mounted correctly with regard to the order of precedence regulations in effect at the time.

Although this medal bar has only two medals (**opposite bottom**), it is a nice example of awards to a young staff member or work leader in the National Labor Service (RAD). A medal bar with a RAD Long Service Award is not often seen. Despite the large number of people that served in the National Labor Service, most of its members were only there for six months of compulsory duty prior to starting their service in the military. Few, actually ever qualified for a long service award. Because the medal bar has the War Merit Cross with Swords, one might assume that this man left the RAD and entered the military. While that is possible, I believe it more likely that he remained in the RAD and won the War Merit Cross for some role in combat support. The RAD originally began as a way to help curb unemployment and boost the economy. The result was a large labor force, available for military as well as civilian construction projects. When World War II began, the RAD was actually considered an auxiliary force to the German Armed Forces. As the war went on, the role of the RAD continued to expand. They were not only involved in construction and repair, but other duties such as supplying frontline troops, manning fortifications, laying minefields, manning anti-aircraft batteries, and guarding prisoners. Some RAD units were even involved in frontline combat, especially in the last several months of the war. So it is by no means unusual that a member of the RAD received an award such as the War Merit Cross with Swords or even the Iron Cross.

The 1939 War Merit Cross is an early-issue type, made of bronze. The RAD 4-Year Long Service Award is made of aluminum and finished in bronze. In my opinion, most originals are the lightweight version made in aluminum. In fact, every example I have owned over the years has been made of aluminum. Reportedly though, there are heavyweight versions of this award as well, probably made of tombak. The reverse of the bar is backed with rose colored wool. The mounting plates are steel and the back plate has an integral hinge/catch setup. The attachment pin is steel wire.

Here is another medal bar (**below**) to a work leader in the National Labor Service. In this case, the man was also a veteran of the First World War. The Iron Cross is magnetic and has silver frames. The Cross of Honor is iron with a bronze finish. On the reverse of the upper cross arm is the stamped marking, "O&B." This marking was used by Ochs & Bonn of Hanau on the Main. The RAD 4-Year Long Service Award is aluminum with a bronze finish. The Defense Wall Honor Award is made of solid bronze. On the reverse, the medal bar is backed with light gray wool felt. The ribbons are padded with white cotton fiber. The mounting plate is zinc, with a brass hinge and catch that are soldered in place. The pin is made of brass wire. A grouping such as this is typical of a RAD work supervisor, who was involved in the construction of Germany's western fortifications. He probably remained in the RAD throughout World War II. I would say that this medal bar was assembled in 1940, based on the fact that Defense Wall Award is bronze rather than zinc, and that most were awarded in that year. The overall look of this medal bar is a good example of what is meant by "consistent aging." This natural look can only be achieved through the passage of time. It would be impossible to create a look like this by artificial means. For a bar such as this, one look is all it takes to know that it is genuine. I can almost hear it saying, "Look at me! I am a real piece of history."

*A four place medal bar to a member of the RAD (National Labor Service). Medals are from (L-R): 1914 Iron Cross Second Class, 1914-1918 Cross of Honor with Swords, 4-Year Long Service Award of the National Labor Service, and the Defense Wall Honor Award. $200-225.*

Medal bar reverse.

*Two examples of Long Service Awards of the National Labor Service. Obverse of the 4-Year Award (left) and the 12-Year Award (right). The 4-Year Award is 32.76mm x 40.64mm and weighs 10.2 grams. $90. The 12-Year Award is 32.86mm x 40.66mm and weighs 9.3 grams. $125.00. Right: Reverse of the 4-Year (left) and 12-Year (right) Long Service Awards of the National Labor Service. Inscription reads, "For faithful service in the National Labor Service."*

Long Service Awards of the National Labor Service were instituted in January of 1938, along with the Faithful Service Decorations and the service awards for the Police, SS, and Luftschutz.[12] The National Labor Service had awards for four, twelve, eighteen, and twenty-five years of service. Design wise, all four awards are the same, except for the color of finish. The 4-Year Award was finished in bronze while the 12-Year Award was finished in silver. The 18-Year Award was also silver, but it had a silver eagle device attached to the ribbon. The 25-Year Award was finished in gold and had a gold eagle device attached to the ribbon. All were worn with a cornflower blue ribbon. There was another version of these awards that was made for women members of the National Labor Service. The women's award did not have the spade on the obverse, and it was worn from a ribbon in bow form. The reverse was identical to the men's award. The inscription on the reverse reads, "for faithful service in the National Labor Service."

All of the originals I have seen are of excellent quality. Most are lightweight and made of aluminum with a plated finish. The finish holds up well over time, so many of these awards look as nice as when they were first made. They are not found often on a medal bar. Over the years, I recall having seen only two original medal bars with a 12-Year Award and none with an 18 or 25-Year Award.

This two-place combination (**below**) is probably the most common medal bar to be seen during the Third Reich Period, at least up until the start of World War II. It is a medal bar belonging to a man that was decorated for bravery in World War I. After the war he returned to a civilian life. Then sometime in the mid to later 1930s, he received his 1914-1918 Cross of Honor with Swords to commemorate his service in World War I. The veteran probably had the medals mounted shortly after receiving the Cross

*Right: In this photograph, the leader of the National Labor Service, Reichsarbeitsführer Konstantin Hierl, is seen wearing his eight-place medal bar. He wears his Bavarian Military Merit Order and Hohenzollern House Order before the 1914 Iron Cross. Courtesy of George Robinson.*

*Two-place medal bar consisting of the 1914 Iron Cross Second Class and the 1914-1918 Cross of Honor with Swords. $65-75.*

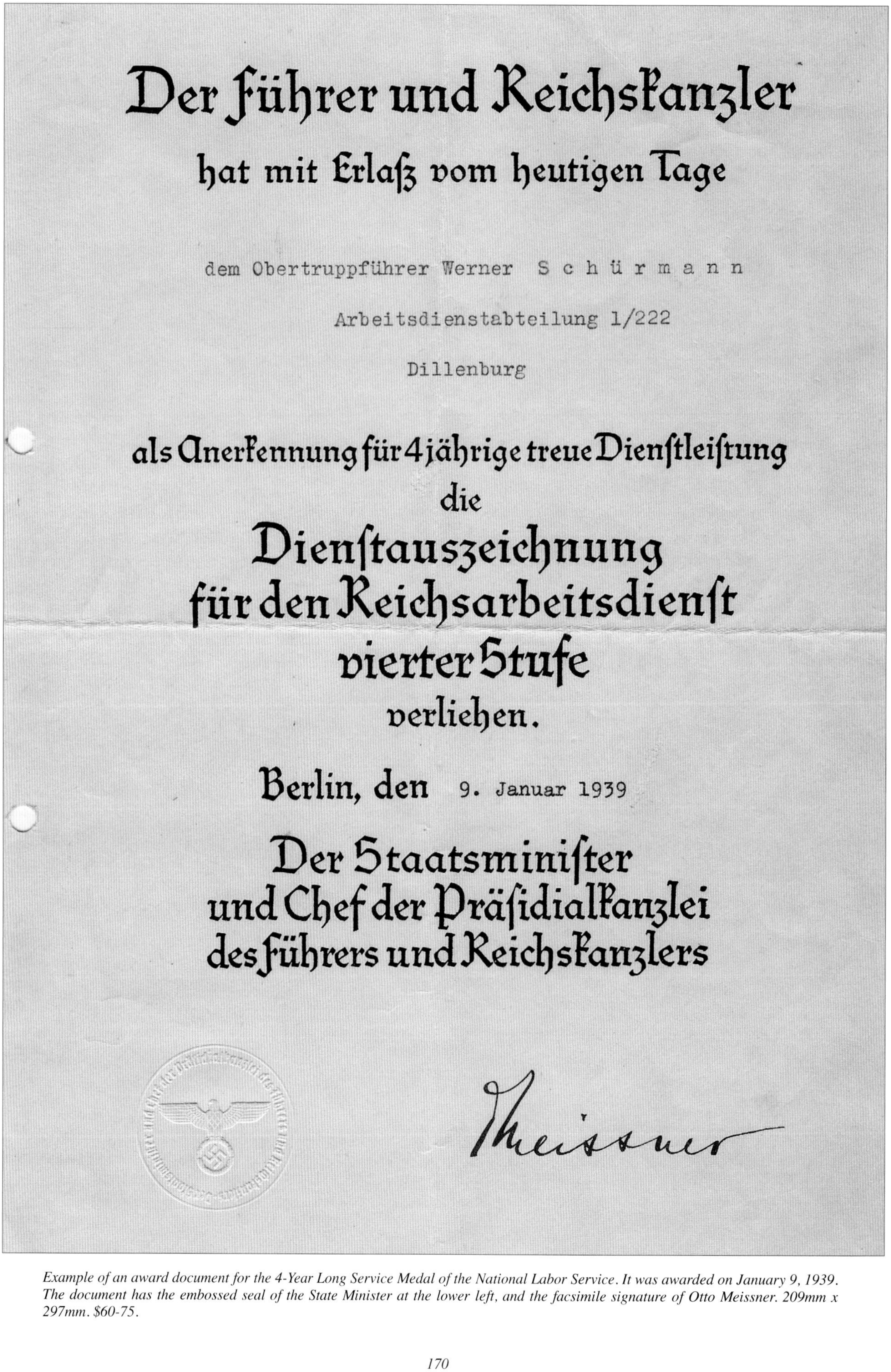

Der Führer und Reichskanzler

hat mit Erlaß vom heutigen Tage

dem Obertruppführer Werner S c h ü r m a n n

Arbeitsdienstabteilung 1/222

Dillenburg

als Anerkennung für 4 jährige treue Dienstleistung

die

Dienstauszeichnung

für den Reichsarbeitsdienst

vierter Stufe

verliehen.

Berlin, den 9. Januar 1939

Der Staatsminister

und Chef der Präsidialkanzlei

des Führers und Reichskanzlers

Meissner

*Example of an award document for the 4-Year Long Service Medal of the National Labor Service. It was awarded on January 9, 1939. The document has the embossed seal of the State Minister at the lower left, and the facsimile signature of Otto Meissner. 209mm x 297mm. $60-75.*

of Honor, so I would say this bar was assembled sometime between 1935 and 1937.

The Iron Cross is a standard three-part type. The core is magnetic and the frames are silver. The Cross of Honor is iron with a bronze finish. Both awards are securely tied down. The Iron Cross is secured with heavy thread, across the lower cross arm. The Cross of Honor is secured just above both of the sword hilts. Because the Cross of Honor is tied down, the maker's mark is not visible. The medal bar has a zinc mounting plate. The hinge, catch, and pin are all made of brass. On the reverse, the red wool backing shows some moth damage.

This three-place medal bar (**below**) was to a World War I veteran that had some duty in connection with the planning and/or running of the 1936 Olympic Games. The bar was probably assembled in the late 1930s. The 1914 Iron Cross has an iron core and the frames are silver. The Cross of Honor is bronzed iron. It has the maker marking, "JK" within a triangle, stamped onto the reverse of the upper cross arm. The Olympic Games

*A three-place medal bar. Medals are from (L-R): 1914 Iron Cross Second Class, 1914-1918 Cross of Honor with Swords, and the 1936 Olympic Games Commemorative Medal. $200-225.*

*A four-place medal bar. Medals are from (L-R): 1914 Iron Cross Second Class, 1914-1918 Cross of Honor with Swords, 1939 War Merit Cross Second Class without Swords, and the 1936 Olympic Games Commemorative Medal. $225-250.*

Commemorative Medal is die-struck iron. It appears that this medal was polished by a previous owner. The polishing has given the medal an almost mirror-like shine, but unfortunately it has removed much of the frosted silver finish. It is always best to leave medals in their original condition. Cleaning and polishing them might make them look brighter, but it also removes original finish. If a medal is cleaned too much, the finish can be worn down to the base metal. Cleaning medals can also remove the natural patina that can only be achieved through decades of time. The idea is not to make the medals look shiny and new, but to allow them to show their natural age. All of the mounting hardware on the medal bar is made of nickel-plated steel. The back plate has an integral hinge and catch. It looks as if someone tried to vault the medal bar so that it would have a neater fit when worn on the uniform. This would explain the crease in the sheet steel back plate.

On this four-place medal bar (**opposite**), the War Merit Cross without Swords is incorrectly placed after the 1914-1918 Cross of Honor. The correct placement would be between the Iron Cross and the Cross of Honor. It seems that this error was made frequently, and it might have been due to confusing the War Merit Cross with the War Merit Medal. The original regulations placed the War Merit Cross before the Cross of Honor and the War Merit Medal after it. In 1942, the regulations were changed, placing the War Merit Medal before the Cross of Honor. This change helped eliminate mistakes since both the War Merit Cross and the War Merit Medal now had precedence to the Cross of Honor. But for that two year period between 1940 and 1942, mistakes could be easily made if the assembler did not realize the difference between a War Merit Cross and Medal. The error in placement leads me to believe that this medal bar was assembled in 1940 or 1941.

*A five-place medal bar. Medals are from (L-R): 1914 Iron Cross Second Class, 1914-1918 Cross Of Honor with Swords, World War I Commemorative Medal for Austria, Prussian 15-Year Long Service Cross, and the World War I Commemorative Medal for Hungary. $150-175.*

The Iron Cross is a three-piece example with an iron core and silver frames. The 1914-1918 Cross of Honor is iron with a bronze finish. The marking, "CEJ" within a rectangle, is stamped into the reverse of the lower cross arm. This marking was used by C. E. Juncker of Berlin. The War Merit Cross is an early issue, made of bronze. The Olympic Games Commemorative Medal is iron with a silver finish. On the reverse, the medal bar has red wool covering the zinc mounting plate. The hinge, catch, and pin are all made of brass.

This is a really nice medal bar to a World War I veteran (**page 173**). He was undoubtedly a non-commissioned officer during the First World War. The medals are neatly mounted and their arrangement is completely within the regulations. No military or civilian service is shown for World War II, so I would assume that the bar was assembled in the mid to late 1930s. The Iron Cross is three-piece and made of the typical materials for the World War I Period. The 1914-1918 Cross of Honor is bronzed iron. The maker marking, "KM&F," is stamped into the reverse of the lower cross arm. This marking was used by Kallenbach, Meyer & Franke of Luckenwalde. The World War I Commemorative Medal for Austria is a non-magnetic base metal with a golden bronze finish. The Prussian 15-Year Long Service Cross is the type awarded between 1913 and 1918. It is tombak with a copper finish. The front of the cross has the imperial crown at the center and the reverse bears the Roman numerals XV. The World War I Commemorative Medal for Hungary is non-magnetic and has an antiqued silver finish. On the reverse, the medal bar has a backing of red wool felt. The mounting plate is zinc, with a soldered on hinge and catch made of brass. The attachment pin is brass wire.

This three-place, World War I veteran's medal bar (**below**) is interesting because it does not conform to the usual assembly methods of the period. It may have been a homemade assembly, done by a family member of the recipient. Despite the non-standard assembly, the work is well done so it could also have been done by a uniform shop. Whether homemade or professionally done, I am convinced that this is an original medal bar. It was most likely assembled in the mid to late 1930s.

The Iron Cross has an iron core and the frames are genuine silver. You will notice that the impression of the Iron Cross' suspension ring is visible through the ribbon. When this medal bar was made, the ribbon was drawn tightly over the suspension ring. With this constant pressure, the suspension ring is actually wearing away the ribbon from the inside out. Eventually, the suspension ring will poke its way through as the ribbon continues to deteriorate. Probably not for several more decades though. Any acidic material that is in constant contact with a ribbon can also have a deteriorating effect. I once owned a medal bar that was in beautiful condition except for one of the ribbons, which was badly deteriorated and falling apart. Looking at the ribbon more closely, I saw that there were paperboard forms underneath that had been used to give the ribbon a nice furled appearance. There is no doubt in my mind that the acid content of the paperboard forms caused the deterioration of the ribbon. I am not sure what that particular ribbon was made of, but I think it was silk. Whatever the material, it certainly had an adverse reaction to acidic paper. The second medal is the Baden Silver Merit Medal. It is made of die-struck silver. The obverse of the medal shows the profile of the Grand Duke of Baden, Friedrich II. The reverse bears the inscription, "for merit." The medal is worn on the ribbon of the Military Karl-Friedrich Merit Order, which means that this example was awarded for merit in combat. According to records, over 100,000 of these medals were awarded between 1907 and 1918.[13] The last medal is the 1914-1918 Cross of Honor, which is made of bronzed iron. On the reverse, it is maker marked in relief, "O.4." The reverse of the medal bar has red wool felt that is stitched in place. The mounting plate is a vaulted piece of brass, and it has an applied brass safety pin of the type that was commonly used on German "tinnies" and "day badges." The matching ribbon bar has steel mounting plates. The back plate has an integral hinge/catch setup with a steel pin. There are some rust stains on the ribbons, caused by moisture and transfer from the rusting steel plates. The crossed swords device is non-magnetic and looks to be made of bronze.

*Three-place medal bar and matching ribbon bar. Medals are from (L-R): 1914 Iron Cross Second Class, Baden Silver Medal of Merit, and the 1914-1918 Cross of Honor with Swords. Medal bar: $110-125. Ribbon bar: $15-20.*

This three-place medal bar (**below**) was to a Bavarian veteran of World War I. It is a nice looking medal bar, but a common grouping of awards to an enlisted man below the rank of Sergeant. I like the fact that it is mounted in the modified traditional style rather than the Bavarian style, which one might think more likely to have been used here. The medals are arranged according to the regulations of the time. I would have to assume that this medal bar was assembled in the mid to late 1930s, shortly after this veteran received his Cross of Honor.

The 1914 Iron Cross is a standard three-part example. The Bavarian Military Merit Cross is bronze with a copper finish. Both the Iron Cross

*A three-place medal bar. Medals are from (L-R): 1914 Iron Cross Second Class, Bavarian Military Merit Cross Third Class with Swords, and the 1914-1918 Cross of Honor with Swords. $100-125.*

and the Military Merit Cross are secured with thread, across the upper cross arms. Black thread was used for the Iron Cross and beige thread was used for the Military Merit Cross. The use of different color threads for securing the medals is actually a good indicator of authenticity. Assemblers tended to use a color that matched the medal being secured, so that the stitching would be less conspicuous at the tie down points. But also remember: It is just as easy for a person putting a fake medal bar together to use different color threads. Evaluate every aspect of the medal bar rather than relying on any particular indicator. The 1914-1918 Cross of Honor is made of iron and finished in bronze. On the reverse of the lower cross arm is the marking "W.R." This marking is in relief and it was used by the manufacturer, Werner Redo of Saarlautern. The mounting plate and catch are steel but the pin is brass wire. Green cotton was used for the backing. There is a deep zigzag cut along the bottom edge of the material.

There are four bravery decorations and three commemorative medals on this World War I veteran's medal bar (**below**). The bar is in excellent condition and shows only subtle signs of age and wear. The 1914 Iron Cross has a magnetic core and the frames are silver. The Brunswick War Merit Cross Second Class is made of bronze. The obverse bears the cipher of Ernst August of Brunswick at the center, a crown on the upper cross arm, and the "1914" date on the lower cross arm. On the reverse is the inscription, "for merit in the war." The cross is worn on a combatant ribbon. (The non-combatant ribbon was yellow with two blue stripes.) The Friedrich August Cross Second Class is made of iron and it has a black lacquer finish. It is also worn on a combatant ribbon. (The non-combatant ribbon for this award was red with two blue stripes.) The 1914-1918 Cross of Honor is iron with a bronze finish. On the reverse is the manufacturer's logo of Wilhelm Deumer of Lüdenscheid. The next award is the Austrian Franz Joseph Bravery Medal (1915 type). It is made of die-struck bronze. The obverse shows the profile of Franz Joseph I and has the inscription, "Franz Joseph I, by the grace of God, Emperor of Austria."[14] The reverse has the inscription, "for bravery." About 950,000 of these were awarded during World War I.[15] The World War I Commemorative Medal for Hungary is non-magnetic and has a darkened silver finish. The World War I Commemorative Medal for Austria is non-magnetic, and this example appears to be bronze gilt. It is interesting the way the crossed swords are attached to the suspension eyelet. The swords were usually attached to the ribbon. I have never seen another example quite like this. The reverse of the medal bar is backed with red wool. The mounting plate looks like brass, but it is actually steel with a gold-colored finish. The pin, hinge, and catch are all made of brass.

*A seven-place medal bar. Medals are from (L-R): 1914 Iron Cross Second Class, Brunswick War Merit Cross Second Class on combatant ribbon, Oldenburg Friedrich August Cross Second Class on combatant ribbon, 1914-1918 Cross of Honor with Swords, Austrian Franz Joseph Bravery Medal, World War I Commemorative Medal for Hungary, and the World War I Commemorative Medal for Austria with Swords. $300-350.*

*Four-place medal bar consisting of from (L-R): 1914 Iron Cross Second Class, 1914-1918 Cross of Honor with Swords, World War I Commemorative Medal for Austria with Swords, and the World War I Commemorative Medal for Hungary. $125-150.*

This First World War veteran's medal bar (**above**) displays a single valor decoration and three commemorative medals. It is a common grouping of awards. The Iron Cross has an iron core and silver frames. The cross is secured with string, across the lower arm. The Cross of Honor is bronzed iron. It is held securely in place by the Iron Cross, so the maker marking cannot be seen. If a medal will not swing up freely, never try to force it. Doing so will only result in damage to the medal bar. The World War I Commemorative Medal for Austria is bronze and the crossed swords device is either bronze gilt or brass. Whereas the previous medal bar has the swords mounted in an unconventional fashion, this example has the swords attached in the usual manner. The World War I Commemorative Medal for Hungary is non-magnetic and finished in darkened silver. On the reverse, the medal bar is backed with red wool felt. The mounting plate is zinc with soldered components. The hinge and catch are brass, but the pin is steel.

This medal bar (**below**) shows combat service in World War I as well as service during World War II in some support role. The 1939 War Merit Cross is an early-issue type, made of bronze. The Hessen General Honor Decoration is made of silver. This particular example was awarded for war merit. There is also an example of this decoration in the previous chapter that was awarded for bravery. The medals are the same except for the inscription on the reverse. The 1914-1918 Cross of Honor is the usual bronzed iron. The reverse is marked, "G19" in relief. On the reverse, the medal bar is backed with gray-green wool. The mounting plate is zinc, with a soldered on brass hinge and catch. The attachment pin is brass wire.

Occasionally, a "frack bar" from the Third Reich Period will be encountered. These were more popular during the Imperial Period, but were still in use during the 1930s and 1940s. I have owned just a few

*Three-place medal bar. Medals are from (L-R): 1939 War Merit Cross Second Class with Swords, Hessen War Merit Medal, and the 1914-1918 Cross of Honor with Swords. $100-125.*

*A three-place "frack mount" medal bar. Medals are (from upper right to lower left): 1914 Iron Cross Second Class, 1914-1918 Cross of Honor with Swords, and the Prussian Cross for War Aid. $100-125.*

of this type over the years. Not only because they are scarce, but more so because I prefer the look of the conventional medal bar. This medal bar (**above**) has a one-piece Iron Cross of excellent quality. The cross is made of a non-magnetic base metal and is finished in black lacquer and nickel-silver. The Cross of Honor is made of iron and has a bronze finish. This example is unlike most as it is has no maker marking on the reverse. The Prussian Cross for War Aid is made of aluminum. It too is an unusual example because most of these were made from zinc. The Iron Cross and the Prussian Cross for War Aid on this medal bar are not World War I production pieces. They were undoubtedly produced in the 1930s as commercial market replacements for the World War I veterans. All of the mounting and attachment hardware is made of brass. Notice that the hinge and catch positions are reversed from that of the conventional medal bar. If the hinge and catch positions were not reversed, and given the way in which the frack bar was worn, the bar could easily fall off the uniform if the pin came unhooked from the catch. The bar is backed with black wool.

*Above: Reverse of the "frack mount" medal bar.*

*Left: This "frack mount" medal bar has a one-piece, 1914 Iron Cross Second Class. The quality is first-rate. Contrary to popular belief, not all original Iron Crosses were made of three parts. An original, one-piece Iron Cross is scarce in relation to the standard, three-piece crosses.*

*Opposite: Four-place medal bar and matching ribbon bar. Medals are from (L-R): 1914-1918 Cross of Honor without Swords, World War I Commemorative Medal for Austria, World War I Commemorative Medal for Hungary, and the World War I Tyrolean Commemorative Medal. Notice that this ribbon bar has a molded plastic back plate. Although scarce, plastic back plates are original to the Third Reich Period. Medal bar: $90-110. Ribbon bar: $15-25.*

This medal bar and matching ribbon bar (**below**) feature four commemorative medals to a non-combatant World War I veteran. The 1914-1918 Cross of Honor is magnetic and made of iron with a bronze finish. On the reverse it is marked "B&N" for Berg and Nolte of Lüdenscheid. The Austrian, Hungarian, and Tyrolean Commemorative Medals are all non-magnetic and have the usual finishes. The medal bar is backed with blue-green wool felt. All of the mounting and attachment hardware is made of steel. The matching ribbon bar is actually my favorite part of this set. It has steel front plates that are clipped into a plastic back plate. The plastic is not Bakelite, but an actual form of polystyrene that was being

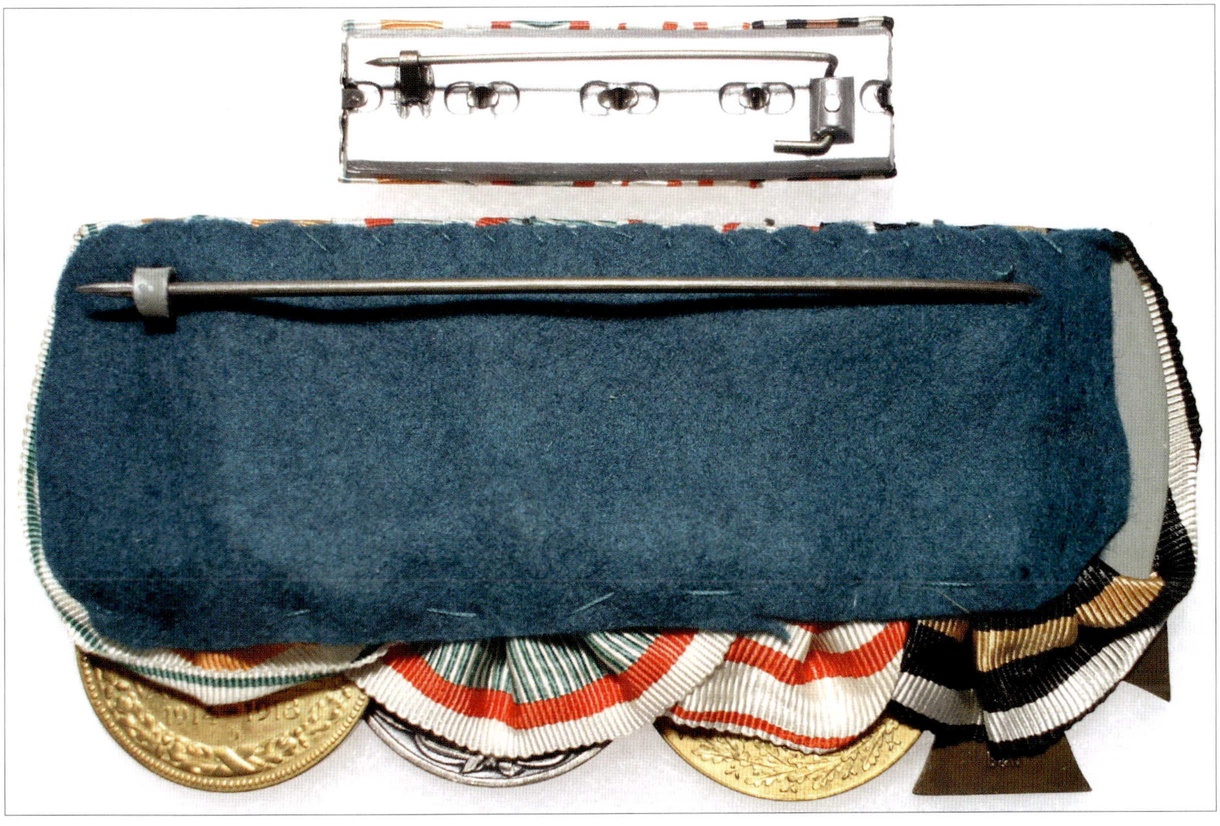

manufactured by the I.G. Farben Company as early as 1931. The back plate has an integral hinge and catch mount. Both the pin and catch are steel. Molded plastic back plates are very scarce, but they are definitely original to the period.

Here is a simple two-place medal bar in excellent condition (**below**). The owner was a non-combatant in World War I and was probably a civilian official at the time Czechoslovakia was annexed in 1938. The 1914-1918 Cross of honor is bronzed iron. The reverse has a stamped marking, "PM." This marking was used by the Berlin manufacturer, Paul Meybauer. The Czech Annexation Medal is tombak with a golden bronze finish. This medal bar has all of its mounting and attachment hardware made of brass. The catch and hinge are separately applied. On the reverse, the bar is backed with gray wool felt.

This two-place medal bar (**opposite top**) is interesting because the 1936 Olympic Games Commemorative Medal is incorrectly placed before the Austrian Annexation Medal. To understand how an error like this could occur, you need to realize that there were actually two different 1936 Olympic awards that could be worn on a medal bar. There was the Olympic Games Commemorative Medal, and there was the Olympic Games Decoration Second Class. (There was also an Olympic Games Decoration First Class, but it was a neck decoration and not worn on the medal bar.) Regulations placed the Second Class Olympic Decoration before the Annexation Medals and the Olympic Commemorative Medal after them. This was confusing and could lead to mistakes if the assembler did not realize the difference between the decoration and the medal.

*Left: In this portrait photo, a member of the NS-RKB (National Socialist War Veterans Association) wears a six-place medal bar. As best as I can tell from the photograph, the medals are from (L-R): 1914-1918 Cross of Honor with Swords, World War I Commemorative Medal for Austria, Austrian Bravery Medal, Austrian Wound Medal, World War I Commemorative Medal for Hungary, and the World War I Tyrolean Commemorative Medal. Below the medal bar, he wears a Wound Badge in Black (1918 type). The cuff title on his left sleeve shows him to be a member from the Donau (Danube) District of the NS-RKB.*

*Below: A two-place medal bar consisting of the 1914-1918 Cross of Honor and the Medal for the Annexation of Czechoslovakia. $55-70.*

*Two-place medal bar featuring the 1936 Olympic Games Commemorative Medal and the Medal for the Annexation of Austria. $175-190.*

This mistake could also occur if the assembler did not read the order of precedence list carefully or completely.

The Olympic Medal is iron with a silver finish. The Austrian Annexation Medal is tombak with a silver finish. On the reverse, the medal bar is backed with green wool. The mounting plate is zinc, with an integral hinge and catch. The attachment pin is steel.

This three-place medal bar (**below**) probably belonged to some sort of government official. The Cross of Honor is bronzed iron and is unmarked. The Olympic Games Commemorative Medal is iron with a silver finish. The Luftschutz Honor Decoration is an early-issue type, made of aluminum. The medals and ribbons are all in excellent condition. The condition leads me to believe that this bar was seldom worn if even worn at all. On the reverse, the medal bar is backed with gray-green wool felt. The mounting plate is zinc, and has an integral catch. The attachment pin is brass. The Luftschutz Medal is incorrectly placed on the medal bar. It should actually be in the center, after the Cross of Honor and before the Olympic Medal. The error in placement may have occurred because the Luftschutz Medal was not specifically mentioned in the regulations. It was one of many medals that fit into the general category of "other long service and national awards." Awards in this category were to be arranged on the medal bar by date of award. The assembler may have mistakenly thought that the Olympic Medal belonged in this general category as well, and since the Olympic Medal was awarded first, it should be before the Luftschutz Medal. The recipients themselves may have also had a hand in

*Three-place medal bar. Medals are from (L-R): 1914-1918 Cross of Honor with Swords, 1936 Olympic Games Commemorative Medal, and the Luftschutz Honor Award Second Class. $200-240.*

some of these period errors. The shops would have to rely on the recipient for providing accurate information as to award dates. There were probably instances too where the recipient told the assembler the supposed proper order in which the medals were to be arranged. Whether or not this input was completely correct, I think in most cases the shop would have done what the paying customer wanted.

The combination of awards seen on this medal bar (**below**) is not only interesting, but scarce. The first three awards are actually common, but the arrangement is interesting because we see another incorrect placement of the War Merit Cross, after the Cross of Honor. The medal bar is considered scarce because of the last medal. While some decorations of the German Red Cross go back as far as 1922, the Medal of the German Red Cross (as seen here) did not exist until 1937.[16] Then in May of 1939, the Social Welfare Decorations were instituted with the intent of replacing the awards of the German Red Cross. So there was only a two year period where the Medal of the German Red Cross could have been awarded.

*Four-place, Red Cross member's medal bar. Medals are from (L-R): 1914 Iron Cross Second Class, 1914-1918 Cross of Honor with Swords, 1939 War Merit Cross Second Class with Swords, and the German Red Cross Medal. $325-350.*

A recipient of a Red Cross award was allowed to continue wearing the award after May of 1939, but if a Social Welfare Decoration of equal status was bestowed, the Red Cross award was no longer to be worn. This medal bar could have belonged to a member of the armed forces in World War II, but it was more likely to a member of the German Red Cross, who received the War Merit Cross with Swords for bravery in a support role. In my opinion this medal bar was assembled in 1940 or1941.

The 1914 Iron Cross has an iron center and silver frames. The 1914-1918 Cross of Honor is magnetic, having a bronze finish over iron. The reverse of the lower cross arm is marked in relief, "№ 44 R.V. Pforzheim." The 1939 War Merit Cross is an early-war example made of bronze. The Medal of the German Red Cross is die-struck tombak with an antiqued silver finish. The front of the medal features opaque white and translucent red enamel. You should be able to see the stippling in the cross arms

*Four-place medal bar to member of the Red Cross or some other social welfare organization. Medals are from (L-R): 1914 Iron Cross Second Class, 1914-1918 Cross of Honor with Swords, Medal for German Social Welfare, and the Medal for the Annexation of Czechoslovakia. $175-200.*

through the red enamel. A separately-applied eagle is at the center of the cross. The eagle has black enamel with gold-finished highlights. On the reverse of the medal bar, there is maroon wool felt backing. The mounting plate is zinc with an applied brass hinge and catch. The attachment pin is also made of brass.

On this four-place medal bar (**page 185**), we see that the owner was a veteran of World War I and worked either for the German Red Cross, or with some other social welfare organization. Since members of the armed forces were eligible to receive the Social Welfare Medal, it is possible that he was back in the military for World War II. However, there are no medals on this bar that actually confirm World War II military service. I would suspect that this bar is an early-wartime assembly, made between late 1939 and early 1941. Because of the excellent quality of the Social Welfare Medal, it is unlikely that this medal bar was assembled later in the war. Also of interest, is the fact that the Social Welfare Medal is incorrectly placed on the bar. It should actually be after the Czech Annexation Medal.

The 1914 Iron Cross is the standard three-part type with an iron core and silver frames. Notice that the top arm of the Iron Cross is secured with string to prevent swaying. The Cross of Honor is bronzed iron. On the reverse, it is marked in relief, "C. Th. D," and also a "D" within a house logo. This marking was used by C. Th. Dicke of Lüdenscheid. The Social Welfare Medal is an early-quality example. It is made of tombak with a silver-plated finish. The Medal for the Annexation of Czechoslovakia is tombak with a matt gold finish. There are steel clips on the front for attaching the medals. On the reverse, the medal bar is backed with gray-green wool felt. There is a small zigzag cut to the bottom edge. The mounting plate is zinc with an applied brass hinge and catch. The attachment pin is also made of brass.

This is an outstanding example of a customs official's medal bar (**below**). The man had at least 12 years of military service, and this time would have counted towards his award for 40 years of loyal civilian service. In addition, he served in some capacity with the Customs Service, either as a uniformed official or as a civilian performing a civil service

*Six-place medal bar belonging to a customs official. Medals are from (L-R): 1914 Iron Cross Second Class, 1914-1918 Cross of Honor with Swords, Kaiser Wilhelm I Centenary Medal, Baden 12-Year Long Service Medal, 40-Year Faithful Service Decoration, and the Customs Service Decoration. Courtesy of George Robinson. $450-500.*

function. The Iron Cross is a standard example made of three parts. The 1914-1918 Cross of Honor is iron with a bronze finish. It is marked in relief on the reverse of the lower cross arm, "32 R.V. Pforzheim." The Kaiser Wilhelm I Centenary Medal is die-struck bronze. This medal was created in March of 1897 to commemorate the 100th birthday celebration of the King of Prussia and first German Emperor. It was awarded to all members of the military in good standing at that time. The 12-Year Long Service Medal of the Grand Duchy of Baden is a non-magnetic base metal with a gold finish. The obverse bears the royal cipher of Friedrich II, the Grand Duke of Baden. The 40-Year Faithful Service Decoration is tombak bronze with a fire gilded finish and black enamel swastika. The last award is the Custom Service Decoration, which is not often seen on a medal bar. The Customs Service Decoration is made of die-struck bronze. It was worn on the traditional cornflower blue long service ribbon, but with the addition of a Customs insignia (eagle/wreath) embroidered in yellow cotton thread. The award was instituted in February of 1939.[17] It could be awarded for an exceptional act of merit, but in most cases it was given for faithful service. Uniformed administrators and border control personnel were eligible for the award after 4 years of service. Civilians working with the Customs Service were required to have 8 years of service.[18] The owner of this medal bar must have been in his 60s during World War II, and no doubt witnessed much history over the course of his long career. On the reverse, the bar is backed with blue-gray wool. The mounting plate looks like brass, but it is actually steel with a gold finish. The pin, catch, and hinge are all made of brass.

*Obverse of the Customs Service Decoration. The cross is die-struck, solid bronze. The Customs Service Decoration is not found often on a medal bar. Courtesy of George Robinson.*

This is truly an outstanding medal bar (**below**) to a well-decorated veteran of the First World War. He was a commissioned officer from Saxony. The owner of this bar was undoubtedly in his late 50s to early 60s during the Second World War. He was probably born around 1880 and must have been in the military around 1900. By the time World War I began, he had been in the military for about 15 years and probably held the rank of *Hauptmann*. He must have served throughout all of World War I, and he would have received double credit for his wartime service. This would have made him eligible for the Saxon 25-Year Long Service Cross for Regular Officers by the end of World War I, or shortly thereafter. By the time he left military service, he was a *Major* or possibly even an *Oberstleutnant*. After World War I, it appears that he had some sort of civil service position by virtue of the Faithful Service Decoration. Since years of military service counted towards years of faithful civilian service, it is unusual that this medal bar displays only the 25-Year Faithful Service

*An extremely rare, Saxon officer's medal bar. Medals are from (L-R): 1914 Iron Cross Second Class, Military Order of St. Heinrich-Knight's Cross, Saxon Order of Albert- Knight's Cross First Class with Crown and Swords, 1914-1918 Cross of Honor with Swords, Saxon 25-Year Long Service Cross for Regular Officers, and the 25-Year Faithful Service Decoration. Courtesy of Edward Maroli. $2500-2700.*

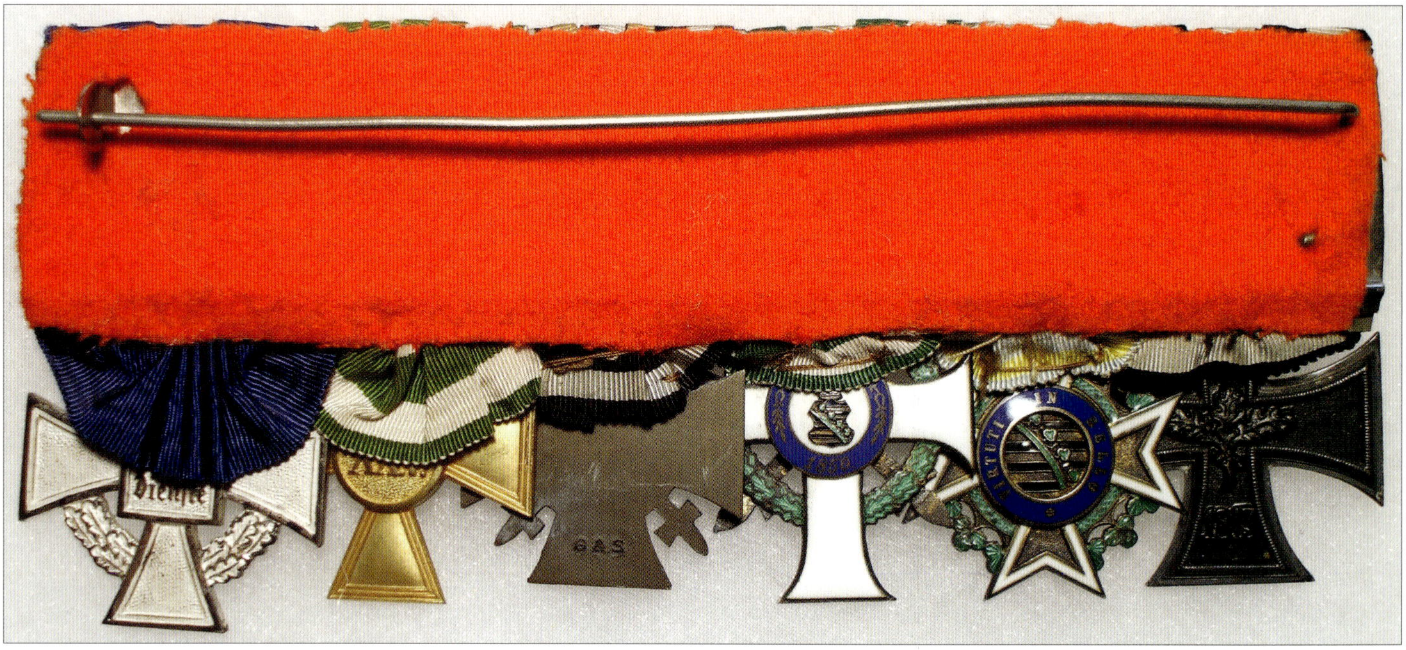

*Above: Medal bar reverse. Courtesy of Edward Maroli.*

*Left: Close-up showing the obverse of the Military Order of St. Heinrich- Knight's Cross and the Order of Albert- Knight's Cross First Class with Crown and Swords. These Orders were struck from silver and finished in gold-plate. The center medallion on the Order of St. Heinrich is hand-painted. The white and blue enamel is opaque. The green enamel is translucent. Both of these examples were made by Scharffenberg of Dresden. Courtesy of Edward Maroli.*

*Close-up showing the reverse of both Saxon Orders. Courtesy of Edward Maroli.*

Decoration rather than the 40-Year Decoration. Accounting for this would suggest that there may have been a break of a few years between military and civilian service. At the time this bar was assembled (late 1938 to early 1939) the owner was probably just short of receiving the 40-Year Faithful Service Decoration.

The Iron Cross is a standard three-piece type, having an iron core and silver frames. The Knight's Cross of the Military Order of St. Heinrich was awarded for bravery to commissioned officers only. It is a rare Order as less than 2,800 were awarded.[19] The Order was struck in genuine silver and finished in gold-plate. It also features white, blue, and green enamel. The white and blue is opaque, but the green enamel should be translucent. There is no marking that can be found on this example. However, the hand-painted artwork to the center medallion confirms that this example was produced by Scharffenberg of Dresden. The Order of Albert- Knight's Cross First Class with Crown and Swords is even rarer. Less than 1,200 of these were awarded during World War I.[20] The large crown at the top signifies that this recipient was actually awarded the Order on two separate occasions. This Order was also struck in genuine silver, and finished in gold-plate. As on the Order of St. Heinrich, the white and blue enamel is opaque, while the green enamel is translucent. On the edge of the lower cross arm is the stamped marking "S" for Scharffenberg of Dresden. The 1914-1918 Cross of Honor is iron with a bronze finish. On the reverse of the lower cross arm is the stamped marking, "G&S" for Glaser and Sohn of Dresden. The Saxon 25-Year Long Service Cross for Regular Officers is made of tombak with a fire gilded finish. It looks to be the single-piece type. (Some of these were made having separate, center medallions.) The Faithful Service Decoration is tombak with a frosted silver finish and polished highlights. The swastika is black enamel. On the reverse, the back plate is covered with red wool. The mounting plates are sheet steel with an integral hinge/catch setup. The attachment pin is also made of steel.

# APPENDICES

**Appendix A**
**Lieferant Code Numbers (official suppliers to the chancellery)**

| # | Manufacturer | Town or City |
|---|---|---|
| 1 | Deschler & Sohn | Munich |
| 2 | C. E. Juncker | Berlin |
| 3 | Wilhelm Deumer | Lüdenscheid |
| 4 | Steinhauer & Lück | Lüdenscheid |
| 5 | Hermann Wernstein | Jena-Löbstedt |
| 6 | Fritz Zimmermann | Stuttgart |
| 7 | Paul Meybauer | Berlin |
| 8 | Ferdinand Hoffstätter | Bonn am Rhein |
| 9 | work group of jewelry craftsmen | Pforzheim |
| 10 | Förster & Barth | Pforzheim |
| 11 | Grossman & Co. | Vienna |
| 12 | Frank & Reif | Stuttgart |
| 13 | Gustav Brehmer | Markneukirchen |
| 14 | L. Chr. Lauer | Nürnberg |
| 15 | Friedrich Orth | Vienna |
| 16 | Alois Rettenmaier | Schwäbisch Gmünd |
| 17 | unknown | |
| 18 | Karl Wurster | Markneukirchen |
| 19 | E. Ferd. Wiedmann | Frankfurt am Main |
| 20 | C. F. Zimmermann | Pforzheim |
| 21 | Gebrüder Godet | Berlin |
| 22 | Boerger & Co. | Berlin |
| 23 | work group for engraving/decorating | Berlin |
| 24 | work group for plaque manufacturers | Hanau am Main |
| 25 | work group of engraver/smith guilds | Hanau am Main |
| 26 | B. H. Mayer | Pforzheim |
| 27 | Anton Schenkl's successor | Vienna |
| 28 | Eugen Schmidthäussler | Pforzheim |
| 29 | Central Mint of Berlin | Berlin |
| 30 | Central Mint of Vienna | Vienna |
| 31 | Hans Gnad | Vienna |
| 32 | W. Hobacher | Vienna |
| 33 | Friedrich Linden | Lüdenscheid |
| 34 | Willy Annetsberger | Munich |
| 35 | F. W. Assmann & Söhne | Lüdenscheid |
| 36 | Bury & Leonhard | Hanau am Main |
| 37 | Adolf Baumeister | Lüdenscheid |
| 38 | unknown | |
| 39 | Rudolf Bergs | Gablonz an der Neiße |
| 40 | Berg & Nolte | Gablonz an der Neiße |
| 41 | Gebrüder Bender | Oberstein |
| 42 | Biedermann & Co. | Oberkassel bei Bonn |
| 43 | Julius Bauer Söhne | Zella-Mehlis |
| 44 | Jakob Bengel | Idar-Oberstein |
| 45 | Franz Jungwirth | Vienna |
| 46 | Hans Doppler | Wels/Oberdonau |
| 47 | Erhard & Söhne | Schwäbisch Gmünd |
| 48 | Richard Feix | Gablonz an der Neiße |
| 49 | Josef Feix Söhne | Gablonz an der Neiße |
| 50 | Karl Gschiermeister | Vienna |
| 51 | Eduard Görlach & Söhne | Gablonz an der Neiße |
| 52 | Gottlieb & Wagner | Idar-Oberstein |
| 53 | Glaser & Sohn | Dresden |
| 54 | unknown | |
| 55 | J. E. Hammer & Söhne | Geringswalde |
| 56 | Robert Hauschild | Pforzheim |
| 57 | Karl Hensler | Pforzheim |
| 58 | Artur Jökel & Co. | Gablonz an der Neiße |
| 59 | Louis Keller | Oberstein |
| 60 | Katz & Deyhle | Pforzheim |
| 61 | Rudolf Karneth & Söhne | Gablonz an der Neiße |
| 62 | Kerbach & Österhelt | Dresden |
| 63 | Franz Klamt & Söhne | Gablonz an der Neiße |
| 64 | Gottl. Fr. Keck & Sohn | Pforzheim |
| 65 | Klein & Quenzer | Idar-Oberstein |
| 66 | Friedrich Keller | Oberstein |
| 67 | R. Kreisel | Gablonz an der Neiße |
| 68 | Alfred Knobloch | Gablonz an der Neiße |
| 69 | Alois Klammer | Innsbruck |
| 70 | Lind & Meyrer | Oberstein |
| 71 | Rudolf Leukert | Gablonz an der Neiße |
| 72 | Franz Lipp | Pforzheim |
| 73 | Franz Mänert | Gablonz an der Neiße |
| 74 | Carl Meurer Sohn | Oberstein |
| 75 | unknown | |
| 76 | Ernst L. Müller | Pforzheim |
| 77 | Bavarian Central Mint | Munich |
| 78 | Gustav Miksch | Gablonz an der Neiße |
| 79 | unknown | |
| 80 | G. H. Osang | Dresden |
| 81 | Overhoff & Cie | Lüdenscheid |
| 82 | Augustin Prager | Gablonz an der Neiße |
| 83 | Emil Peukert | Gablonz an der Neiße |
| 84 | Carl Poellath | Schrobenhausen |
| 85 | Julius Pietsch | Gablonz an der Neiße |
| 86 | Paulmann & Crone | Lüdenscheid |
| 87 | Roman Palme | Gablonz an der Neiße |
| 88 | Werner Redo | Saarlautern |
| 89 | Rudolf Richter | Schlag bei Gablonz |
| 90 | August Richter | Hamburg |
| 91 | Josef Rössler & Co. | Gablonz an der Neiße |
| 92 | Josef Rücker & Sohn | Gablonz an der Neiße |
| 93 | Richard Simm & Söhne | Gablonz an der Neiße |
| 94 | unknown | |
| 95 | Adolf Scholze | Grünwald an der Neiße |
| 96 | unknown | |

| | | |
|---|---|---|
| 97 | unknown | |
| 98 | Rudolf Souval | Vienna |
| 99 | Schwertner & Cie | Graz-Eggenberg |
| 100 | Rudolf Wächtler & Lange | Mittweida/Sa. |
| 101 | Rudolf Tham | Gablonz an der Neiße |
| 102 | Philipp Türk's widow | Vienna |
| 103 | August Tham | Gablonz an der Neiße |
| 104 | Heinrich Ulbricht's widow | Kaufing bei Schwanenstadt |
| 105 | Heinrich Vogt | Pforzheim |
| 106 | Brüder Schneider | Vienna |
| 107 | Carl Wild | Hamburg |
| 108 | Arno Wallpach | Salzburg |
| 109 | Walter & Henlein | Gablonz an der Neiße |
| 110 | Otto Zappe | Gablonz an der Neiße |
| 111 | Ziemer & Söhne | Oberstein |
| 112 | Rust & Hetzel | Vienna |
| 113 | Hermann Aurich | Dresden |
| 114 | Ludwig Bertsch | Karlsruhe |
| 115 | unknown | |
| 116 | Funcke & Brüninghaus | Lüdenscheid |
| 117 | Hugo Lang | Wiesenthal |
| 118 | August Menze & Sohn | Vienna |
| 119 | unknown | |
| 120 | Franz Petzl | Vienna |
| 121 | unknown | |
| 122 | J. J. Stahl | Strassburg |
| 123 | Beck, Hassinger & Co. | Strassburg |
| 124 | Rudolf Schanes | Vienna |
| 125 | Eugen Gauss | Pforzheim |
| 126 | Eduard Hahn | Oberstein |
| 127 | Moritz Hausch | Pforzheim |
| 128 | S. Jablonski | Posen |
| 129 | Fritz Kohm | Pforzheim |
| 130 | Wilhelm Schröder & Co. | Lüdenscheid |
| 131 | Heinrich Wander | Gablonz an der Neiße |
| 132 | Franz Reischauer | Idar-Oberstein |
| 133 | unknown | |
| 134 | Otto Klein | Hanau |
| 135 | Julius Moser | Oberstein |
| 136 | J. Wagner & Sohn | Berlin |
| 137 | J. H. Werner | Berlin |
| 138 | Julius Maurer | Oberstein |
| 139 | Hymmen & Co. | Lüdenscheid |
| 140 | Schauerte & Höhfeld | Lüdenscheid |
| 141 | Sohni, Heubach & Co. | Oberstein |
| 142 | A. D. Schwerdt | Stuttgart |

## Appendix B
## LDO Production Code Numbers (firms licensed to sell commercially)

| Code | Manufacturer | Town or City |
|---|---|---|
| L/10 | Deschler & Sohn | Munich |
| L/11 | Wilhelm Deumer | Lüdenscheid |
| L/12 | C. E. Juncker | Berlin |
| L/13 | Paul Meybauer | Berlin |
| L/14 | Friedrich Orth | Vienna |
| L/15 | Otto Schickle | Pforzheim |
| L/16 | Steinhauer & Lück | Lüdenscheid |
| L/17 | Hermann Wernstein | Jena-Löbstedt |
| L/18 | B. H. Mayer | Pforzheim |
| L/19 | Ferdinand Hoffstätter | Bonn am Rhein |
| L/21 | Förster & Barth | Pforzheim |
| L/22 | Glaser & Sohn | Dresden |
| L/23 | Julius Maurer | Oberstein |
| L/24 | Fritz Zimmermann | Stuttgart |
| L/25 | A. E. Kochert | Vienna |
| L/26 | Klein & Quenzer | Idar-Oberstein |
| L/50 | Gebrüder Godet | Berlin |
| L/51 | E. Ferd. Wiedmann | Frankfurt am Main |
| L/52 | C. F. Zimmermann | Pforzheim |
| L/53 | Hymmen & Co. | Lüdenscheid |
| L/54 | Schauerte & Höhfeld | Lüdenscheid |
| L/55 | Rudolf Wächtler & Lange | Mittweida/Sa. |
| L/56 | Funcke & Brüninghaus | Lüdenscheid |
| L/57 | Boerger & Co. | Berlin |
| L/58 | Rudolf Souval | Vienna |
| L/59 | Alois Rettenmaier | Schwäbisch Gmünd |
| L/60 | Gustav Brehmer | Markneukirchen |
| L/61 | Friedrich Linden | Lüdenscheid |
| L/62 | Werner Redo | Saarlautern |
| L/63 | G. H. Osang | Dresden |
| L/64 | F. W. Assmann & Söhne | Lüdenscheid |
| L/65 | Dr. Franke & Co. | Lüdenscheid |
| L/66 | A. D. Schwerdt | Stuttgart |

# GLOSSARY

While typing out the text for this book, I have tried to keep the use of German words down to a minimum. When a German word is used, I have put the English meaning in parenthesis, immediately following the word. In this way, I hope to avoid confusion. As a collector though, you should have at least some basic understanding of German words with regard to the German Armed Forces of World War II, and the terminology concerning orders, decorations, and medals. This glossary should provide some assistance.

| German | English |
|---|---|
| Abzeichen | badge |
| Altsilber | old silver (darkened nickel-silver) |
| Aluminium | aluminum |
| Ausführung | manufacture/version |
| Auszeichnung | decoration/award |
| Band | ribbon |
| Bandring | ribbon/suspension ring |
| Bandspange | ribbon bar |
| Bandspangen | ribbon bars |
| Baumwolle | cotton |
| Beamte | official |
| Blech | sheet metal |
| Bronze | bronze |
| Buntmetall | colored metal (bronze, brass, tombak, etc.) |
| Cupal | copper-plated aluminum |
| Dienst | service |
| DRGM | abbreviation for: German Empire registered design |
| DRK | abbreviation for: German Red Cross |
| Eisen | iron |
| Eisernes Kreuz | Iron Cross |
| farbig | colored |
| Feldspange | field clasp/ribbon bar |
| Feinzink | fine zinc |
| feuervergoldet | fire gilded |
| Gebrüder | brothers |
| Gold | gold |
| Haken | hook/catch |
| Hakenkreuz | hooked cross/swastika |
| Heer | German Army |
| Hoheitsabzeichen | national insignia |
| Kreuz | cross |
| Krieg | war |
| Kriegsmarine | German Navy of World War II |
| Kriegsmetall | war metal (a crude, wartime zinc alloy) |
| Kriegsverdienstkreuz | War Merit Cross |
| leichte Ausfuhrung | lightweight manufacture/version |
| Leichtmetall | lightweight metal |
| Lieferant | supplier |
| Luftschutz | air defense |
| Luftwaffe | German Air Force |
| Medaille | medal |
| Medaillon | medallion |
| Messing | brass |
| mit polierten Kanten | with polished edges |
| mit Schwertern | with swords |
| Nadel | pin |
| Neusilber | new silver (nickel-silver) |
| NSDAP | National Socialist German Workers Party (Nazi party) |
| NS-RKB | abbreviation for: National Socialist Veterans Association |
| ohne Schwerter | without swords |
| Orden | order/medal |
| Ordens | orders/medals |
| Ordenschnalle | single-place medal bar |
| Ordenschnallen | single-place medal bars |
| Ordensschnalle | multi-place medal bar |
| Ordensschnallen | multi-place medal bars |
| Ordenspange | single-place medal bar/clasp |
| Ordenspangen | single-place medal bars/clasps |
| Ordensspange | multi-place medal bar/clasp |
| Ordensspangen | multi-place medal bars/clasps |
| Öse | eyelet |
| poliert | polished |
| Polizei | police |
| RAD | abbreviation for: National Labor Service |
| Ritterkreuz | Knight's Cross |
| Rotes Kreuz | Red Cross |
| schwere Ausführung | heavyweight manufacture/version |
| Silber | silver |
| Sohn | son |
| Söhne | sons |
| Spange | clasp |
| Spangen | clasps |
| Stoff | material/fabric |

| | |
|---|---|
| Tapferkeit | bravery |
| Tombak | a brass alloy having a high copper content |
| Tuch | cloth |
| unpoliert | unpolished |
| Verdienst | merit |
| vergoldet | gold-plated |
| vernickelt | nickel-plated |
| versilbert | silver-plated |
| Waffenfarbe | arm/branch of service color |
| Wehrmacht | German Armed Forces of World War II |
| Weltkrieg | world war |
| Wolle | wool |
| Zink | zinc |

# NOTES

**Chapter 1**

[1] J. Rex Reddick, *F.W. Assmann & Söhne Sales Catalog* (Denison, Texas: Reddick Enterprises, 1992), 137.

**Chapter 2**

[1] Roger J. Bender and Warren W. Odegard, *Uniforms, Organization and History of the Panzertruppe* (San Jose: R. James Bender Publishing, 1980), 68.

[2] Gordon Williamson, *The Iron Cross: A History 1813-1957* (Denison, Texas: Reddick Enterprises, 1994), 14.

[3] John R. Angolia, *For Führer and Fatherland: Military Awards of the Third Reich* (San Jose: R. James Bender Publishing, 1976), 337.

[4] Mike Miller, "General der Flieger Rudolf Bogatsch," *Axis Biographical Research*,http://www.geocities.com/~orion47/WEHRMACHT/LUFTWAFFE/General/BOGATSCH_RUDOLF.html.

[5] Christopher Ailsby, *A Collector's Guide to: World War 2 German Medals and Political Awards* (London: Ian Allan Publishing, 1994), 49 & 53.

[6] Angolia, *Military Awards*, 306.

[7] Ibid.

[8] John R. Angolia, *For Führer and Fatherland: Political and Civil Awards of the Third Reich* (San Jose: R. James Bender Publishing, 1978), 77.

[9] Ibid.

[10] Emilie C. Stewart, *German Military Award Documents 1939-1945* (New Jersey: Emilie C. Stewart, 1991), 111.

[11] Ailsby, *World War 2 German Medals*, 125.

[12] Angolia, *Military Awards*, 55.

**Chapter 3**

[1] John R. Angolia, *For Führer and Fatherland: Political and Civil Awards of the Third Reich* (San Jose: R. James Bender Publishing, 1978), 22.

[2] Ibid., 12.

[3] David Danner, "Principality of Lippe-Detmold," *Decorations of the States of the German Empire*, http://home.att.net/~david.danner/militaria/lippe-detmold.htm#2.

[4] John R. Angolia, *For Führer and Fatherland: Military Awards of the Third Reich* (San Jose: R. James Bender Publishing, 1976), 300.

[5] Ibid., 61.

[6] Angolia, *Political and Civil Awards*, 164.

[7] Ibid., 167.

[8] Michael Shackelford and Hendrik Meersschaert, "Medals of Austria-Hungary," *Great War Primary Documents Archive, Inc.*, http://www.gwpda.org/ medals/austmedl/austria.html.

[9] Megan C. Robertson, "Medals of Bulgaria," *Orders, Decorations and Medals*, http://www.medals.org.uk/bulgaria/bulgaria.htm.

[10] David Danner, "The Hanseatic Crosses," *Decorations of the States of the German Empire*, http://home.att.net/~david.danner/militaria/ hansastaedte.htm.

[11] Ibid.

**Chapter 4**

[1] John R. Angolia, *For Führer and Fatherland: Military Awards of the Third Reich* (San Jose: R. James Bender Publishing, 1976), 66.

[2] John R. Angolia, *For Führer and Fatherland: Political and Civil Awards of the Third Reich* (San Jose: R. James Bender Publishing, 1978), 12.

[3] Andreas M. Schulze Ising, "Manufacturers of the Albert Order," *Imperial German Orders, Medals and Decorations*, http://www.medalnet.net/Albert_Manufacturers.htm.

[4] Michael Shackelford and Hendrik Meersschaert, "Medals of Austria-Hungary," *Great War Primary Documents Archive, Inc.*, http://www.gwpda.org/medals/austmedl/austria.html.

[5] Angolia, *Political and Civil Awards*, 122.

[6] Edward Maroli, personal communication to author, July 20, 2007.

[7] David Danner, "Friedrich August Cross," *Decorations of the States of the German Empire*, http://home.att.net/~david.danner/militaria/oldenburg.htm.

[8] David Danner, "General Honor Decoration," *Decorations of the States of the German Empire*, http://home.att.net/~david.danner/militaria/hessen.htm.

[9] Andreas Altenburger, "4. leichte Division," *Lexikon der Wehrmacht*, http://www.lexikon-der-wehrmacht.de/Gliederungen/ leichte%20Panzerdivisionen/4leDiv.

[10] Michael Shackelford, "Medals of Finland," *Great War Primary Documents Archive, Inc.*, http://www.gwpda.org/medals/finmedl/finland.html.

[11] Ibid.

[12] Michael Shackelford, "Medals of Imperial Germany," *Great War Primary Documents Archive, Inc.*, http://www.gwpda.org /medals/ medalshome.html.

[13] Marcus Wendel, "Silesian Eagle," *Axis History Factbook*, http://www.axishistory.com/index.php?id=1823.

[14] Mark Piersall, "Crusade against Communism Medal 1942-1944," *The Piersall Collection of Orders, Decorations, and Medals from Around the World*, http://www.marksmedals.com/romanian_medals_files/crusade.html.

[15] Ibid.

[16] Angolia, *Political and Civil Awards*, 162 & 163.

[17] Brian L. Davis, *German Army Uniforms and Insignia 1933-1945* (New York: Arco Publishing Company, Inc., 1977), 59 & 157.

[18] Christopher Ailsby, *A Collector's Guide to: World War 2 German Medals and Political Awards* (London: Ian Allan Publishing, 1994), 128.

[19] Edward Maroli, personal communication to author, August 25, 2007.

[20] Richard Lundström, via e-mail messages to author, February 28, and March 1, 2005.

[21] Mike Miller, "Generaloberst Otto Deßloch," *Axis Biographical Research*, http://www.geocities.com/~orion47/WEHRMACHT/LUFTWAFFE/Generaloberst/DESSLOCH_OTTO.html.

[22] Ibid.

[23] Ibid.

[24] Ibid.

[25] Ibid.

[26] Andreas M. Schulze Ising, via e-mail message to author, July 14, 2007.

[27] Photograph can be seen online, http://www.ritterkreuztraeger-1939-45.de/Luftwaffe/Startseite-Luftwaffe.htm.

[28] Miller, "Generaloberst Otto Deßloch."

[29] Herzovision, "Medaille des Militär- St. Heinrichs- Orden," *Sachsens-Orden*, http://herzovision.de/sachsens-orden/kategorie3/24a6bc968e0897f02/ index.html.

[30] Herzovision, "Ritterkreuz II. Klasse," *Sachsens-Orden*, http:// herzovision.de/sachsens-orden/kategorie1/24a6bc96710f3b507/index.html.

**Chapter 5**

[1] John R. Angolia, *For Führer and Fatherland: Political and Civil Awards of the Third Reich* (San Jose: R. James Bender Publishing, 1978), 216.

[2] Ibid.

[3] Ray Cowdery, *Nazi Para-Military Organizations and Their Badges* (Minneapolis: Northstar Commemoratives, Inc., 1985), 28.

[4] Ibid., 26.

[5] Angolia, *Political and Civil Awards,* 139.

[6] Ibid., 141.

[7] Christopher Ailsby, *A Collector's Guide to: World War 2 German Medals and Political Awards* (London: Ian Allan Publishing, 1994), 140.

[8] John R. Angolia, *For Führer and Fatherland: Military Awards of the Third Reich* (San Jose: R. James Bender Publishing, 1976), 306.

[9] Andreas M. Schulze Ising, "Manufacturers of the Albert Order," *Imperial German Orders, Medals and Decorations,* http://www.medalnet.net/Albert_Manufacturers.htm.

[10] Richard Lundström, "1940 Rules and Regulations," *Guide to German Ribbon Bars 1914-1945,* http://www.wehrmacht-awards.com/related/ribbons/regulations/rules_regulations3.htm.

[11] David Danner, "Grand Duchy of Baden," *Decorations of the States of the German Empire,* http://home.att.net/~david.danner/militaria/baden.htm.

[12] Angolia, *Political and Civil Awards,* 151.

[13] Danner, "Grand Duchy of Baden."

[14] Michael Shackelford and Hendrik Meersschaert, "Medals of Austria-Hungary," *Great War Primary Documents Archive, Inc.,* http://www.gwpda.org/medals/austmedl/austria.html.

[15] Ibid.

[16] Angolia, *Political and Civil Awards,* 108 & 118.

[17] Ibid., 171.

[18] Ibid.

[19] Wikipedia: The Free Encyclopedia, s.v. "Military Order of St. Henry," http://en.wikipedia.org/wiki/Military_Order_of_St._Henry.

[20] Herzovision, "Ritterkreuz 1. Kl. mit Krone u. Schwerter- 1918," *Sachsens-Orden,* http://herzovision.de/sachsens-orden/kategorie1/ 24a6bc96710f40f0d/ 24a6bc96710f46a16/index.html.

# BIBLIOGRAPHY


Ailsby, Christopher. *A Collector's Guide to: World War 2 German Medals and Political Awards*. London: Ian Allan Publishing, 1994.

Altenburger, Andreas. *Lexikon der Wehrmacht*. http://www.lexikon-der-wehrmacht.de/inhaltsverzeichnis1.htm.

Angolia, John R. *For Führer and Fatherland: Military Awards of the Third Reich*. San Jose: R. James Bender Publishing, 1976.

Angolia, John R. *For Führer and Fatherland: Political and Civil Awards of the Third Reich*. San Jose: R. James Bender Publishing, 1978.

Bender, Roger J. *Air Organizations of the Third Reich: The Luftwaffe*. Mountain View, California: R. James Bender Publishing, 1972.

Bender, Roger J., and Warren W. Odegard. *Uniforms, Organization and History of the Panzertruppe*. San Jose: R. James Bender Publishing, 1980.

Cowdery, Ray. *Nazi Para-Military Organizations and Their Badges*. Minneapolis: Northstar Commemoratives, Inc., 1985.

Danner, David. *Decorations of the States of the German Empire*. http:// home.att.net/~david.danner/militaria/states.htm.

Davis, Brian L. *German Army Uniforms and Insignia 1933-1945*. New York: Arco Publishing Company, Inc., 1977.

Davis, Brian L. *Badges and Insignia of the Third Reich 1933-1945*. Poole, Dorset: Blandford Books Ltd., 1983.

Forman, Adrian. *Forman's Guide to Third Reich German Awards and Their Values, 2nd Edition*. San Jose: R. James Bender Publishing, 1993.

Forman, Adrian. *Forman's Guide to Third Reich German Documents and Their Values, Volume 1*. San Jose: R. James Bender Publishing, 1995.

Forman, Adrian. *Forman's Guide to Third Reich German Documents and Their Values, Volume 2*. San Jose: R. James Bender Publishing, 1996.

Fowler, E. W. W. *Nazi Regalia*. London: Bison Books Ltd., 1992.

Hayden, Mark. *German Military Ribbon Bars 1914-1957*. Atglen, Pennsylvania: Schiffer Publishing Ltd., 2001.

Hayes, A. *SS Uniforms, Insignia & Accoutrements: A study in Photographs*. Atglen, Pennsylvania: Schiffer Publishing Ltd., 1996.

Herzovision. *Sachsens-Orden*. http://herzovision.de/sachsens-orden/index.html.

Lumsden, Robin. *A Collector's Guide to Third Reich Militaria: Detecting the Fakes*. New York: Hippocrene Books, Inc., 1989.

Lumsden, Robin. *A Collector's Guide to: Third Reich Militaria*. New York: Hippocrene Books, Inc., 1987.

Lundström, Richard. "1940 Rules and Regulations." *Guide to German Ribbon Bars 1914-1945*.http://www.wehrmacht-awards.com/related/ribbons/regulations/rules_regulations3.htm.

Mallmann Showell, Jak P. *The German Navy in World War II: A Reference Guide to the Kriegsmarine*. Annapolis: Naval Institute Press, 1979.

McCarthy, Robert. *World War II German Military Collectibles*. Paducah, Kentucky: Collector Books, 1980.

Miller, Mike. "General der Flieger Rudolf Bogatsch." *Axis Biographical Research*. http://www.geocities.com/~orion47/WEHRMACHT/LUFTWAFFE/General/BOGATSCH_RUDOLF.html.

Miller, Mike. "Generaloberst Otto Deßloch." *Axis Biographical Research*. http://www.geocities.com/~orion47/WEHRMACHT/LUFTWAFFE/Generaloberst/DESSLOCH_OTTO.html.

Niemann, Detlev. *Bewertungs-Katalog: Orden und Ehrenzeichen Deutschland 1871-1945*. Hamburg, Germany: Niemann Verlag Hamburg, 2004.

Pia, Jack. *Nazi Regalia*. New York: Ballantine Books, 1971.

Pia, Jack. *SS Regalia*. New York: Ballantine Books, 1974.

Piersall, Mark. "Crusade against Communism Medal 1942-1944." *The Piersall Collection of Orders, Decorations, and Medals from Around the World*. http://www.marksmedals.com/romanian_medals_files/crusade.html.

Reddick, J. Rex. *F.W. Assmann & Söhne Sales Catalog*. Denison, Texas: Reddick Enterprises, 1992.

Robertson, Megan C. "Medals of Bulgaria." *Orders, Decorations and Medals*. http://www.medals.org.uk/bulgaria/bulgaria.htm.

Schulze Ising, Andreas M. *Imperial German Orders, Medals and Decorations*. http://www.medalnet.net/German_Orders.htm.

Schulze Ising, Andreas M. "Manufacturers of the Albert Order." *Imperial German Orders, Medals and Decorations*. http://www.medalnet.net/Albert_Manufacturers.htm.

Shackelford, Michael. "Medals of Imperial Germany." *Great War Primary Documents Archive, Inc*. http://www.gwpda.org/medals/medalshome.html.

Shackelford, Michael. "Medals of Finland." *Great War Primary Documents Archive, Inc*. http://www.gwpda.org/medals/finmedl/finland.html.

Shackelford, Michael, and Hendrik Meersschaert, "Medals of Austria-Hungary." *Great War Primary Documents Archive, Inc*. http://www.gwpda.org/medals/austmedl/austria.html.

Stewart, Emilie C. *German Military Award Documents 1939-1945*. New Jersey: Emilie C. Stewart, 1991.

Wendel, Marcus. *Axis History Factbook*. http://www.axishistory.com.

Williamson, Gordon. *The Iron Cross: A History 1813-1957*. Denison, Texas: Reddick Enterprises, 1994.

Williamson, Gordon. *The Iron Cross of 1939*. San Jose: R. James Bender Publishing, 2002.